THE
CHRISTMAS
LOVER'S
HANDBOOK

Lasley F. Gober

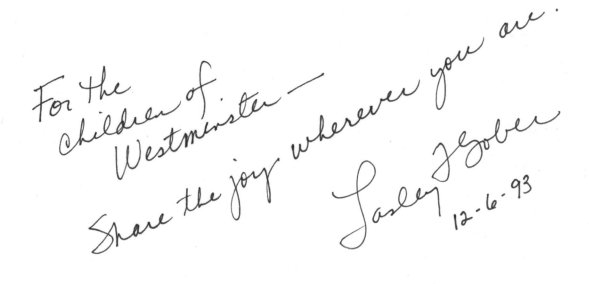

For the
children of
Westminster —
Share the joy wherever you are.

Lasley F Gober
12-6-93

BETTERWAY BOOKS

Cincinnati, Ohio

Illustrations by Charles Peale
Typography by Park Lane Publication Services

The Christmas Lover's Handbook. Copyright © 1993 by Lasley F. Gober. Printed and bound in the United States of America. All rights reserved. No part of this book may be reproduced in any form or by any electronic or mechanical means including information storage and retrieval systems without permission in writing from the publisher, except by a reviewer, who may quote brief passages in a review. Published by Betterway Books, an imprint of F&W Publications, Inc., 1507 Dana Avenue, Cincinnati, Ohio 45207. 1-800-289-0963. First edition.

97 96 95 94 93   5 4 3 2 1

Library of Congress Cataloging-in-Publication Data

Gober, Lasley F.
    The Christmas lover's handbook / Lasley F. Gober. -- Rev. ed.
      p. cm.
    Includes index.
    ISBN 1-55870-313-6
    1. Christmas decorations. 2. Christmas cookery. 3. Christmas.
  I. Title.
  TT990.C4G63 1993
  394.2'663--dc20
                                           93-23917
                                             CIP

This book is dedicated to:
Mom and Dad—the best Mr. and Mrs. Claus a kid ever had
Jim—my enthusiastic partner in holiday espionage, giving, and sharing
Geoffrey, Linley, and Zack—elfin keepers of the magic

Acknowledgments

Special Thanks to ... Ginny and Dave Fick without whose help and encouragement, grammatical and lyrical corrections, and expert assistance in putting together the "Tools" segment, not to mention 40-odd years of nurturing, this book might never have gotten finished.

Justina Poe ... a true Christmas lover, for her holiday inspiration and wonderful help in conceptualizing *The Christmas Lover's Handbook*. Justina's sketches were also the basis of many of the book's illustrations.

Kathy Kirkman ... who is always feeding me fun ideas and resources, and whose severe case of Peter Pan Syndrome at Christmastime makes celebration a joy for all those who know her, her family, Ken, her dogs, and the Bears.

And to all my friends and family, who helped me follow this project through to the end, in spite of themselves.

To them all—Merry Christmas! and many, many more!

Contents

Introduction

I admit it. I'm a Christmas fanatic.

While others may groan at the first appearance of red and green in the middle of October, I get a tremendous surge of enthusiasm. I love it!

BECAUSE CHRISTMAS IS—

Handel, Bing Crosby, and Elvis ...
Roasting marshmallows and a fire (even when it's 72°)
Wearing antlers and drawing a chuckle from perfect strangers ...
Evergreens and ribbon tied to the luggage rack of station wagons ...
Reflections of tree lights in baby's eyes ...
Traditions ...
Making a snowflake costume for the school play ...
Red and green Hershey kisses ...
Santa grabbing a burger at McDonald's ...
Sending and receiving cards from faraway family and friends ...
Memories ...
Singing "The Twelve Days of Christmas" and remembering all the words ...
Overhearing a seven-year-old explain why he "kinda believes in Santa ... "
Gladly writing a check for the Empty Stocking Fund ...
Parties, family reunions, outrageous Christmas feasts ...
Grandparents ...
Cinnamon sticks, candy canes, gingerbread, eggnog, and pfeffernuss ...
Mistletoe ...
The Salvation Army bellringers and brass quartet ...
An opportunity to be generous, creative, cheerfully gluttonous, high-spirited, festive, reflective, surprising, and absolutely jolly ...
Christmas is ... everything that makes life grand!

Everyone celebrating should love Christmas. Everyone.
Instead of groaning when the first string of big fat multi-colored

bulbs goes up the day after Thanksgiving, completely boxing your next door neighbor's house, everyone needs to learn how to love Christmas, not dread it. Everyone should know how to make a merry Christmas, without shame (that you photocopied your Christmas letter), without guilt (that you bought all your cookies at the bakery), without panic (that you forgot to get a gift for Aunt Agnes, again), without fear (that your homemade wreath will fly apart with the first winter breeze), without anger (that the crazy woman up the street actually looks forward to school letting out for the holidays), without paranoia (that *everybody but you* has Christmas under perfectly lovely control).

When you make Christmas your own and that of your family and friends, stripped of expectations aroused by magazine editors, idealized memories of Christmas Past ... and those super-celebrants who chime in excessively with eight uniquely decorated trees, gifts wrapped in yards of gold lamé tied up with miles of French-wired ribbon, a table elegantly set and groaning with enough to feed seventy of their nearest and dearest friends, and all of this done by December first (right!) ... when you can make Christmas your own, according to your own ideas and expectations, you can sit back and enjoy.

And love it ... this most wonder-filled and marvelous of holidays.

To borrow a phrase from the '60s, "Do your own thing." To go back even further, to Thoreau, "Do what you love, pursue your life."

Once you get your priorities in order, choosing what you as a family want to do, pursue it. And enjoy.

Do what you love. Pursue YOUR Christmas.

How to Use this How-to Book

The *Christmas Lover's Handbook* is a reference book of celebration—of the holiday itself and the creative spirit nurtured within its keep. Open to any page and something may just jump out and pull you in for a closer look, simply for the fun of it.

What began as a small effort to collect ideas for myself and my family—when we were very young—grew into a six-year project of research, observation, experimentation, and lots and lots of listening.

What do people like about Christmas? What drives them nuts? What makes it seem so difficult? What are the very best traditions, the not-to-be-left-out's? What makes it worth repeating, year after year after year?

I compiled simple instructions, helpful hints, Christmas trivia and holiday history, recipes and fun foodstuff, plus a sleighful of organized reminders regarding the basic how's, what's, when's, and where's of creating a happy, want-to-do-it-all-again-next-year Christmas.

Basically, I looked for and put down the answers to all my own questions: how do you roast a goose? make gravy? wassail? those neat molded chocolate leaves? how do you preserve and arrange greenery? tie those big fat bows? what did my true love give on the seventh day of Christmas?

I needed to find out EVERYTHING! Over time, I created this crash course in Christmas, for myself and, eventually, for others equally intimidated by revisionary memories of Grandma and slick magazine opulence.

And because, in those days, there *were* the babies and little ones, a great deal of the material I sought and devised pertained to young families newly embarking on the magical calendar of days.

Like a good wine, however, with age our holidays have become richer and mellowed. The babies are teenagers (gasp!) and I look at Christmas with a different perspective now. The tree has emerged from the playpen with little danger of being pulled down by a two-year-old. The traditional baking of sixteen kinds of homemade cookies has "gone to waist" since we don't get the exercise we once did chasing small fry all over the house. No

Christmas comes but once a year ... but it does come year after year after year. There will be countless opportunities to make the most of your holiday celebration. You don't have to do it all at once.

As we race toward the 21st century, our lives race along as well, compelling us to organize time and energies wisely. Clearly, a moderate amount of organization, without becoming extremely compulsive, makes more time for fun.

Also, as we have to work to make more time for ourselves, we have to work to put our free time to its best use. *The Christmas Lover's Handbook* takes a lot of the guesswork out of how to do many things in the most efficient, most effective, most enjoyable ways possible.

All of us work full time, whether at home, school, or the office. Make the most of whatever free time you can make for yourself, doing whatever it is you love to do.

The Christmas Lover's Handbook has *lots* of projects and activities to choose from. Don't be overwhelmed by the offerings. Simply pick and choose to create your own very special Christmas celebrations ... and LOVE every minute of it.

construction paper bells trailing gobs of glitter come home from "art" anymore. And work, school, and other of life's distractions have curtailed many of the creative activities so therapeutic during those tender years.

All of which is to say that the new, updated, and revised version of *The Christmas Lover's Handbook* is even more realistic, more comprehensive, sometimes more sophisticated, and decidedly more "'90s" than before. The original intent to inspire an even greater love of and for the season, to encourage every Secret Santa to make Christmas his or her very own (without the trappings of guilt, over-reaching enthusiasm, hysteria, or paranoia), to make it easier on everyone to "make" a happier holiday ... all of this remains in the text.

What has been added is a broader spectrum of celebratory possibilities (for all of us lacking the "little ones" purportedly requisite for maintaining the childlike wonder), an even more "environmentally-correct" focus on the preservation and use of natural resources and the recycling of old treasures into new, a modernized approach to facilitating that "good old-fashioned Christmas" with high-tech (time-creating) conveniences, and more, simply, of everything: decorating, recipes, traditions, gift ideas, handcrafting techniques ... still, with the accent on "simply."

Liberal use of the following punctuation " ..." means, "here are a few ideas, now see what you can come up with yourself." Tips, gentle nudges, and basic procedures should make creative endeavors a little easier.

The boot 🥾 is my own holiday version of the footnote: additional information and references.

Because a sense of humor is mankind's greatest asset during the good times as well as the challenging, seemingly impossible ones, I couldn't resist including a few Christmas anecdotes (told by various survivors of adversity), entitled "*Someday, we'll laugh about this.*"

Each chapter has "*Make it easy on yourself*" shortcuts for those who haven't the time or the inclination to go all out in that particular area of celebration.

The final chapter, "Making Merry: Handcrafting a Merry Christmas," is found in THE BACK OF THE BOOK for easy reference, with specific instruction regarding tools, materials, techniques, and a lot of nifty ideas for year-long enjoyment. Activities and crafts particularly suitable for children are listed in the Index under "Children, activities for ."

You can pull it all together and get organized with "The Twelve Lists of Christmas," a chapter including strategies for managing your celebration.

Don't think that you have to do everything every year to make a wonderful Christmas. You can't ... and you won't.

Just ... *do what you love.* Pursue your Christmas!

ONE

May Your Days Be Merry and Bright
Getting Everyone into the Spirit

It was always said of him, that he knew how to keep Christmas well if any man alive possessed the knowledge.
— Charles Dickens

You're busy, possibly even frantic. Only one week until Christmas. Suddenly, all the kids are home and you have moments when you'd like to stuff each one of them into a gift-wrapped parcel bound for Alaska.

The excitement and tension in the holiday air are bound to get to us at one time or another. And the only way to deal with it is constructively, making plans for activities to keep everybody happy and release all that energy.

Look for events you can enjoy together, things you can do with the children on a one-to-one basis, as well as things the kids can and should do by themselves, with minimal guidance from adults. Allow some time for plain and simple family fun, and …

May your days be merry and bright!

If you are lucky enough to have grandchildren/grandparents living nearby, spend as much time together as possible over the holidays. Share the past, present, and future experience of the season doing simple things that will make your celebration most memorable.

A FAMILY CHRISTMAS

The season and spirit of Christmas say "family." If you are lucky enough to have one, make your holidays together worth remembering. These memories will stay with your children wherever life takes them, and most surely will lay the foundation for happy family lives of their own in Christmas Future. And don't even try to make *everything* perfect, thus

Sometimes, no matter how hard you try, the Christmas spirit seems a hundred miles away from anywhere you and the kids find yourselves together. Be realistic about your "merry Christmas." Try to relax and make the best of times until (on the "not so merry" days) you finally get them all nestled snug in their beds (early!).

Charles Dickens and Prince Albert, who brought many German customs to his marriage to Queen Victoria, are perhaps more responsible than any others for the popularity of the Christmas celebration. They began the revival of that warm, generous, sentimental celebration of the day.

Said Dickens of the holiday, "Christmas is a good time; a kind, forgiving, charitable, pleasant time; the only time I know of, in the long calendar of the year, when men and women seem by one consent to open their shut-up hearts freely, and to think of other people below them as if they really were fellow passengers to the grave, and not another race of creatures bound on other journeys."

laying the groundwork for one more generation with unrealistic expectations. Unwrap your sense of humor well before December 25!

Communities celebrate Christmas in many ways. Check the newspaper, local magazines, church bulletins, and cultural organization calendars for lists of special events:

Bazaars and Festivals
Storytellings or Poetry Readings
Live Nativity Scene or Play
Puppet Show
Concerts
Home Tours
Visits to Nursing Homes and Hospitals

Caroling
Special Church Services
Visit with Santa
Outdoor Tree Lightings
Department Store Promotions
    (Breakfast with Santa, Santa's
    Secrets Shop ...)

Favorite Christmas Events

The Messiah choral performance. Composed by George Frederick Handel in 1741 using the text from the New Testament, this work was completed in 23 days. Traditionally, the audience stands at the opening of the "Hallelujah Chorus."

The Nutcracker ballet. Tchaikovsky wrote the music for E.T.A. Hoffmann's story, "The Nutcracker and the Mouse King." The first performance was given in 1892 and this colorful fantasy is a thrill to watch and listen to, especially through the eyes and ears of young children.

Amahl and the Night Visitors opera. Composed by Gian-Carlo Menotti, this is the story of a young crippled boy who welcomed the Three Wise Men on their journey to Bethlehem, of the wonderful gift he gave to the Christ Child and the magical gift he received in return. First performed in 1951, this award-winning contemporary opera is fast becoming a Christmas classic.

A Christmas Carol drama. Charles Dickens' beloved tale has been adapted to everyone from Mr. Magoo to Kermit the Frog, with numerous television and cinematic versions in between. A timeless piece with the warmest of spiritual messages.

When attending performances such as these, read the story and familiarize yourself with the music in advance of the event, as a family, to make the production even more meaningful.

You recognize the commercialism of these, but children see them as one more wonderful event that says, "Christmas is coming!" Let them enjoy the magic as much as they can for as long as they can.

Read Together During the Holidays

"A Child's Christmas in Wales," Dylan Thomas
"The Fir Tree," Hans Christian Andersen
"The Gift of the Magi," O. Henry
"A Visit from St. Nicholas," Clement Clarke Moore
"Yes, Virginia, There is a Santa Claus," Francis Church, *The New York Sun*
"A Christmas Carol," Charles Dickens
"A Christmas Dinner," Charles Dickens
How the Grinch Stole Christmas, Dr. Seuss
The Littlest Angel, Charles Tazewell
The Bible, Luke 2:1-20 and Matthew 2:1-23

Sing Together Favorite Christmas Carols

Organize a group to go caroling in the neighborhood, at a home for the elderly or orphaned, or on an open street corner or shopping mall. If you have access to a truck and a reasonable amount of hay, a family hayride staged annually with a group of friends could become an unforgettable tradition, especially if you top it off with hot chocolate and pizza.

"Silent Night" was written on Christmas Eve in 1818, in Oberndorf, Austria, by Minister Josef Mohr and schoolteacher Franz Gruber.

"Away in a Manger" is attributed to Martin Luther, who also is reputed to have decorated the first Christmas tree.

"Deck the Halls" is a Welsh carol; "Angels We Have Heard on High" comes from 18th century France.

"The First Noel" and "Hark! The Herald Angels Sing!" were written by Charles Wesley.

"Joy to the World" and "O Come All Ye Faithful" are 17th and 18th century carols; "The Twelve Days of Christmas," "The Holly and the Ivy," and "O Tannenbaum" date back to the Middle Ages.

An insurance executive, William Chatterton Dix, wrote the words for "What Child Is This?" to the 16th century tune "Greensleeves."

"We Three Kings," "O Little Town of Bethlehem," and "I Heard the Bells on Christmas Day" (the last by Henry Wadsworth Longfellow in honor of his son wounded in Civil War battle) are American-born songs of the season.

Popular Songs We All Know and Love

"The Christmas Song" Chestnuts roasting on an open fire ... written by Mel Tormé and Robert Wells.

"Here Comes Santa Claus" by Gene Autry and Oakey Haldeman.

"Jingle Bells" (1857) by J. Pierpont, uncle of J.P. Morgan, one of America's wealthiest industrialists.

"Rudolph, the Red-Nosed Reindeer" is a character conceived by Robert L. May of Montgomery Ward as an advertising gimmick. In 1949, Johnny Marks put the story of Rudolph to music, and Bing Crosby and

Gene Autry were among the many vocalists to record the song.

"White Christmas" by Irving Berlin was written for the movie *Holiday Inn* and became one of Bing Crosby's biggest hits.

"All I Want for Christmas is My Two Front Teeth"

"Frosty the Snowman"

"I Saw Mommy Kissing Santa Claus"

"Sleigh Ride"

(And, of course, my personal favorite, Bruce Springsteen's version of ... "Santa Claus is Comin' to Town!")

Pick Out the Tree

Make this a family outing, and a group decision, as to which lucky tree gets to come home and be yours. Plan to stop at a donut shop or special dessert place for cocoa and a celebratory treat—and to warm toes and fingers after that discriminating walk through the tree lot.

Stopping by Woods ... on a Snowy Evening

Memories are made of the family excursion into the woods with an ax, saw, length of rope, and thermosful of hot chocolate (and perhaps another of hot milk and kahlua!). Getting permission to roam an over-grown pine forest or visiting a "cut-your-own" tree farm in search of *your* tree will bring all of you a valued experience. Research commercially-operated tree farms in the area for information.

Going to See Santa

Even the bigger kids who coolly profess to know there's "no such thing as Santa Claus" can't help but be a bit skeptical when they face the jolly old fellow on the department store throne, handing out candy canes and Ho!Ho!Ho!ing in a quite convincing way.

Don't we too, even as adults, feel a trifle in awe of this figure ... smile our warmest smiles, stand straight at our best behavior, lest he skip our chimney this year?

It's the man as the symbol we love, and children deserve as much exposure to his goodness as possible. Be excited with and for them as you approach the visit, but don't be surprised if the littlest angels scream and kick the old fellow in the shins, so frightened are they of this imposing figure. Don't force them to love Santa. They will.

 Bring lots of music into your Christmas celebration—a daily dose of Handel, Bach, Bing, and Bruce (even Alvin and the Chipmunks) adds such life to the holidays. Start a collection of Christmas music you can add to each year. Or simply tune your radio to the most spirited of local stations.

Go ahead and have the screaming-meany picture taken. Let this be another episode in your "someday we'll laugh about this" book of memories.

Over the River and Through the Woods: to Grandmother's Condo, Disney World, Vermont ...

If you travel at Christmas, be sure to wrap bows and garlands around the luggage rack of the station wagon, take plenty of pre-moistened towelettes, tissues, activity books, packaged fruit juice, snacks, extra pillows and blankets — and probably a trailer for everything else (including the kids!).

Leave a note for Santa with explicit instructions as to where you will be the night before Christmas.

Church Activities

Affiliation with a church can be doubly rewarding at Christmas. The celebrations are so uplifting and beautiful one can't help but see through all the glitter and gift wrap to the true meaning of Christmas.

Church services I enjoyed most as a child were the Christmas Eve midnight services at a local Episcopal church. The pageantry, color, and song and the cold starry night of promise are rich Christmas memories to me still.

My own church celebrated with a "Love Feast" early each Christmas Eve, and this informal service was also an event to warm the holidays—with beeswax candles, spiced tea, and carols.

Even if you are not a regular churchgoer, consider finding a church with special Christmas activities for your entire family to enjoy.

One event our church in Atlanta has organized for children is the "Secrets Workshop." Moms and Dads plan gift-making activities and gather all the materials. Then, one December Saturday morning, all the children come to make handmade "secret" gifts for family and friends. Following the workshop, each excited child brings home a sackful of personally wrapped surprises to put under the tree. This is a successful effort to take out some of the commercialism and restore some of the simple pleasure of Christmas giving.

Other church festivals, nativity plays, live outdoor nativity scenes, family suppers, caroling get-togethers, and many more events are scheduled to bring the holiday celebration into the heart of the community

Make it Easy on Yourself

• Avoid too many sweets. Sugar can turn even the mildest personality hyperactive.

• Stick to routine as much as possible during the holidays.

• Give the kids plenty of chances to exercise away excess energy, and incorporate a "calming hour" before bedtime — quiet music, stories, and other "non-exciting" material.

• Have a couple of new coloring books, drawing pads, or crossword puzzle books around to pull out before Christmas for creative activity and distraction. Show home movies or rent a restful video.

• When you find yourself pushing the kids away so you have more space and time to create *their* merry Christmas, it's time to call the sitter. Take advantage of out-of-school teenagers who would probably like to earn some Christmas money, and give yourself one long uninterrupted afternoon or evening to get things done so you can relax and enjoy the kids again.

• Co-op with a friend. Agree to take his or her children for a couple of hours in return for keeping yours.

Compile a list of local family activities at Christmas. Allow each family member to select one you will all attend, or that he would like to attend along with one or both parents, as a "Very Important Individual" treat. It's amazing, sometimes, how special attention tames the wild "beast" in just about anyone.

On Christmas Eve Day, when the children are little and anticipation is at its pitch, Justina uses this point system: give points for helpful, positive behavior. Subtract for uncooperative, negative displays. An accumulation of 5-10+ points wins a chance to open one gift at bedtime.

and away from the shopping malls. If you and your family can enjoy such activities together, your holidays will be all the richer for it.

Other Family Activities

Make just about anything in this book together: cards, decorations, gift wrap, gifts, cookies ...

Check out lots of Christmas books, music, and videos from the library and enjoy them together.

Exercise away tension, cabin fever, excess energy, and Nana's fudge:

1. Take a nature hike to collect greenery and pine cones.
2. Dance or exercise to Christmas music. (Let small children act out *The Nutcracker*, if you have seen it recently.)
3. Do a slow easy jog through the neighborhood to view decorations.
4. Go ice skating wherever and whenever possible.

Rehearse an improvised nativity play with family performances scheduled for Christmas Eve. (You will love the various versions of the Christmas story as interpreted by little ones.)

Build a giant snow castle, replicas of each family member, or an igloo fort out of your "white Christmas" snowfall.

Have an old toy and clothing round-up for the joint purpose of cleaning the house and finding "gently worn" outgrown things to give away to those less fortunate.

Throw a party! See the Entertainment section for ideas.

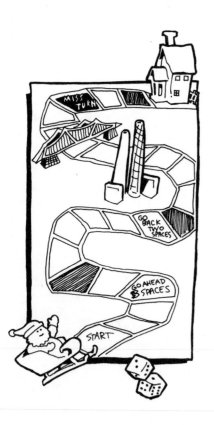

Things Kids Can Do by Themselves—Creating Creativity

Invent a Christmas board game. Provide heavy cardboard, crayons, cutouts, glue, markers, a pair of dice or a spinner from an old game. Use shapes, colors, numbers, words, obstacles, animals, chance ... as suggested themes.

Paint faces on old white gloves or directly onto fingers for a finger puppet show. Or make puppets from socks, paper bags, paper plates.

Make homemade finger paint: pour liquid starch into jars and add food coloring to desired color. Let little fingers stir to mix up the paint, and finger-print on moistened shelf paper or wax paper. Instant chocolate pudding is another fingerpaint that makes clean-up finger-lickin' good!

Write a Christmas story. Mom or Dad can take dictation from the little ones and each child can illustrate his or her original tale. If needed, give a headstart with suggested characters, plots, or first lines, and let the child finish the story. Bind each "book" in a special binding or scrapbook for safekeeping. (One year our Geoffrey wrote *A Very Scarey Christmas*, illustrated with lots of green and red monsters. We'll keep our copy forever—or at least until it comes out in paperback!)

Record an audio or videocassette greeting to keep or send to faraway grandparents, cousins, or friends. Sing carols, read stories and poems, relate recent news of the family ... a fabulous gift for a lifetime of sharing.

Cut out pictures of things beginning with each letter of the word CHRISTMAS. Glue into a scrapbook to share with toddler brothers and sisters.

Use old greeting cards for a number of projects: a Christmas collage placemat (laminated or covered with clear Contact paper); glue to cardboard backings and cut in jigsaw style to make puzzles; make cutout paper dolls with gift wrap cutout clothing ...

Make a Christmas village with construction paper, milk cartons, scissors, crayons, and glue.

Keep your family Christmas scrapbook full of favorite family photos, school art, greetings, letters to Santa, special event ticket stubs ...

SOMEDAY WE'LL LAUGH ABOUT ...

A Christmas memory vivid to me still is the time my parents took me to *The Nutcracker* as a child. I can still see the colorful ballerinas dancing around the enormous stage filled with costumed children, fanciful characters, and a dreamy living room Christmas scene.

When my daughter Linley was born, it was all I could do to wait until she was old enough for us to travel together back in time, to experience "The Nutcracker" magic again through her eyes.

This little character was a perfect candidate for the ballet. For her birthday, Granny had given her a cassette of "the sugar plum fairy and those other guys," and Linley passed many happy hours dancing around the living room before a captive audience of dolls and bears.

In the beginning of her fifth year, we went all out, purchasing the best tickets we could get to see the Atlanta Ballet perform *The Nutcracker* on stage at the Fabulous Fox. As Christmas approached and the tree went up, so did the intensity of excitement and anticipation in our own little "sugar plum" fairy.

Finally, the big day arrived and we dressed in our holiday finest— this bouncing curly-haired little girl in her Victorian batiste dress with the wide burgundy satin sash ... a picture to melt the heart even of Ebenezer Scrooge.

Unfortunately, it was pouring rain that day. But no matter. Nothing could dampen our spirits. As well, we got to be in a bit of a rush somehow, at the last minute. But we were on our way. This was it, finally our big day.

Traffic was awful and it took some doing, but we eventually achieved a parking space, hurriedly plunging through mud puddles, braving bone-chilling gusts of wind and rain, and finally reaching our destination—a little muddy, a little soggy, yet ever eager. The show would go on.

I brought along a lollipop, in case Linley got hungry or restless, but Curly-Locks Holmes spied it out in a minute. Before the first curtain rose, before the first note sounded, the lollipop was history, written into the folds of that lovely dress with sticky fingers now reaching out for

something to drink. "I'm awful thirsty," she said.

Well, thirst quenched, we settled in to study our program and wait for the music. Finally, the strings started tuning, and the overture began.

The curtain rose. Everything colorful and fantastic saturated our senses, and for a few shining moments, my mother-daughter fantasy came to life, as the young girl Clara danced about the stage as Linley had so often twirled across the living room floor. I looked at her. She looked at me. And we squeezed hands in mutual entrancement.

But what followed oh so closely on the heels of those first dance steps ... an increasing inability to sit still, inescapable need to go to the bathroom even before intermission, my poor judgment in allowing the sugar-plum angel to buy a chocolate bar in the lobby, and the LOUDLY whispered "Not *again*!" when a ballerina reappeared for one more pirouette ... these combined to bring the fantasy back to real life.

Yet now I can laugh about the wearying discomforts of that adventure. And sustain a wistful smile remembering those few wonder-filled moments when we — my daughter and I — were one in a warm and glowing Christmas memory.

TWO

The Twelve Lists of Christmas
Planning the Best Christmas Ever

*Making a list and checking it twice
Santa Claus is coming to town.*

The history of the list dates back to the earliest days of Santa him-self and has been with us ever since. We check it once, twice, a thousand times—adding, subtracting, revising, and holding onto it for dear life. For losing a list is tantamount to losing our minds. The list does what our minds seem incapable of—it keeps track of all we have to re-member to do when, where, how, and with whom.

Somehow, when that jumble of worries and wonderings dancing in my head is reduced to an organized list, neatly committed to paper, the weight on my shoulders automatically lightens—if only just a little.

Keeping Christmas lists together in one place is the best safeguard against losing them. Consider using a three-ring binder, card file box, or computer disk. (Has no one yet invented a software package for holiday planning, Christmas card cataloging, recipes … ?) Portability is nice, in some form or fashion, so you can keep up with yourself when you're out somewhere, trying to remember what you're doing there in the first place.

But before you even get started, you must remember this: unless you particularly enjoy going through a really depressing post-Christmas "bud-get-blues" period, think first about how much you are going to spend this year and where the money will come from. Another list …

In order to have sufficient time to fulfill your Christmas dreams, make as much room as possible in your holidays for FUN! Begin in July or August, simplifying your December by getting routine jobs out of the way: home repair and redecorating, doctor's appointments, major cleaning duties, silver polishing, winter clothing repair …

TIGHTENING SANTA'S BELT

Aside from the holly and mistletoe, the tree and stockings, one of the less jolly constants of Christmas is the budget. We wish our pockets of silver were bottomless during the holidays, perhaps more than at any other time of the year. Unfortunately, this is rarely the case.

Budgeting for Christmas is no fun, but it is critical. When January comes, so do the bills, yet everyday life goes on. There will be those nagging plumbing repairs, doctor visits, and new basketball shoes for each of the kids. So you just can't burden your future with overwhelming commitment and debt (attention, U.S. government ...).

The best way to avoid trouble with the credit office is to plan carefully—well in advance—what you think you can spend on Christmas, and make your lists accordingly. Determine your spending priorities: gifts, cards, decorations, a twelve foot tree, cocktail party for one hundred, or that silky new dress. Allow room for error by underestimating your allowance, so any last-minute "necessities" or that irresistible gilded angel ornament will be affordable.

Christmas can be a very expensive production, especially when feelings of generosity fill our hearts so completely. It's wonderful to be generous, but only within your means. There *are* ways to maximize your spending capacity by planning carefully, shopping wisely, and utilizing other resources, such as time and found objects (natural greenery, recyclable toys and clothing, your own talent for making "something from nothing") that will stretch your budget.

Consider opening a holiday savings account and putting something in each month during the year. It's easiest to save when you deposit the same amount each month. You forget to miss it. But if this is impossible, put in as much as you can whenever you can.

Another way to lighten December spending is to buy for Christmas all year long. Not only do you spread out the monetary output, but you ease the stress of shopping for everything at once in crowds. A summer vacation spot may be a good place to find interesting things—museum shops are wonderful sources for gifts and ideas. Spring and fall bazaars and festivals are also great mall alternatives.

Other Christmas Budgeting Tips

Arrange to take care of major expenses (automobile tuneups, dental checkups, new appliances, etc.) at times other than near the holidays, freeing up fixed expense money for a seasonal splurge.

Conduct a fall garage sale. Clean out all the old junk and make money and room for the new.

Start a small "cottage industry" to raise extra spending money: handmade ornaments, homemade jellies and jams, holiday babysitting service, summer house- and pet-sitting, gift-shopping service ...

Gather a group of creative friends and craft all year long, culminating with a show and sale in the fall, with unique gift items, hand-printed cards, funky gift wrap, decorative items with your own personal flair.

LIST #1: GOALS AND OBJECTIVES

The very first thing is to determine your priorities. Before you send out the first card, make those first (of many) trips to the mall, or begin to create the most extraordinary greenery arrangement ever, make a list of the things that are *most important* to you and your family, *in order of importance*:

On the first day of Christmas (July 1), I addressed my cards ...

On the second day of Christmas (July 22), I made 12 jars of pepper jelly ...

On the third day of Christmas (August 3), I started to needlepoint stockings ...

On the fourth day of Christmas (September 9) ...

1. Take each of the children to a Christmas production *individually*.
2. Needlepoint new stockings.
3. Get shopping and wrapping done by Nov. 30.
4. Have the in-laws for Christmas Eve dinner.
5. Card to printers by Nov. 15.

Begin Christmas organization by organizing your thoughts, as a family. Devote one November dinner conversation to polling the family on their interests and feelings (because these will change dramatically as the years go by, don't rely too heavily on last year's experience).

Then read through the following eleven lists to get some ideas. Look through your collection of decorations to decide what you need this year. Consider what kind of entertaining you might want to do, what meals you will serve, any baking ...

Above all, abandon all "should's." Embrace only the "would-love-to's." Retire tired traditions, hold on to the very best, and freshen up your holidays with something new and completely different. But remember, the best-laid plans are helpful, flexible, even dispensable, if something better comes along.

Chapter 3 "Greetings!" is a cele-bration of card-sending: how to buy or make your own cards, how to photograph your family portrait for card enclosure, how to write an enthusiastic greeting and/or Christmas letter, and detailed specifics on having your card printed professionally or at home.

LIST #2: CHRISTMAS CARD ADDRESS LIST

Keep this list alphabetized with each name and address on individual 3 x 5 cards in a file box, or commit it to the memory of your computer. You can add and pull cards or databases without entirely obliterating your original organization.

Kirkman, Kathy & Ken
816 Willow Point
Anywhere, USA 45601

Rumplestiltskin 3/14/86

'88   '89   '90   '91   '92

I like to keep a list of children's names and birthdays, if possible, so I can refer to them in notes on the card. Old friends you can't keep up with except through Christmas correspondence will appreciate your astounding "memory" and thoughtfulness. Keeping records of when I sent cards to others and when we received one from them helps when it's time to trim down the list (as the cost of cards and postage climbs toward astronomical).

On the back of each file card, or beside a name, you might want to jot reminders during the year of news to share with certain individuals in a personal note (whom you saw at homecoming, who's had a new baby, and various other events of the year past). Likewise, record information derived from their previous notes (he's studying for a doctorate in physics, she just started a new business) so you have a store of pertinent material to keep your correspondence personal and lively, as well as meaningful and deeply appreciated. Some people, like Great Uncle Henry, love to see a picture of the children, so note on his card to send him one each year.

Christmas card address lists need to be revised each year—add a husband, subtract a wife, change an address. When you receive cards, check return addresses against your current list. Add and subtract names as you lose touch with one friend, make a new one, or simply raise or lower your goals in correspondence.

Updating is a year-round effort, but if done diligently your list will be ready and waiting when you begin to address envelopes or pull your labels off the printer.

LIST #3: GIFT LIST

Another list that should be an all-year project is the gift list. Have a card, notebook page, or file for each recipient—family and friends—and divide the list into categories:

Gober, Fred		Birthday: April 30
Gift Ideas	**Birthday**	**Christmas**
golf balls	'90 picture of kids	'90 golf balls
Cross pen set	'91 picture of kids	'91 shirt
jogging shoes	'92 picture of kids	'92 tie
	'93 picture of kids	'93 paperweight

Keeping a running list of gift ideas keeps you from running around like an idiot trying to think of something brilliant when the retailers are selling nothing less than sensory overload. Recording past gifts prevents constant duplication ("Oh, wonderful, *another* box of golf balls!") while reminding you of the things most successful with that particular recipient. This is especially helpful with family members to whom you enjoy giving frequently.

List clothing sizes, favorite styles and colors, and any other information needed to find the absolutely-just-right thing. Listen for hints, innocent or otherwise. ("Gee, aren't those copper gelatin molds swell?" or "I sure could use that gorgeous blue sweater, L.L. Bean, page 52, adult medium ... ")

Young children will be full of hints, starting around January 1 (or sooner). "*Next* Christmas, I want ... " But don't take these premature requests too seriously. Annie will change her mind 25 times between the two-wheeler, football uniform, or electronic robot who does housework. Only you can decide how frantic to get over last-minute mind changes, when everything is wrapped and under the tree, but keep these lists as up to date as possible. You will have your own ideas about what each child needs and she will provide you with enough wishes to fill an entire Sears catalog. (But go ahead and get Annie the robot anyway. If she gets tired of it there is probably someone else who might find some use for it.)

BOONE		
Wants	**Have Bought**	**Stocking**
bike	bike	bear mug
soccer ball	football (returned)	marbles
marbles	soccer ball	water pistol
oil paints	Michael Jordan poster	

Chapter 4 "Giving—The Greatest Gift of Christmas" is a wholehearted attempt on my part to help everyone *enjoy* the act of giving over the holidays: how to match each recipient with the perfect gift, how to buy for children, how to shop, how to wrap, and how to ship or deliver gifts. There is also a generous listing of particularly pleasing ideas for buying or making unusual presents for any and everybody. You just may find that when it comes to giving, you will have Christmas in the bag!

Chapter 6 "Decking the Halls!" contains many decorating theme ideas, detailed information about greenery preservation and arrangement, how to make wreaths and swags, how to force bulbs in time for Christmas bloom, how to make the most of outdoor as well as indoor resources, in addition to a huge assortment of decorating suggestions utilizing the many symbols and traditional elements of the season.

LIST #4: DECORATIONS AND DECORATING

Try keeping a list of decorating accessories as you accumulate them from year to year, so you will have a guide to future needs and developing themes. (Believe me, this is a lot easier than pulling out all the boxes in late September.) Record everything as you pack up this January and simply update from year to year.

Planning decorating over the years, replacing a well-worn life-sized stuffed Santa, making wreaths for each of the doors, or adding new ornaments to the tree will enhance the overall appearance of your Christmas home, creating a most festive holiday environment. The list will give you easy reference when you start needlepointing pillows in June or when you want to buy up the after-Christmas decorations at a great sale price (a must for all true Christmas-lovers).

Make a brief outline of what you want to do this year to make the family home look especially dramatic, clever, unique, colorful, and/or just plain jolly to live in over the holidays.

DECORATIONS	
Have	**Need**
porcelain crèche	papier-mâché stars for
3 grapevine wreaths	chandelier
topiary forms	battery-powered lights
etc. etc. etc.	

LIST #5: MAKING MERRY—HOLIDAY HANDCRAFTING

Don't suffer needlessly, enviously annoyed by what *everybody else* makes at Christmas. If the mood strikes you, make merry yourself. Whether it's cards, gifts, decorations, or a miniature Victorian dollhouse completely decked out for the holidays that you hope to make this season, get on the ball early with a good plan of action.

Allow plenty of time and energy to enjoy the making itself, by limiting yourself to what you can reasonably do, in terms of schedule and capability. Check to be sure you have all the necessary materials. There is nothing worse than finally setting aside time to work on a project and coming up short of the essentials.

Make	Materials Needed
Caroline—smocked dress	fabric, thread, floss, buttons
Tedescos—stenciled tray	tray, stencil paper, green paint
Hunters—stenciled frame	wood frame, 8 x 10 non-glare glass
Gobers—stenciled toy trunk	rust remover, blue & red paint

Consolidate these Materials Needed with other shopping requirements added to List #10—the Master Shopping List.

Chapter 11 "Making Merry!" is a reference section for even the most timid of craftspersons. From "Don't Be Intimidated by Tools," to simple instructions on such techniques as papier-mâché, dough clay, painting, finishing wood, cutting metal, and many other nifty crafting procedures, this section is guaranteed to bring a lot of pleasure and satisfaction to your Christmas and all through the Happy New Year as well.

Anyone can be creative with just the slightest inclination or desire to do so. Patience and perseverance almost always forge a path to inspiration. And hidden talents *must* be sought. Exercise your imagination; try your hand and mind at any one of the myriad creative possibilities Christmas provides.

 See page 70 for more tips on shopping in order to render this often frustrating, frenzied, and fatiguing aspect of your holidays a little less so.

Chapter 8 "Eat, Drink, and Be Merry!" outlines some of the basics for happy party-planning, with specific tips and theme ideas. Virtually no stone has been left unturned. Any one of these sparks should light a fire under the most sedentary imagination — to come up with all kinds of new and delightful ways to share the holiday spirit with family and friends.

LIST #6: HOLIDAY ENTERTAINMENT

If you haven't done much entertaining in the past, you need to know that this is an area where lists—multiples of them—are essential.

Even the most confident and practiced of hosts get "stage fright" at the last minute, wondering if the entire production will actually come off without a hitch. If entertaining is something you are considering this year, keep a section open in your organization file for this express purpose. You might even begin a year-round record of entertaining notes—who you invited, who came, what you served ... even mistakes made and lessons learned.

3/16/92		Chili Party
	Guests:	Caughmans, McKnights, Purvises, Poes
	Menu:	chili, salad, rolls, mudpie, beer, bleu cheese bites, champagne grapes
	Next time:	Have extra salad dressing on hand
12/20/92		Christmas Wassailing and Caroling
	Guests:	Neighborhood—45 came
	Menu:	cookies, pound cake, cheesecake, chocolate fondue, wassail, spiced tea
	Next time:	Don't use goldfish bowl to serve wassail!

Fanatic magazine and newspaper clippers should add an envelope or a box for various cutouts: unusual table decorations, menus, outrageous party themes, recipes, how to make white chocolate snowflakes ...

LIST #7: BAKING AND MEAL PLANNING

Here's your grocery list—from whence cometh six pounds of butter, ten pounds of sugar, and at least five pounds onto your hips and thighs … each!

Another area in which organization can rein in your budget as well as your sanity, meal planning begins as early as November, with the Thanksgiving feast, and runs through at least five batches of Chex party mix, twelve loaves of almond bread, and 57 varieties of Christmas cookies.

Go through Christmas recipes (a separate section in your recipe box?) and cookbooks, deciding which wicked treats will tantalize the tastebuds of family and friends this year:

To Make	Ingredients Needed
Shortbread (3 batches)	5 lbs. of butter
Gingerbread People	10 lbs. of sugar
Pound Cakes (2)	raisins
Pepper Jelly (8 jars)	pectin, green peppers

Chapter 9 "A Festival of Feasting" is a truly delectable collection of recipes, food serving and garnishing tips, kitchen crafts, and kitchen gift ideas for the holidays. All with a large serving of EASY. You will find just about everything there but fruitcake … which is still being passed around from fridge to fridge. (I think Uncle Billy has it now … no, Cousin Sue … well, it's out of *my* hands.)

Meal planning doesn't include formal entertainment—that's part of your Entertainment file—but involves only family meals and food you would like to have on hand for spontaneous hospitality.

You might be saying to yourself, "Uh oh, she's getting a little obsessive here." (It's okay to talk to yourself … Christmas Lovers are wonderful company.) But for those of us who groan every evening at 5:00, "What are we gonna have *tonight*?" this is salvation, especially during the busy holidays when we're in and out, shopping, wrapping, baking, partying … and can't stand the thought of another Quickie Burger, fries, and Alka Seltzer.

So if you've never done it before, consider meal-planning during the holidays. Give it a try. Keep holiday life as simple and uncomplicated as possible, leaving time for the things you want to do. You can keep an inexpensive calendar taped inside a cabinet door and fill in menus by the week. Make a shopping list directly from this, to be sure all ingredients are on hand. Believe me, you *will* save money and time.

Monday:	tacos, black bean salad, orange wedges
Tuesday:	grilled cheese sandwiches, tomato soup, gingerbread
Wednesday:	roast turkey, wild rice, asparagus casserole
Thursday:	vegetable soup, cheese toast, curried fruit
Friday:	I'm going out—get your own dinner!

Chapter 7 "All Decked Out" is a special feature dedicated to self-ornamentation — holiday dress-ups with a few ideas for making something new from something old, and all kinds of festive suggestions to "suit" the whole family.

LIST #8: HOLIDAY CLOTHING NEEDS

Last-minute parties for which you have "nothing to wear!" can really throw a wrench into the holiday schedule. Who has the time or the inclination to run all over town searching the racks for something sparkly, gorgeous, and unique to wear? Besides, by December, the sparkly, gorgeous, and unique are typically faded, picked over, and lost between the cruisewear and early spring lines.

No doubt you have some idea what parties you will be attending and what kinds of things you will wear. If "thrift" is your middle name, there *are* ways to make maximum use of the things you already have and to coordinate these with others you need or want to buy.

What to Wear?	Need to Buy!
Office Party:	
Jim—tux	cufflinks, Christmas tie
Lasley—black strapless	goldtone earrings
Johnson's Open House:	
Jim—suit	Geoffrey—red sweater
Lasley—red suit	Zack—green sweater
	Linley—Christmas dress

Chapter 1 "May Your Days Be Merry and Bright" highlights activities children can enjoy on their own, as well as things the family can do together, with a few reminders about the spirited traditions in cultural entertainment available all through the season.

LIST #9: FAMILY ACTIVITIES

If you have small children, planning some things for them to do over the school holidays (especially *before* December 25) is imperative for mental health maintenance—yours *and* theirs. No doubt they will be wild with excitement (well, aren't you?). But craziness needs an outlet, or you will all be bouncing off the walls ... in unison.

You have much to keep you busy, but budget some time for yourself and the children to enjoy a few relaxed and pleasant moments together. Those few quiet times will likely make the remainder of your days together a lot easier too. A little special attention goes a long way.

Channel elfin spirits creatively, involve them in the preparations, and if they're old enough (walking), there is bound to be something they can do to help—be it emptying the trash (not in the *toilet*, Cody!), baking bread and cookies, or sorting outgrown toys for needy children.

When Santa Claus is watching ... who knows? Planning wisely and supervising patiently (you *can* get the two pounds of flour out of Mandy's hair!), you will all enjoy the holidays—together.

Dec. 19:	String popcorn and cranberries for bird's tree
Dec. 20:	Make gingerbread people
	Sort through toys for "Empty Stocking" donation
Dec. 21:	Sends kids to movie with sitter
Dec. 23:	Make Christmas placemats
Dec. 24:	Deliver gifts

LIST #10: MASTER SHOPPING LIST

Actually, any expectations of compiling a complete and final "Master Shopping List" are grand delusion at Christmas. You will no doubt think of one or two (or twenty) items you have forgotten along the way. But your ultimate goal is to organize and plan as best you can to minimize those last-minute treks through blizzards of snow and multitudes of other last-minute shoppers.

Consolidating your many lists of "needs"—gifts, wrapping and decorating supplies, crafting materials, exotic recipe ingredients—into one master shopping list will be something of an effort, but again, a highly rewarding one.

Once you pull it all together, map out your itinerary: this mall and that, hardware store, drug store, intimate apparel boutique ...

Estimate the amount of time needed in each place, their locations relative to each other, items you need to purchase early in the season and those that can wait until the next paycheck. Cutting down on drive-time and position-jockeying in parking lots saves many a headache and allows more time and energy for the jollier aspects of the holidays.

Leave plenty of room for additions, as you will inevitably think of something else you need. And make two copies, one for your file and one more for the road. As you shop, you won't likely find everything you need the first go-round ... or you may need to take a reconnaissance tour before making up your mind.

As you shop, keep notes of things the store is out of, items you discover but are not quite ready to buy, ideas you get from displays, numbers and kinds of batteries and other accessories you'll need for various toys and electronic gifts, questions you have concerning sizes ...

It's not even a bad idea to file your completely checked-off lists, keeping a record of what you have already bought, where you got it, and where you hid it—or you may end up with *two* mountain bikes stashed away somewhere in the house!

Master Shopping List

FARMER'S MARKET	CRAFT STORE
rice flour	paintbrushes
crystallized ginger	stencil board
ivy topiaries	gold paint pen
HARDWARE	LENOX SQUARE
walnut stain	Bookstore
polyurethane	Walkman
tree lights (sale ends Sat.)	3 pr. Levis
INTIMATE APPAREL	
something red & slinky!	

LIST #11: DECEMBER CALENDAR

Are you beginning to feel listless from making so many lists? Relax, you're almost through. We've finally arrived at the Master Plan—the organization of all organization.

Draw up a special calendar just for the holidays—yours may include all twelve months of things to do, just the few pre-holiday months, or even only December.

Here is Creative Life Planning at its best—all your days reduced to neat little squares containing neat little notes of schedule, reminders, deadlines, and guidelines. You can handle it. Everything's right there on paper.

What's that? You say you can't stand regimen, a fixed time and place for everything and everyone? It stifles your sense of freedom and creativity? Stop. Read no further. Forget I mentioned it. This section is definitely not for you. Move on to the next chapter. And enjoy. Do what you love.

Now, for those of you remaining—those paragons of punctuality and nitpicky perfection (no offense intended—I need it all on paper just like you, and I'm not even a perfectionist), let me remind you that Christmas is no time for paranoia. If you slip off schedule, don't do all you planned, or meet with unexpected demands from job, school, family, or friends, don't panic, don't whine, and don't give up.

I can't emphasize enough the importance of *comfortable* enjoyment of the holidays. When the activities and plans you have made become overly tedious and deflating of spirit STOP! Pour yourself a cup of tea or a glass of Chablis and reflect on your true purpose:

To enjoy ... share ... love ... create ... excite ... sing ... decorate ... grow (pleasantly plump, doesn't everybody?) ... TO CELEBRATE!

Whew. Just make a casual chart, a simple and flexible schedule with these things in mind: to plan is to be organized, to be organized is to get it done effectively and efficiently, and to get it done happily is ... CHRISTMAS!

8	9	10	11	12	13	14
Festival of Trees	Pick up tux hardware			Buy tree	Go see Santa	Decorate tree
15	16	17	18	19	20	21
Wrap gifts			School's out	Amy's friends over to string popcorn	Shopping w/ Dad	Jason to symphony Christmas concert
22	23	24	25	26	27	28
Gingerbread making party	get sitter so I can finish wrapping	Deliver gifts				

LIST #12: NEXT YEAR, I'M GOING TO ...

Can you believe it? Here we are just getting started on this Christmas, and already she's shoving us into *next* year. But no Christmas book dedicated to helping you plan and organize your best Christmas ever would be complete without a wholehearted attempt at making next Christmas even better.

Work on this list sometime around New Year's, or soon thereafter—maybe while you're taking down the decorations. Evaluate the holidays lightly with an eye and ear for how they might be improved upon next year. (Learning by mistakes has always been my primary source of knowledge!)

Evaluation of 19____
I wish I'd spent more time _____ _____
I wish I'd spent less time _____ _____
Things I needed but forgot to get _____
Things I didn't need to do but did (and shouldn't have) _____
Gift, card, decoration, entertaining ideas for next year _____ _____ _____
New recipe ideas _____ _____ _____
Leftover supplies _____
After-Christmas sale purchases for next year _____ _____
Things I want to do next year _____ _____ _____
Great gift ideas I thought of December 26 _____ _____

Begin a new file for Next Year, and put this list inside. When it's time to do it all over again—there will *always* be another Christmas—you'll be ready to go.

THREE

Greetings!
Selecting or Making Your Cards

My best wishes for your merry Christmases and your happy New Years ...
—Charles Dickens

Despite ever-increasing postal and printing costs, cards are still the least expensive way to send your heartful of Christmas spirit to friends and family near and far. In many cases, season's greetings are our only correspondence with long-distance friends each year, our only way of knowing who's doing what and with whom.

Whether you make your own or buy them, sending cards, along with a new photo of the kids (or dog) can be a gratifying holiday experience—a loving tradition you just can't quit.

MAKING A LIST ... CHECKING IT TWICE

No doubt (that is, I hope) you've already revised this year's card list, as per recommendations in List #2 of the "Twelve Lists of Christmas." You likely have added the names of new friends and subtracted others, for whatever reasons. Because postage is so high, you may decide not to send cards locally, or simply delete that part of your list containing friends you often see.

If you live in a small community, however, and distances aren't too great, hand-deliver your messages throughout the neighborhood, at the office, in the health club locker room ...

 Whether you make your own cards or buy them, it's fun to save a copy each year as a history of your greetings. Your children and grandchildren will love looking through the collection grown from year to year.

The Tradition of Card-Sending …

is said to have begun in 1843, when the first Christmas card known was printed in England. Approximately one thousand copies were sold of the elaborate card designed by John Calcott Horsley.

Sophisticated printing processes came into use during the latter half of the nineteenth century. Fans, stars, crescents, embossed, iridescent, even jewel-studded … cards were available to the well-to-do greetings sender. Today more than a billion Christmas cards, of all shapes, sizes, and adornments are sold each year in the U.S. and Great Britain alone.

Christmas seals are the brainchild of a Danish postal clerk, Einar Holboell, who in 1904 conceived of a stamp to be sold for a penny, with the proceeds going to charity and hospitals. Jacob Riis brought this idea to the U.S. under the auspices of the National Tuberculosis Association. Riis had lost six brothers to TB. Seals are supportive today of many charitable causes, and attaching them to your cards is an outward and visible sign of your sharing and caring.

Postal issues of Christmas stamps originated in Austria in 1937. The U.S. Postal Service issued its first Christmas stamp in 1962—a Christmas wreath and candles pictured on a small red and green background. Protests of religious involvement by the government were overcome, and each year, holiday scenes, both religious and secular, are issued by the Postal Service (though we were never asked to choose between a young slim Santa or an aging stout one!).

SELECTING CARDS AT THE STORE

Choosing your Christmas cards can be a real spirit-lifter early in the season when selection is at its best. Take a little time to read the messages, evaluate the artwork, and consider the space you need for writing personal notes.

My friend Kathy, most at home in a zoo, never fails to send a card covered with marvelous animals—crowding in a sleigh, sliding down banisters, or enjoying a Christmas feast. She truly asserts the innermost depths of her wildly crazy personality (naturally incorporating the greetings of Rumple, Shar-Pei with antlers) with every card she sends.

Your card should be a personal expression of your feelings, be they spiritual, joyous, aesthetic, or humorous. Select one that says you "cared enough to send the very best" representation of *you*, the greeting you and your family wish to convey.

Consider, too, sending a card made of recycled paper. You'll be doing the environment of reindeer and other forest creatures a friendly service.

Getting an Early Start

When you come home with your purchase—hopefully it's still early in the season—why not go ahead, address the envelopes and affix the stamps. Get this part over with so you will have plenty of time to write each card as the mood hits you. You might even run address labels off your computer, straight from your carefully keyed-in list. If you hate the taste of stamps, give this job to an enthusiastic five-year-old or a damp sponge. And save yourself from writer's cramp by ordering (six weeks in advance) some return address labels (very cheap, yet effective) or splurge on an envelope embossograph with your name and address ($15-20 in most stationery stores). These will be useful all year long, especially for those bulk mailings like January bills and February valentines.

PHOTOCOPYING YOUR PERSONAL NOTE

You want to send a detailed letter about the previous year's goings-on, but haven't the time nor the energy to write 75 times about your master's thesis, the new baby, or your triumph in the Boston Marathon (you finished!). There are many occasions when a photocopied or computer printout letter of recent family history is perfectly appropriate (even if Miss Manners might disapprove), especially if you add a personal line or two to each recipient at the end.

Usually it's fairly easy to gauge which of your greeting recipients would be thrilled to receive all your family news. Plan what you'll say and try to make the narrative as lively yet humble as possible. Not many people harbor the desire for lengthy epistles, but a light and witty pageful of family news, ideas, and future plans will be welcomed by good friends. And if you think you're incapable of witty, just write in a breezy conversational style as if you were chatting on the phone.

Frankly, this is an area that opens itself up to lots of creative possibilities. Stand-up comedians' careers have been made poking fun at the burdensome boasting of the stereotypical family Christmas letter. So don't fall into that claptrap. Try twisting annual family history into a "borrowed" narrative form for a lighthearted chuckle. Reinterpret "The Raven," Dickens' "Christmas Carol," the Addams Family, or the Brady Bunch … inserting yourselves as characters. Be a satirist for a day regarding the past year's events. Or emulate Bombeck, Cosby, and other comical authors. All in good fun, and quite a comic relief from the standard brag sheets still shamelessly fluttering about out there.

FAMILY PHOTOS

Far-flung family members and old friends would probably love to see an updated family photo: everyone around the tree (put up in October for "authenticity"), you and Bowser, the kids in green and red striped pajamas … A picture *is* worth a thousand words.

But there's a science to taking good pictures. Consider the following suggestions to keep it as elementary as possible:

Rule #1: Start early. Shoot in October. Getting back proofs and having reprints made takes time you won't want to spend in December. And you need to allow for the possibility, however grim, that none of your photos turns out even remotely the way you hoped. Plan for this to happen, and keep your fingers crossed you won't have to schedule a retake. (It makes me "shutter" just thinking about it.)

Rule #2: Have scene and clothing needs mapped out in advance. Unless you like the casual thrown-together look in a family photograph, decide where everyone will sit or stand, what they will wear, and what background props you will use IN ADVANCE OF THE ACTUAL PHOTO SESSION. (My own family can vouch for the utter hysteria of gathering 30 or so kids, moms, dads, and grandfolks together in one place and *then* trying to decide who sits where with whom beside what!)

Rule #3: Take several shots and poses.

Rule #4: Use a reputable developer who won't lose your negatives, make a mess of your prints, or take forever to return them. You'll want a quality print on quality paper and enough copies to show off to everybody.

The styles of bordered cards for inserting photos have certainly improved since the old days and may be just the thing for suitably framing your family portrait as a holiday greeting. Ask the developer about these.

Say "Cheese!" …
In preparing her family portrait for Christmas card enclosure, one friend of ours built a fire in the fireplace, hung stockings, decorated the mantel with greenery and bows, decorated her daughters in candy-cane nightgowns, and shot this whole holiday scene in early October. The younger girls were slightly confused for a few days, but come December these pictures made a fantastic addition to their greeting (without the last-minute rush!).

If the photo actually turns out to be pretty great, have a few prints made for carrying around and giving to proud grandparents, aunts, and uncles …

A "Sticky" Subject ...

If you're attaching a family photo to your Christmas card, it's best to use rubber cement, spray fixative, or double-stick tape. The recipient can then peel it off the card to save and enjoy. Write who's who on the back with the date and any other pertinent information you like.

A folded card with a cutout window (use a mat knife for this) and decorative border makes a nice frame for the family portrait.

A Picture Worth a Thousand Words

Whether you are shooting for your card enclosure or photographing the whole gang on Christmas Day, here are a few ideas for family settings to effect "higher art form" family portraits. One of the most important aspects of true artistry is unity. Expand your photographic perspective by experimenting with metaphorical scenery and props to make a dramatic (or clever) statement regarding your subject matter.

- Gather the family somewhere outside, where the background attractively highlights the scene—around a great big tree, perched on a split-rail fence, sitting on various levels of a garden terrace ...
- Take everybody to a park and seat the children by age coming down a slide, swinging on swings, peeking through steps of natural wood climbing equipment, hanging from either side of a ladder ...
- Capture the family in motion (with high-speed film) — depicting yourselves participating in the family hobby or sport: everybody on bikes, fishing, swinging tennis rackets, mountain-climbing ...
- Gather round the front steps of a new house, the new deck or patio ...
- Indoors, select a spot that complements the family grouping: a not-too-busy background effectively highlighting the coloring and features of each "model" — a comfortable place that depicts "Home Sweet Home": by the fireplace, on and around a favorite sofa or chair, sitting around the Christmas tree, standing on your heads in the exercise room ... Decorate minimally to give the scene a holiday feeling with stockings, greenery, a few wrapped gifts, mantel decorations ...
- Coordinate clothing colors with the background. A bevy of bright pullover sweaters, nightgowns and robes, cheerful Christmas outfits, or Rudolph noses all make for superbly attractive photographs ...
- Be creative. Do something totally unexpected, outrageous, even out of character! Surprise!

Do-It-Yourself Tips on Photography

- Get as close to your subjects as possible.
- Avoid busy backgrounds.
- Use a good automatic camera that adjusts quickly and the proper speed film for the lighting and action. Fast film captures the flames of a crackling fire so you don't have to use a flash (ASA 400 or 1000).
- When photographing small children, get down on their level to take your shot (and take *several* to be sure you capture at least one simultaneously spirited pose!).
- Keep the shooting situation simple and natural.
- When photographing outdoors, early in the morning and late in the afternoon are usually the best times to prevent squinting, a too-deep contrast, and other lighting problems. Cloudy days often produce the best lighting situation.
- Special filters are available to correct and enhance many photographic situations. (They're not terrifically expensive either, and

would make great stocking stuffers for shutterbugs.)

All this may seem like a lot of trouble for one picture, but if you can get a gorgeous portrait of your family, however formal, casual, or hilarious, you will treasure the captured moment for many years to come. And relatives and friends will appreciate the effort when they receive a copy of their own.

About Receiving Pictures of Other People's Families

If you go to all the trouble to send pictures to your friends, you know the time and trouble they took to send photos to you. A fun way to keep these past the week or so of card display is to hang a "Friends" board somewhere in the house year round. The frequent pleasure of seeing faraway friends is worth the space and effort.

Add photos all through the year—of friends who visit, candids of the kids with this week's best buddy, and new baby portraits that occasionally come your way. Cousins, aunts, and uncles who never see each other will enjoy keeping the family connections.

Whether in the kitchen, in the hallway, down a stairway, or even in magnetic frames on the fridge, having friends and kinfolk "hanging around" all the time is fun for the whole family.

MAKING YOUR OWN CARDS

> How utterly ridiculous you'd feel,
> How damned unpleasant,
> If you sent just a card to us
> And *we* sent *you* a present.
> In order that no such thing
> Can happen to you, comma,
> This card is all you'll get from Ring,
> His kiddies or their momma.
> —Ring Lardner, from *Two Kinds of Christmases*
> H. Jack Lang, ed. World Publishing Co., 1965

Ring Lardner. What a card. And though he downplays the generosity of sending "just a card," his personalized greeting is a gift of himself, his time, and his talents, therefore a veritable treasure to those who appreciate the "thoughtfulness" of homemade.

Making your own Christmas card is a terrific way to personalize holiday greetings, saying just what you want to say to your family and friends. Creative energies and good plain fun emerge as you experiment with the many techniques of card-making.

I honestly enjoy designing our cards myself—making a yearly expression of the family's holiday spirit. Frequently frustrated that they don't turn out just the way I had hoped, I continue to make the annual attempt to come up with something stunning and inspirational or at least incredibly witty.

Dear Doting Grandparents:

Why not try to gather all your grandchildren at some point during the year, if at all possible, for a Grandkids Group Shot. Enclosing this in your Christmas card is one of your best chances to show off the best-looking kids in the world!

When Preparing Copy for the Printer ...

Use the following supplies, available at stationery and art supply stores, to make preparation of camera-ready printer's copy efficient and professional looking:

spray fixative (to protect artwork), non-reproducible pen, technical pen, rubber cement, drafting tape, graph paper.

Many Ways to Make Your Own Cards

Consider these things before having a printer reproduce your card professionally:

❄ DRAWING UP THE DESIGN

As you begin the work of creating a design, you will need to decide:

1. Size of card. Measure out your card size on scratch paper, with the size of the envelope, dimensions of the design, and space needs for greetings and personal messages as your guide. If you're using a standard size envelope, make the card slightly smaller, for a comfortable fit.
2. Sketch various designs on the measured scratch paper, until you come up with exactly what you want.
3. For the final draft use a clean piece of white paper and a blue non-reproducible pencil or pen (available at art supply stores). This will guide your spacing, measuring, and design—and won't show up in the final print.
4. When you have the design mapped out in blue, use a black pen or felt-tip marker to draw your card and fill in the lettering. If you make a mistake, relax. Attempt to cover it up with a cutout replacement rubber-cemented onto the original. Or use Liquid Paper pen and ink correction fluid lightly, letting it dry thoroughly before continuing, and correct the mistake. If done neatly, this shouldn't show up in the final print. Discuss any questions, fears, and tremblings with the printer.

❄ LETTERING

Now that everybody has a sister or an uncle who does calligraphy, there are many lettering possibilities for your message. You don't even have to be a pro to do it yourself. How-to books and calligraphy pens are available at art and office supply stores. Practice. With patience.

Or consider other lettering possibilities: a bold script, your own handwriting, tiny printing, or whatever style suits your card. The library has books on lettering and, with practice, you could duplicate just about any style imaginable. Use the non-reproducible pencil to keep your lines straight, even, and neat. You can draw all sorts of grids with this that will never show up on the final print. Of course, if you are doing something wild, like this: **MERRY CHRISTMAS!**

Don't worry about precision and straight lines.

 If making cards doesn't appeal to you, don't forget the little artist in your house who just might enjoy designing the family greetings.

❄ TYPESET MESSAGES

Your printer can and will typeset the lettering for you, or he can reproduce pre-set copy found elsewhere. Some even have books (called clip-art books) of pre-set messages you can reproduce onto your cards. Explore all these possibilities when creating your camera-ready copy.

❄ PREPRINTED BORDER TAPES AND BORDER BOARDS

Available at art and office supply stores, these are transparent matte-finish printed tapes that are great for applying onto cards and other printed materials as graphic borders. Many designs, including holly, stars, bells, and geometric shapes, can add a clean professional look to your own design. Also available are border boards, ready-sized framed borders, as background for a pasteup layout. Check stores for many other graphic design supplies to give a great look to your greetings.

❄ PAPER AND ENVELOPES

Select paper stock and envelopes in accordance with available printing ink colors. The printer will have his own stock, or you may have better luck with variety at a commercial paper supplier. See THE BACK OF THE BOOK for notes on paper selection and quality. Let the Yellow Pages lead you to a good paper supply company.

You might consider using pre-packaged stationery cards, such as the stock stationers use for monogramming and embossing. These are more expensive, but you can get attractive colors, border trims, and fancy envelopes if these options are unavailable in bulk elsewhere.

❄ CHOOSING INK COLORS

Black ink is less expensive than colors. The cost of two colors or more is considerably higher. Some print shops have special "color" days or holiday sales, when colored ink is available at a lower rate. They can print red all day without having to clean the press. Check the Yellow Pages for printers who make this offer. Shop around by phone for the best deal.

❄ MY FRIEND, THE PRINTER

Pamper your printer—you need him to do a good job for you. Ask all the questions you can think of, present him with a camera-ready makeup sheet of your card (black ink on clean white paper), and give him detailed instructions as to what you want, possibly even written directly on the original with the blue non-reproducible pencil: ink color choice, paper stock, where the paper is to be cut and/or folded, lettering style, and number of copies needed. Always ask to see the typesetting before final printing is done.

Have your card printed well ahead of mailing time. It's so easy to make mistakes; even the best printers slip up on occasion.

Plan Ahead

If your card is small, you can get two prints on each sheet of standard-sized paper and the printer can cut and fold them for you.

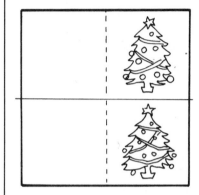

If you want to print both the cover and inside greeting of the card, make two separate print copies, each to be run separately on front and back. The least expensive way to have a folded card with copy inside and out is as illustrated:

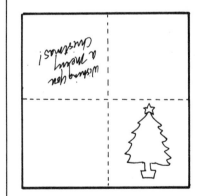

Plan carefully how the copy will reprint, how the card will fold, and where your design will appear on the printed card. Most printers, especially those set up for small jobs such as this, will be glad to show you how to make up your design for best printing results.

If I be a poet, I surely don't know it.
—Anonymous

❆ OTHER ITEMS FROM THE PRINTER

When you're doing your cards, you might want to have other items printed at the same time, for your own use or as gifts:

printed stationery
party invitations
gift enclosure cards
holiday postal cards

personalized notepads (great for thank you's)
gift tags
all-occasion greeting cards

Writing Your Message

While it's true that a picture is worth a thousand words, you'll likely want to add a phrase, quip, wish, greeting, poem, or highly philosophic discourse to your personally-designed card.

"Merry Christmas" is nice. Adding "Happy New Year" even nicer. But perhaps you're looking for something a bit more original, straight from the heart. Accompany your design with the appropriate complement—something inspirational with your Madonna and Child, wistful with your country snow scene, jolly and rib-tickling with your fat little Santa, wickedly scathing with your political cartoon ...

Consider the mood. Is it religious and inspirational? seasonal? aesthetic? lyrical? sentimental? cutesy? political? hilarious? Look for a Biblical passage, line from a carol or hymn, passage from fiction or poetry, or a self-composed rhyme, blank verse, solemn yet touching expression of holiday inspiration, comical quip, burst of humor, or simply warm and personal wish for health and happiness.

What you say is what you share with these special friends and family, near and far—your greeting. Consider it lovingly. Make it clever and unique. Keep a pencil and pad by your bed—inspiration strikes at the strangest times.

A Child's Christmas Card

Our friend Nathan McKnight, an extraordinary artist from an early age, has been doing his family's card for several years now. Nathan's natural creativity and gift for artistic expression have produced memorable greetings from his family.

Your child need not be a budding Michelangelo to design the family Christmas card. Sometimes the crudest renderings are the most touching and effective (particularly in the eyes of grandparents and doting aunts and uncles). Consider having the little ones pour out their spirit with the ink of a felt-tip pen and have this work reprinted as your card. The child will feel special, you will be nurturing creativity and expression, and there will be a recorded artifact of growth and development in the family scrapbook. To get the children started, measure the space within which the card should be drawn. Allow and encourage several drafts (over an equal number of days, so as not to dishearten). Praise highly for positive effort. He will proudly continue to improve with your encouragement.

We solved the problem of competition between three wise guy artists one year by letting each draw his or her interpretation of an angel floating over a heavenly blue cardstock field. Hilarious. And one of our very best cards ever.

If you prefer not to use the child's artwork on your card, how about letting a drawing be the design for printed notecards or stationery as a gift for grandparents, aunts, or uncles?

PRINTING CARDS AT HOME

Print cards, gift wrap, stationery, and fabric at home. Some home printing techniques are very easy, some are difficult, and some seem nearly impossible. But mostly, printing is fun, incredibly energizing, and exciting—you show off previously untapped talents to less resourceful friends and neighbors (or more important, yourself).

Nathan McKnight, Age 7

Stamp-Printing

For kids and adults alike, this is an entertaining and easy way to print on paper or fabric. There are several materials available to make the stamps and several inks useful for transferring your designs onto a surface.

❋ POTATO PRINTS

Everybody's heard of this, but have you tried it? Kids are especially fond of carving a half-potato (wipe off juiciness with a paper towel). A sharp knife works best, so carefully supervise the carving. Or you can cut the shapes, and let younger children dip them into tempera or acrylic paint, or an inked plate, and stamp onto paper or fabric. Bobby pins, toothpicks, combs, kitchen tools ... add distinctive textural effects to all these printing techniques.

❋ STAMPING BY THE FOOT DOCTOR

Dr. Scholl has provided us with many a comforting foot aid, but his adhesive foam can also be cut into shapes for making neat little wood block stamps for printing. Use a sharp mat knife, or an X-acto knife, and small *sharp* craft scissors to cut shapes and designs from the adhesive foam, which comes in sheets. Peel off the paper backing and attach to a small wood block.

Caution, cutters: the foam will tear easily, so practice on scraps, use a *sharp* knife, and take your time. These stamps will last and last, and make cute stocking stuffers with names, initials, logos ...

 A book by Edna Barth, *A Christmas Feast*, Houghton/Mifflin Clarion Books, is full of whimsical Christmas poetry, wishes, and greetings, and should be a rich source from which to draw lines of inspiration for your homemade cards.

❄ OTHER MATERIALS FOR STAMP-PRINTING

Carve, cut into shapes, or use as is: fruits/vegetables
gum erasers   textured household items
sponges   cookie cutters
corks   rope or string
textured fabrics   pasta shapes

(for the designing man and/or woman, glue one or more of these to a woodblock to create unusual effects)

❄ USING INK OR PAINT TO PRINT

Tubes of ink are available in many colors, marketed specifically for linoleum block printing (art supply stores). Spread ink with a brayer (roller) on a smooth glass or acrylic surface. Dip stamp into the ink and transfer to the paper or fabric printing surface.

Pour liquid acrylics, tempera, or poster paints into a pie tin and dip stamps. Acrylic is best for fabric printing, as it won't wash out once it has dried.

Use an inked stamp pad (office supply stores) with homemade or purchased stamps. The colors are not as bright, but it's easy and ready when you are.

❄ PRINTING SURFACES

tissue paper   paper bags
stationery or notecards   muslin
rice paper   cotton
construction paper   linen
shelving paper   raw silk
white/brown craftpaper   any absorbent fabrics

See page 245 for instructions on printing fabrics.

❄ UNUSUAL TECHNIQUES FOR STAMP-PRINTING

The more you experiment, the more unusual effects you will come up with in stamp-printing. Practice on scrap paper using different stamp shapes singularly or together. When using several colors, let one color dry before adding another. Mix media, using more than one technique on the same surface. Add special effects with a multitude of found "objets d'art" whose shapes and textures you can superimpose on your print.

❄ FINGER-PRINTING

This is great sport for kids and provides an enormous number of Christmas card and decorative possibilities for witty grownups as well.

See Chapter 12 "Making Merry" for specific information regarding use of different papers, coloring tools, and creating designs and lettering.

Press a finger against a stamp pad or an inked surface and transfer to paper. Now, with just a few added lines, curls, squiggles, dots from a felt tip pen … you can create people, animals, and other crazy things.

You needn't limit the prints to fingers or thumbs either. Add a palm, side, or heel of the hand, all fingers or toes together to expand the never-ending variety of possibilities.

Fingerprint art is fast, fun, and an almost inexhaustible resource for youngsters of all ages. Rainy days are brightened merely by providing each child with a stamp pad, paper, and pen. Proceed with caution, however. Stamp-pad ink is fairly indelible. Supervise the younger and messier of your crew, and have a soapy washcloth ready for removing finger ink immediately—or you may find renditions of this high art form on permanent display all over your house.

Thumbs-up for a one-of-a-kind finger-printing technique …

❄ HOME PRINTING AS A TIMELESS ART FORM

Linoleum block printing is an art form that dates back much further than Gutenberg cares to remember. While somewhat tedious, this process produces extremely satisfying results when exercised intelligently, knowledgeably, and innovatively. Materials needed, and available at art supply stores, are:

linoleum block (comes in various sizes)
linoleum cutter (a gouging tool)
block printing ink (tubes)

brayer (rolls out the ink)
glass or smooth inking surface
printing paper (see "Papers for Creative Use" page 221)

The design is carved out of the linoleum. The uncarved areas will obviously be those that print, so rather than carving *out* a design, you are, in effect, carving *around* it.

Crucial to the technique is the fact that your picture will print backwards, so you need to draw your design with a soft lead pencil on a piece of paper, lay it over the linoleum block (design side down) and transfer the design to the block by rubbing pencil lead across the entire backside of the paper. When you lift the paper, the lines of your drawing should be transferred backwards to the linoleum block and thus will print as you originally intended.

Now, carefully carve (shave) out the spaces around the inside of the transfer which are *not* to be printed.

When the carving is complete, put ink on the glass inking surface, roll the brayer in ink and then onto the linoleum block. To ink the block evenly, roll ink up and down, then side to side, then up and down one more time. Arrange the printing paper on top of the block, exactly where you want the print to transfer. Press down, rolling a drinking glass or spoon over the entire surface to uniformly press the paper onto the inked design.

"Borrow" graphic and illustrative designs from printed cards or gift wrap, quilt and stencil patterns, famous artists, a child's drawing, reference books …

How to Make Your Own Envelopes

Make an outline of your folded card on a large piece of paper selected for your envelope. Measure with a ruler the side, top, and bottom flaps as shown in the illustration:

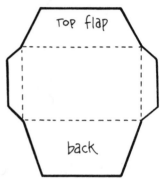

Cut as shown (you may cut several at once with a steady hand and good sharp scissors). Fold side flaps in first, then the bottom flap up, gluing the bottom flap to the side flaps with rubber cement or white glue. Fold top of envelope down, inside for hand-delivered correspondence, or glued around the top flap, for mailing. Be sure envelope is secure and dry before mailing. Dry the glued seam by pressing under a heavy book to ensure your card's safety while traveling through rain, hail, sleet, or snow ...

This is truly a lovely technique and deserves your attention if you are interested in learning the art of block printing. Much time, practice, and patience (as with all good things) are required, and I suggest you read more extensively about the how-to's of the process, or discuss your ideas with a skilled block printer, before attempting it yourself. Taken all into account, the final product will be well worth this extra effort.

MORE IDEAS FOR THE ENTERPRISING CARD-MAKER

How to Score Paper for Folding

To make a neat, professional-looking fold, draw a sharp tool (end of scissors, stylus, or table knife) along the straight edge of a ruler to make the fold line. Fold and press the side of the tool up and down the fold to put in a hard and fast crease.

Enlarging and Reducing Designs

If you plan to reproduce someone else's design (as long as you don't sell it, it's usually okay), use the grid method of enlarging and reducing. See page 226 in THE BACK OF THE BOOK for details.

Fun-Flavored Stamps

Cut pictures from a magazine in stamp-like squares. Lay face down on wax paper. Heat 1 t. flavored gelatin in 2 t. water, stirring until dissolved. Remove from heat and cool slightly. While still warm, coat onto the backs of magazine cutouts with a paintbrush. Let dry two to three days. Lick 'em and stick 'em on all letters to Santa and hand-delivered greetings. (Not acceptable to U.S. Postal Service!)

NOT FOR KIDS ONLY—MORE CARDS YOU CAN MAKE

If you haven't done anything like this since fifth grade art class, you will remember what you've been missing—it's creative, therapeutic, and just plain hands-on FUN! Make individually crafted cards for Very Important Persons with:

Stickers (sold individually or by the yard) for a bright focal interest attached to ink or crayon drawings.

Crayons, construction paper, color, and cutouts.

Paper doll Christmas characters, with an extra outfit or two (don't forget the tabs!).

 Making and sending postal card greetings saves you money—no envelopes and a cheaper stamp.

Paper colored with several different wax crayons. Cover over all with the side of a black crayon, and scratch out a colorful drawing with a toothpick.

A "leaded" frame made with black mat board or construction paper cut out to reveal "stained glass windows" of multicolored cellophane.

A collage with fabric, magazine cutouts, old card cutouts, photos, colored paper, Contact paper, wallpaper ...

Aluminum foil or papier-mâché sun, moon, and stars; shiny balls; cotton balls or popcorn to make snow; dyed or natural seeds and dried flowers glued on in a bouquet.

Doilies, fabric, ribbons, bows, lace, buttons, braid ... and other leftover sewing or upholstery/decorating materials to give dimension to Christmas trees, angels, snowmen, and monsters (a four-year-old's favorite Christmas character!).

Wrapped candy, gum, or lollipop attached with rubber cement.

Bright copper pennies, shiny nickels and dimes as favorite "tree" decorations. Attach with rubber cement.

Crisp green bills rubber cemented or stuck into a "pocket," "window," or slot.

Shiny adhesive tape or Contact paper cut into shapes and patterns, arranged on a slick paper background.

A 3-D card with paper fold-outs, popsicle sticks, fabric, trim ... that can hang on the tree.

A design colored with wax crayons on rough sandpaper and ironed over to heat-transfer onto paper.

An early American papercut or stencil affixed to a solid background.

Decorated brown paper lunch bags with a treat inside: "Here's hoping you've got a jolly Christmas ... in the bag!"

An Advent calendar sent Thanksgiving weekend for little ones to enjoy all December long ...

FOUR

Giving
The Greatest Gift of Christmas

It is in giving that we receive ...
—St. Francis of Assisi

Who can say it's selfless to be generous when we get such a tremendous kick out of the very act of giving? Creative generosity is a challenge bringing a world of fulfillment.

The idea that "it is more blessed to give ... " is irrefutable, and that's what makes Christmastime so blessedly joyous. After all, the birthday child Himself endowed our world with this fine and true sentiment from Acts 20:35.

No one should dread, resent, fear, or even hate Christmas shopping. It is, and should be, such a pleasure—looking to find that certain something that will bring a grin to the face of someone you love. An eager, anticipatory, generous, and happy attitude toward buying, and even better, making gifts for others makes it easier to discover just the right thing for each person on your list.

Simply remember that generosity is rarely measured in terms of money spent except by those too young or too unwise to know the difference. Gift-giving *should* be fun, especially at Christmas. But it is often easy to go overboard when you plunge into the spirit. Not only can an overabundance of giving be expensive, but it takes its toll in other ways. A huge gift list is formidable; the time required to shop, make, wrap, and deliver your many presents here, there, and everywhere will wear you out, diluting your best efforts and mushrooming every year when you don't know where to draw the line.

At Christmas, family comes first. Your best efforts and energies need to be directed inward, among those you love best. Sometimes we get so caught up trying to please and impress relative strangers that there's nothing left for the most important people in our lives, our immediate families. Lavish your best on these loved ones, particularly your time and attention, and branch out from there, expressing your fondness and appreciation as best you can.

Don't feel guilty if you can't give to everyone, or if what you give (in your opinion) isn't much. Remember, it really *is* the thought that counts.

I Will Never Forget …

the year my brother, Duncan, and I, as youngsters, compiled a scrapbook of our poems, art, and writings to give Mom and Dad as our special Christmas gift. We worked long and hard — well into the wee hours of December 25—preparing our grand presentation.

In all likelihood, I didn't sleep a wink that night. For the first time, I was too full of myself and the energy of eager anticipation —not about what Santa had in store for me, but what we had so lovingly prepared to give.

Not every Christmas will find us with an extraordinary gift to give, but if you have ever known the pride and joy of even one moment of superior generosity and thoughtfulness — whether your gift was a saggy dough ornament with sparkles or a multi-carat sparkler from Tiffany's — you remember the feeling and try to bring it back every holiday season.

Give as generously of yourself as you are able—confidently, happily, and in the best of the Christmas spirit.

CREATIVE KINDNESSES—GIVING OF YOURSELF

Some nice things you can do to make you and someone else feel extra-good at Christmas and put the true meaning of the season into perspective:

- Offer to help someone who's extra-stressed about the holidays, by sharing an hour or two of your time.
- Visit a shut-in or nursing home. Take a poinsettia, some cookies, or simply a few words to brighten a lonely day. And try not to forget these new friends the rest of the year.
- Share a pot of soup or a casserole with someone who deserves a break.
- Offer to babysit so a young mother can shop, address cards, decorate, wrap … or nap.
- Drive an elderly person or a non-driver to the shopping center and back home again. If you have time, help with the shopping.
- Offer to house-sit or dog-sit for traveling friends or neighbors. Take a paper bagful of simple games, gum, and a juice box for each child going on the trip.
- Adopt a family and give them a Christmas when they would ordinarily have none. Check social service agencies for names of the deserving.
- Share some quiet, reflective time with those who have lost loved ones during the year. The first Christmas without a beloved family member is bittersweet. If you are comfortable and close, encourage fond memories to lift the heart of the grieving.
- Try not to ask "What can I do?" Examine the situation at hand and look for the best way you can help ease someone else's burden, brighten a lonely time, or simply MAKE SOMEONE HAPPY.

MAKING GIFTS—A LABOR OF LOVE

Unless you really enjoy making things, *don't* feel inadequate because you don't. Confusing guilt with love (feeling the only worthy gift is a handmade one) will leave you frustrated, resentful, and smarting with a hammered thumb as well as a shoddy gift impatiently made to give.

Show your love in your own way, be it needlepointing a pillow, painting a picture, taking a photograph, writing a poem, buying a soft, furry teddy bear, or simply giving a great big Christmas bear hug!

If you *are* making all or most of your gifts, it's sometimes easiest and most satisfying to settle on an annual giving theme, making the same kinds of things for everybody—painted picnic baskets, personalized coffee mugs, dried flower wreaths … And if you have always wanted to make a papier-mâché floor lamp with hand-sculptured dough clay finials and a cross-stitched lampshade ... (really?), Chapter 12 in THE BACK OF THE BOOK contains how-to's on many craft techniques to bring your creative imagination to life.

HOW DO I DECIDE WHAT TO GIVE TO WHOM?

If you think you've got problems, how about that big order Santa has to fill? (In order to get through any difficult situation, imagine all the ways it could be worse.) It *is* overwhelming to begin the long process of Christmas shopping and giving. But an organized plan of action can alleviate fears of forgetting someone or not knowing what to get Grandad, and keep you from being "malled" to death during the holiday season. Keeping List #3 of the Twelve Lists of Christmas will be a big help in getting you on your way to developing the graceful ...

Art of Giving

> *It's not the gift, but the thought, that counts.*
> —Anonymous

"Anonymous" was absolutely right. Thoughtful giving is an art and a gift. Few people are as gifted in this art as my mother. While she may agonize unnecessarily often over "just the right thing" for any and everybody, she rarely misses.

All year long she listens for intended and unintended hints, keeps an eye and ear open for needs, mentally notes interests and enthusiasms, and gives accordingly. Yet Mom would modestly insist this is an accumulated talent—one you must perfect over years and years of trying. And that things were not always so wonderful. She occasionally misjudged over the years (like the time she gave me cookbooks and two chairs the year I was getting married, and what I really still wanted was a "toy" ... though the happy ending to that story is that Jim, later that sadly all-grownup afternoon, drove up the driveway and climbed out of the car with a life-sized teddy bear!).

All in all, Mom always works hard at it and works at it still, with the grandchildren. Her formula, in the early years, when there were fewer of us, was this: assemble a collection of items that fill a variety of specific gift categories.

GIFTS FOR THE GIVING

Terrific gifts come in all varieties and sizes. Perhaps a review of these will get your thinking in gear. The categories of items Mom used to spoil us rotten include the following:

Luxuries: Absolute non-necessities. Something you would never buy for yourself.

Practical Items: Something you need and can use that's not too terribly

No act of kindness, no matter how small, is ever wasted.
— Aesop,
"The Lion and the Mouse"

It is always so pleasant to be generous, though very vexatious to pay debts.
—Ralph Waldo Emerson, *Essays*

boring yet not so essential you have already bought it for yourself.

Toys: Not for kids only. Even the cookbook year, Mom and Dad gave each of us post-adolescents at least one silly plaything.

Clothing: Something frivolous or practical (if the shoe fits the style and personality, buy it).

Hobby or Sports Implements and Equipment: Accessories for active types.

Collectibles: Things you know will become dear to the heart of a collector.

Special Events/Special Interests: Something endearingly appropriate to commemorate an event of the past or to pave the way for future explorations and experiences (memorabilia, tickets, trips, subscriptions ...).

Books, Records, Art: Treasures for a culture lover's collection of favorites.

Pets: Gifts that can bring years of delight to the recipient (as long as they're accompanied by a signed permission slip from the eventual feeder, bather, flea picker, and house trainer). See "Giving Pets" page 53.

Humorous Gifts: The kind that require the most thought of all—only your best friends are allowed to laugh at you.

Money/Stock/Gift Certificates: Impersonal, yet rarely exchanged the day after Christmas, and even more rarely returned with a "no thanks."

Keeping the Year-Long Vigil for Ideas

A thoughtful giver is the Sherlock Holmes of Christmas—forever seeking clues for that very special gift. *Listen* when your recipient expresses dreamy desires, covets things in shop windows, mentions interests and needs. Recognize a hint when you hear it.

Look at what they buy for themselves, the kinds of things they have, what they like to do, favorite colors, books, music ... thoroughly examine tastes. Pay attention!

Stop! Immediately. Write down your findings on your permanent gift list.

TRISTAN: Braves baseball cap, dinosaur sipper cup, hooded sweatshirt (Duke blue), backpack for preschool ...

CAROLYN: miniature pitchers, recipe card box, red cotton sweater, *The Christmas Lover's Handbook*!

BETTY: photo album, ball for Sally, green sofa pillows

Giving Money—Passing the Buck

Though not much fun to shop for, money is a gift that will rarely be returned. Make the giving of this gift more personal and fun by hiding it inside a special envelope (usually available at banks and stationery stores). On the other hand, crisp new bills and shiny "silver" are happily found inside an interesting container: a piggy bank, new wallet or change purse, jewelry case, decorative box, personalized toothbrush travel case ...

Our Papa always draped the tree with envelopes to be opened and enjoyed by us all at the end of gift-giving. And Nana gave us a collection of coins minted the year of our birth. The older we get, the more valuable these become.

Buying Clothes as Gifts

Be absolutely certain about sizes. Carefully note color and style preferences, as indicated by what the recipient usually likes to wear. You might exercise remarkable stealth with a sneak and peek into the recipient's drawers and closet. Keep all receipts, tags, and care instructions.

Humorous Gifts

These are the most fun of all. Sure, they take a little more time and energy to create, but it's almost always worth it. There's nothing like a good sense of humor, and a clever way of showing it indicates a superior level of intelligence in my book.

Some ways to poke good-natured fun: concoct a slogan to be printed on a T-shirt; have a personalized bumper sticker printed for select friends; make a soap box for your favorite demagogue (filled with a good soap); design and make unusual clothing items—a horny baseball cap, Rudolph the Red-nosed jock strap (on page 57), handpainted boxers; print an appropriate quote or poem and have it framed or decoupaged onto a plaque or box; record a ridiculous audio or video exercise tape! What fun!

Giving Pets

You must realize from my writings that I'm an animal lover, though I admit that, as a much younger mother of three "monkeys," I preferred inanimate creatures as pets—at least during that particular phase of life. As head zookeeper, I found my own children most at home on the range, in the refrigerator, or hanging from the exercycle. That was enough animation for anybody! Cuddly stuffed creatures, at that critical stage, had enough personality for our household, even displaying a good-natured flexibility with regard to the external world that I envied myself. During those toddler years, we were satisfied to train the children to come when called, fetch the slippers, and acknowledge their excitement

**Make a Potentially
Unexciting Gift Fun ...**

• Add a "tacky" homemade bow tie to the collar of a new shirt.
• Put extra pizzazz into your gift wrap.
• Fill new socks with inexpensive "stocking stuffers."
• Put a sachet in the box with a flannel nightgown.
• Add a personalized bookplate to a copy of the year's bestseller.

Give a book or pamphlet of proper care instructions, a few days worth of food, bowl, pillow, toy ... and any other accessories to give your pet present a healthy start.

in some way other than jumping on our bed. I always felt, however, that the picture of the all-American family has a pet in it, and knew that someday our Prince would come.

So when Geoffrey turned nine and Zack and Linley were six, we got Sylka (of the one-of-a-kind Humane Society variety) and, frankly, she's been my most consistently obedient and trusted "offspring" ever since!

Clearly, for most people, it's necessary to reach a certain station in life before a pet will be welcomed into the household. And because I do care so much about animals (what mother of three+ wouldn't?), I think it's imperative they receive proper love and care from *willing* "parents."

Consider the following before buying or giving a pet at Christmas (or anytime):

1. How old is the child to whom you are giving the pet? Preschoolers cannot be expected to be fully responsible for an animal's care. Are the parents willing and able to supplement the time, energy, and expense of care?
2. What kind of living conditions will the pet have? An Irish setter doesn't belong in an apartment or even a small house. Select an animal appropriate to the surroundings: fish, birds, hamsters, and sometimes cats and small dogs are best suited to confined dwellings.
3. Will the pet receive the maximum amount of TLC in its new home? Don't subject any creature to an unfriendly, irresponsible, or non-receptive environment.

Another important factor to consider is the nature of Christmas itself. Christmas morning, particularly in the homes of small children, is a bright and lively time, rarely calm, never peaceful. Introducing a young puppy, kitten, or other sensitive young animal into the confusion may make for a bad start to the new relationship. Sometimes it's better to bring the pet into the family after the holidays when things have slowed down a bit, so the animal will receive the full attention newborn family members require and deserve.

Just What I Always Wanted ...

Consider some of these ideas for Christmas gifts to various age and interest groups. The possibilities are actually endless, and you should use the white space on this page to mark in ideas of your own. Just give it some extra thought and seek out the ...

❄ GIFTS JUST ABOUT ANYBODY WOULD LOVE

Christmas decorations and ornaments (give in advance of December 25 so they can be enjoyed that very season and forevermore)

Food and drink (see "A Festival of Feasting")

Decorative collectibles

Framed photographs

Tickets, subscriptions, coupons for special services, gift certificates

Personally-designed or printed notepaper, notecards, notepads, gift enclosure cards
Starter items or additions to a collection (china, silver, antique books ...)
A copy of *The Christmas Lover's Handbook*! (deliver in July!)

❄ LUXURY GIFTS (FOR THE PERSON WHO HAS EVERYTHING—YOU COULD AFFORD TO GIVE THEM!)

New Year's Eve champagne and caviar
Basket of gourmet treats
Foaming bath oil, a bottle of wine, and a good paperback
Tray of fully-prepared hors d'oeuvres
Anything from the fabulous Neiman Marcus, Horchow, or Metropolitan Museum of Art catalogs!

Baskets-Full

It takes a good deal of caring to fill a basket, stocking, or other container with uniquely appropriate gifts. But oh, what a treat for the lucky recipient!

Basket of Balls—tennis, golf, ping-pong ...
Gift Wrap Basket—Thanksgiving week, give a basket or giftbag full of Christmas gift wrap supplies: curling ribbons, gold cord, recycled paper, tissue, gift enclosure cards, tape ...
Bath Basket—soap, bubble bath, natural sponges, cream, powder, facial masks, a back brush ...
Gardener's Basket — soft work gloves, hand spade and fork, seed indicator or lanky stem stakes, special seeds or bulbs, perennials ...
Breakfast Basket—homemade jellies and jams, pancake or muffin mix, biscuit cutter, crepe pan, favorite recipes, country ham ...
Kitchen Basket—cookie cutters, wooden spoons, wire whisks, dish towels, small kitchen aids, his and her aprons or chef's hats ...
Artist's Basket—brushes, paint, sponge, palette ...
Picnic Basket—tablecloth, napkins, plastic plates, eating utensils, acrylic wineglasses, corkscrew, candleholders, plastic ants, bug spray ...
Crafter's Basket — see "Craft Workbasket" on page 226, and gather a collection of unusual supplies ...
Mother of Young Children—(to keep *her* from becoming a basket case) rainy day activities and art supplies, coping manuals, babysitting coupons, a night or weekend away from it all ... any kind of luxury gift that says, "Hang in there, Mom!"
Wine and Cheese Basket—bottles of wine, two wine glasses, corkscrew, specialty crackers and cheese, fruit, dessert wafers ...
Bread Basket—warm loaf or braid wrapped in a colorful new dish towel accompanied by a crock of herb butter, honey, jam ...
Gourmet's Basket—windowpots of fresh spices and herbs, mustards, international sauces, unusual kitchen accessories, pickled octopus ...

Write a funny or sentimental line or verse to accompany gift collections—for a personally loving touch ...

This is one Jim's anything but sluggish sense of humor came up with the year he gave my sister, Hilli (who wastes no love on slimy creatures), a can of escargots (snails!):

This present's for you since I like you so much:
Some snails, grubs, and slugs so smooth to the touch.
You won't have to swallow, they're still crawling around ...
Just place in your mouth—they'll find their way down!

Bill Collector's Basket—empty basket to hang near the door for incoming bills until they cry out to be paid (attach a card that says "May this be ever empty and your pockets ever full!")

Coupon Basket—brightly painted and filled with a package of lovingly clipped (unexpired) coupons, a "widget" for future clippings ...

Sewing or Needlework Basket—special sewing scissors, handmade pincushion, needles, thread, floss or yarn, specialty accessories ...

New Apartment or Newlywed Basket—Scotch tape, masking tape, stapler, large scissors, hole punch, multi-use tools ...

Host and Hostess Basket—coordinated paper, linen, or cloth napkins; coasters; napkin rings; ruffled toothpicks; glass stirrers ...

"My Favorite Grownup Kid" Basket—a fun collection of little toys and mind games for fun-lovers of all ages ...

Promises! Promises! Basket—special service coupons, gift certificates, promises (to be kept) for future adventure and fun ...

Basket of Baskets—a basket holding a nesting of more of the same ...

Use peach baskets, grocer's mushroom baskets, recycled Easter baskets, handmade vine baskets ... to make your baskets-full. Paint or stain them, line with cloth (Spanish moss, sphagnum, cellophane, colorful tissue ...), tie on a bow, and fill with your clever thoughtfulness and generosity.

Just for Fun

How do you deal with the spouse who always spends lots of money on something you're just dying to return but haven't the heart? How do you convince Ethel that you don't need *another* bathrobe this year? How do you give Harve that shot in the arm he needs to find you something really imaginative and exciting for Christmas? (My good friend, Ruthie Watts, says, "Give me anything ... as long as I don't have to plug it in!") For an ounce of prevention to the age-old problem of the generously inept gift-shopper, here are a few suggestions regarding ...

How to Tactfully Hint at Christmas (Is She Kidding?)

- Record a cassette tape of your "wants" and play it under his pillow at night so his subconscious will assimilate the list like a Berlitz Italian lesson.
- Needlepoint a pillow with your "would love to have's" artistically worked into the design and put it on the loveseat at the office. If your loved one doesn't notice, maybe the secretary will—and possibly this is the person who does all the shopping anyway (shame on any secretary who would!).
- Serve fortune cookies at dessert weekly starting in early December. Insert "You will buy your spouse _____" filling in the blank as indicated), making sure that particular prophecy hits your mate's plate.
- Make up your own words to "My Favorite Things" (from *The Sound of Music*) and sing loudly and passionately each morning in the

shower.

- Enlist the children to take him/her shopping. Dress each in T-shirts silk-screened with your sizes, color preferences, and selected gift hints.

Seriously now, be as thoughtful and generous to your spouse as you wish your spouse to be with you. Maybe conversion will occur by osmosis. And don't be afraid to blurt out your wants and needs. Or write a letter to your own Santa Claus. Nobody should be expected to read minds at Christmas or any other time.

Perfect Gifts for Husbands/Wives

— who deserve something frivolous, extravagant, practical, beautiful, stunning, fun … from their spouse and greatest friend (one and the same). He or she deserves the very best of your giving energies and thought:

clothing (if you've had success selecting this)

jewelry and accessories

interesting collectibles (start a collection if he/she doesn't already have one: animals, beer mugs, antique spoons, birds, unicorns, old books …)

gourmet utensils

plants or flowers, photos, decorative accessories for home or office

cook's book (for writing in favorite recipes, entertaining notes …)

desk calendar/daily organizer

personalized notepaper coupons for "free time," massage, manicure, tennis lessons …

tickets and dinner—a night on the town

hotel weekend away in bleak January (Wrap gift certificate in a slinky nightie! "He" might even enjoy receiving this from "her.")

hobby accessories

sports or exercise equipment

art, music, books

electronic gadgets or "toys"

old college mementos (Duke basketball, Princeton jogging shorts, Indiana sweatshirt …)

Call a best friend, work partner, decorator or fellow sports or hobby enthusiasist for a little help if you're stumped for ideas.

Gag Gifts

Add laughter to the smiles on Christmas morning. Every package opening needs some of these—a joke or memory shared between just you two, a clever gadget or "fun" item (tacky Christmas underwear or tie, argyle socks, a "How to Successfully Fry Chicken" cookbook, "We interrupt this marriage to bring you the football season" plaque …).

Gag Gifts Add Fun

Make a Rudolph the Red-Nosed Jock Strap: To an athletic supporter, add craft eyes, brown felt antlers, a red felt tongue on a painted-on mouth, and a large red pompom for the nose! Great fun!

An Offer They Can't Refuse

Everybody can use a little help now and then. Be on the lookout for ways to lighten someone's load: be it yardwork, home repair, baby-sitting, elderly parent care, legal advice, chauffeuring, tax preparation, house-sitting ...

Perfect Gifts for Grandparents and Great-Grandparents

—who want nothing, deserve the world.

photographs and/or frames
recorded audio or videocassette of the kids (singing, reading, reciting)
scrapbook of the children's art, writing, school photos ...
plaster handprints
framed children's artwork, poetry
paperweights
placemats
bookmarks or bookplates
painted clay pot and plant
child's drawing reproduced as stationery or notecards
framed family tree
bound genealogical family study
Christmas wreath, doormat, mailbox decoration
Christmas tie, sweater, or socks
painted mailbox (and the promise of lots of letters)
garden seed indicator stakes
needlework supplies
hand-painted ceramic plates or mugs
hand-painted linen napkins
back-rub rollers
gourmet foods
jogging shoes

Perfect Gifts for Friends and Neighbors

—the boy/girl/cup-of-sugar supplier next door.

any and all kinds of foods and kitchen treats
sweets-filled cookie jar or canister
baskets-full of ...
printed and personalized "to and from" gift enclosure cards
calligraphed or hand-painted quotes (framed or on plaques)
gingerbread house or gumdrop tree
ornaments or decorations
weekly family activity calendar/shopping list pad/chores organizer
secretly shot candids of their kids, pets ... enlarged and framed
Advent calendar or wreath
Christmas breakfast goodies
matching aprons (his and hers) or other his/hers items
Christmas travel activity bag: crayons, drawing pads, highway bingo, all-day suckers, juice boxes, gum ...
two or three hours of babysitting, yardwork, house-painting ... coupons
busy holidays supper basket or pizza delivery coupon

Perfect Gifts for Secretaries and Bosses

—to seal a good working relationship.

food and/or drink
tickets or gift certificates for special services
office and desk accessories
personalized memo pads, stationery, stamps
plants or flowers
entertainment or restaurant coupon books
desk-side cookie or candy jar (filled)
collectibles
perfume
wardrobe accessories
jewelry
baskets of potpourri
baskets-full of ...
One friend gave her secretary an appointment for a "color evaluation" for planning makeup and wardrobe. She loved it!

Perfect Gifts for Special Service People

—an extra thank-you for hairdresser, housekeeper, babysitter, yardman, paperboy ...

money envelopes or gift certificates
food gifts (Christmas turkey, ham, wine, fruit ...)
gifts personalized to the profession (often available in catalogs and gift shops, these might also originate from your highly creative mind)
office or shop decoration
vanity car tag or bumper sticker
special service coupons "at *your* service"

Perfect Gifts for Teachers

—give an "A" for loving attentiveness.

fancy foods and baked goods
containers or baskets-full of ...
small luxury items
art, books, music
poinsettia or other plant (attach a note written by your child, saying, "Thank you for helping me grow!")
personalized apple ornament

"Fantastic Friend" Tree Ornament

Insert a looped ribbon in between and glue the backs of two small mirrors together. Attach a hand-printed card with the following verse:

Hang this mirror on your tree
For you and all your friends to
    see ...
If you look in it carefully,
You'll see someone who's dear to
    me!

—Emily Fennel

The twelve days of Christmas originated in medieval England, where the royal court indulged in unparalleled merry-making, feasting, and the presenting of gifts to the king.

Twelve Days of Christmas Candle

To be delivered on the twelfth day before Christmas ... Paint (with acrylics) the numbers counting off to Christmas Day (12, 11, 10, 9, 8 ...) at equal intervals down the side of a stout candle. Insert in a candleholder wrapped in cheerful Christmas ribbon and present to special friends with this note:

Place this little candle
Where your family gathers 'round,
And count the days 'til Christmas
As you watch it burning down.
Light your Christmas candle
On the thirteenth of December,
Then burn each day that follows ...
Don't forget, now, to remember!
By the time you reach the candle's
   end,
It will then be Christmas Day
But you'll never reach the end
Of the love we send your way!
             The Poes

---

ribboned basket of fresh crisp apples
ornaments or holiday decoration
handmade bookmark or bookplates
craft smock or apron
potpourri or pomander (see page 107)
homemade flower press (see page 98)
Make your own bath salts: Let little hands mix Epsom salts (from a drug store) with a few drops of food coloring to tint and a few drips of perfume to scent. Present in an apothecary jar or other clever container.

Perfect Gifts for Newly-Graduated Singles

—just getting started.

date book or calendar (filled with all family birthdays/anniversaries)
picture frame or scrapbook
personalized stationery with new address
travel accessories
"house" warming supplies
subscription to favorite publication
tickets to concert, show, sports event, dinner ...
holiday decorations
baskets-full of ... tools, home accessories, kitchen aids, paper supplies

Perfect Gifts for Newly Marrieds

—on a shoestring budget.

starter tool set (or other household starter items)
dinner for two or theater tickets
picture frame and candid wedding shot
his and hers items
silver, crystal, china pattern items
houseplants
kitchen tool "bouquet" or wreath
holiday decorations (get them started with a memorable first Christmas)
picnic basket
herb, spice, tea, flavored coffee ... collection
frivolous decorative accessories

Perfect Gifts for the Newly Pregnant

—expecting at least one little surprise.

maternity clothes
parenting and birthing books
pickles and chocolate ice cream
small picture frame for nursery photo

gift certificate for future family photo
"Mom" and "Dad" mugs, T-shirts, visors ...

Perfect Gifts for the Due-ly Pregnant

—give something for Mom—the baby will get plenty.

(same as above)
expanded Christmas apron ("How 'bout a kiss for old jelly belly!")
hospital "necessaries" (champagne, paperbacks or magazines, lingerie
   suitable for nursing, bath powder, new travel kit filled with overnight sundries ...)
coupons for a full dinner to be delivered soon after delivery
coupons for babysitting, baby nurse, diaper service, disposable diapers
fancy pink and blue bows for the mailbox (maybe she'll have one of each!)
baby book (with a promise you will fill it in the first two years)
film and a photo album

Who's Next?

Many Christmas customs and superstitions were related to marriage and romance. According to Swedish tradition, the girl who finds a ring hidden in the Christmas rice pudding will be the next to marry.

SPECIAL INTEREST GROUPS

Sports Fans—tickets to a game, bleacher seat cushions, lap blanket,
   thermos and sandwich carrier, sports publication subscription, favorite team souvenirs ...
Golfers—Lucite boxes or a mug filled with colorful tees (glue a golf ball
   on top with a craft eye attached; write "Keep your eye on the ball!"
   on the side with a permanent marker), knitted club covers, glove,
   golf cap, personalized golf balls ...
Fishermen—flies, hooks, fly-tying kit, metal tape (for measuring the one
   that got away!)
Tennis Players—handpainted visor, heavy cotton socks, handmade rac-
   quet covers, colorful sweatbands, tennis ball wreath ...
Swimmers—professional-style goggles, ear plugs, large raft for "aprés-
   swim," waterproof radio, ribbon display board or trophy shelf ...
Skiers—silk or thermal underwear, wool socks, gloves, ski mask, sun-
   glasses, coupons for lift tickets, sunscreen ...
Doctor, Lawyer, Indian Chief—professional specialty gifts, office accessories, subscription to professional publications ...
Book Lovers—illustrated coffee table book, antique books, handmade or
   personalized bookmark or bookplates, miniature reading lamp ...
Music Lovers—coveted compact discs or cassettes, stereo equipment or
   accessories, concert tickets, decorative instruments or musical
   prints, pertinent literature (Pavarotti's bio or subscription to *Stereo
   Review, Rolling Stone* ...)
Art Lovers—membership to a national or local museum, antique frame,
   numbered and signed print, art book, art supplies, prepared canvas,
   specialized lamp, easel ...
Fitness Fanatics—health club membership, warmup suit, tote bag, exercise or instructional video, weights, first aid kit ...

Record-Keeping

Always keep a record of what you have already bought. Picking up things here and there during the year and hiding them away may find you with an excess for one child, not enough for another. You may forget you already bought the oil paints last summer on sale, or just exactly where it is you hid the marbles. And at Christmastime, the last thing you want to do is lose your marbles.

It's good to keep these lists over the years, for posterity, if there is room in your files. They provide a fun history of growing up, of changing interests and changing minds. An older child's previous list may give you some ideas about what younger brothers and sisters might like when they reach the same age. Or when yours are suddenly teenagers and your mind has been vacuumed of ideas for tiny nieces and nephews, a look back can refresh your memory.

Vegetarians—juicers, food dehydrator, subscription to *Vegetarian Times*, salad spinner, miniature herb garden, vegetable steamer …
College Students — telephone credit card, subscription to hometown newspaper, small coffeemaker, clock radio, cassette player, money …
Handypersons — hardware store gift certificates, tuition for a special course, box of household adhesives, special interest book or magazine, multi-drawer cabinet, heavy-duty extension cord …
Photographers — special lens filters, film and batteries, picture frames, camera bag, developing gift certificates …

YOU DON'T HAVE TO GIVE A GIFT TO EVERYONE WHO GIVES YOU ONE

Assume, though it may not always be true, that one who gives a gift is giving out of the pure goodness of his heart, and not in expectation of a gift in return. A sincere and gracious thank-you will often suffice in return for an unexpected, unreciprocated Christmas gift.

If, however, you feel uncomfortable with this, have a few "staple" gifts in your Santa's bag to give to unexpected gift-givers. These can be kept around year-long for holidays and other times you have the urge to be generous. Start a gift collection now:

- Tie a current issue of a popular magazine in a ribbon and give as a promise of a one-year subscription (don't forget to mail in the subscription card!).
- Pack an assortment of cookies or candies in decorative tins and have on hand for spontaneous giving.
- Order extra poinsettias and use in a cluster decoration. Present one from the grouping as needed.
- Decorate a small tree or bare branches with homemade ornaments, miniature toys, cookies, potpourri bags … and offer a choice from the tree to expected as well as surprise guests.
- Tie the bottles in a wine rack with red ribbons. These can serve as decoration, and if needed, make lovely ready-to-go gifts.
- Hang a large "Santa's bag" by the chimney with wrapped "funstuff" inside. Offer your guests a reach into your Christmas "grab bag" for a friendly holiday treat.
- Keep small decorative boxes, hospitality accessories (cocktail napkins, cheese slicer, coasters …), notepaper, jellies and preserves, attractive baskets, fancy soaps … on hand for anyone's enjoyment.

Be on the lookout for super sales year round. See "Tasteful Presentations," page 193, for more "staple" gifts.

WHO'S NAUGHTY AND NICE?

Perhaps the only thing that's more fun than being a child at Christmas is being a child's parent. Jim and I always have a ball going from toy store to sporting goods store to record store, trying to keep ourselves from buying EVERYTHING we see. Maybe the "kid" in us still loves toys as much as any five-year-old. But it's also the excitement we get anticipating the surprised look on early Christmas morning faces (though, now that we have teenagers, the Christmas morning faces are sometimes grumpy because *we* couldn't wait for *them* to get up!).

While I find the most difficult aspect of shopping for kids to be "What should we put back?", some folks need a gentle nudge to remember what it was like to be three. Though, just as with snowflakes, no two children are alike, there are basic characteristics of age groups that can give some idea about when to buy the Louis Pasteur chemistry kit, finger paints, or personal computer with full set of software. Whether shopping for your own children or grandchildren, nieces and nephews, or little neighbors, consider the following guidelines for buying and making the "most favoritest" gifts of all.

Along with the store-bought kind, teach little ones by example to treasure their earth by recycling the old into something new and completely different.

Infants

Stimulate brand-new senses with awakening experiences in movement, color, sound, touch ...

mobiles	toy mirror
teethers	crib gym
squeeze and squeak toys	cloth blocks
noisemakers/rattles	tub toys

For the very young, be particularly careful about toy safety. Look for objects that are washable, too big to swallow, and that have no removable parts smaller than 1¼" diameter and 2¼" deep (federal guidelines). Edges should be smooth, paints and dyes non-toxic, and any cord or string should be no longer than 8-10 inches.

Give young babies clean colorful plastic lids and coffee scoops in a coffee can. A great homemade toy to give hours of holding and chewing pleasure.

My sister-in-law, Jean, gave her daughter Lexi a wonderful first Christmas gift—a lovingly handwritten and illustrated "book" about the wonders of their new life together. Beautiful, and certain to be a treasure to Lexi always.

Twelve to Eighteen Months

Test newly-acquired skills, encourage safe adventure and discovery. Continue to stimulate with color, shapes, textures, and sounds ...

Someday We'll Laugh About ...

the surprising culmination of weeks playing Santa.

It seems a universal phenomenon — we spend hours upon hours fighting the crowds in toy stores, department stores, boutiques, and gift shops. Everything is painfully assembled. Gifts are carefully wrapped, tied, and bowed. The assortment under the tree is awesome and exciting. Will she squeal with delight when she sees the hand-painted dollhouse (I even made tiny cushions to match the exquisite hand-sewn draperies)? Will he be ecstatic over the shiny new bike? I can't wait to see him setting up this neat electric train set. The automatic robot is fantastic!

And the entire day, from Christmas morning 'til night, what does he play with? What gift never leaves his hands, even during breakfast, lunch, and dinner? Which single item is tucked neatly against his breast as he finally settles down for another long winter's nap?

It's the $1.98 Matchbox car I picked up on Christmas Eve — just to have one more stocking stuffer. Who would have guessed???

Santa Claus

The tradition of gift-giving during the holiday season began even before there was a Christmas. Ancient Romans exchanged gifts during the winter festival of Saturnalia. This custom, in addition to the giving of gifts by the Three Wise Men and the legend of a popular fourth century saint named Nicholas, have contributed to the current presence of gaily-wrapped gifts under our tree.

Saint Nicholas was Bishop of Myra (now Demre, Turkey) in the days of Diocletian's anti-Christian rule. It was said that one night, on hearing the sad tale of three unmarried daughters of a poor man, Bishop Nicholas secretly dropped three bags of gold into their window as they slept. They discovered the miraculous gift of a dowry the moment they awoke.

The tale of this and other acts of generosity by Nicholas endeared him to Christians near and far. During Nicholas' reign as Bishop, Constantine came into power, and in 313 A.D., the Edict of Milan finally allowed tolerance of Christianity. After his death, Nicholas was made a saint, and the legend of the secret giver of gifts spread throughout Europe. St. Nicholas Day, December 6, is still a favorite holiday in some countries where children await the arrival of a kind and generous old fellow in dignified Bishop's robes bringing longed-for surprises. Due to its proximity to Christmas, St. Nicholas Day's gift-giving was moved to December 25 in many countries as part of the holiday celebration.

indoor riding toys	rock and stack toys
large soft balls	surprise pop-up books
push/pull toys	colorful animals

Thread wooden spools on a thick string. Give a net bagful of plastic cups and spoons for the tub. Scooping and pouring out are favorite pastimes of this youthful crowd.

Eighteen Months to Two Years

Exercise that boundless energy, challenge skills, aid the intense desire to imitate grownups and older siblings …

play phone	Sit 'n Spin
hammering bench, tools	shape sorter
climbing equipment	grocery cart
riding toys	doll stroller

Fill an old pocketbook or briefcase with costume jewelry, a wallet, handkerchief, fat crayons, and newsprint pads … Put an assortment of play equipment (binoculars, thermos, outdoor tools) in a backpack.

Two to Three Years

Encourage learning and awareness of the world around them, coordination and imagination development … (A busy "two" is rarely terrible!)

functional moving toys	trucks and cars
lock and snap blocks	dolls/puppets
musical instruments	modeling clay
wheelbarrow	cardboard "brick" blocks
color and shape games	sing-along videos

Attach furniture casters or wheels to a wooden crate. Sand, paint, and tie on a pull string for a funky little red wagon. Load up with plastic soda bottles filled with noisemakers (large jingle bells, wood blocks, plastic dinosaurs …).

Three to Four Years

Fine motor and more sophisticated language skills are beginning to sharpen. There is a conflict between the desire to be independent and a fear of getting too far away from security. Possessions are carried everywhere. Also, threes are usually happy to play dress-up …

tricycle	medical kits
plastic tea set	crayons/scissors
Legos	puzzles
costumes/hats	records/tapes/videos
hardwood blocks	cuddly soft animals

A decorated cardboard box, personalized plastic container, or hand-stitched bag would thrill this age—anything useful for carrying around all their "stuff." Fill a change purse with play money, or stitch up a fake fur sleeping bag to take to Grandma's.

Four to Six Years

Begin the age of collections ... passive and aggressive personalities tend to define themselves sharply ... continue to stimulate creativity, fantasy, and imagination ...

games	plastic bat & ball
Etch-a-Sketch	Tinker Toys and Legos
bike with training wheels	miniature figures (whatever is the
easel/chalkboard	latest craze!)

Make sock puppets with old socks, felt, craft accessories. Paint a playhouse on a huge cardboard box or stitch to a card table cover that hangs to the floor.

Six to Ten Years

Enter the age of outrageous sexism, when peer pressure also begins to play a tremendous role in likes, dislikes, and "hates"! Don't force a child one way or another, but provide and encourage all options ...

two-wheeler bike	easy-reader books
puppets	discovery "toys": microscope, mag-
ant farm	nets, butterfly net, "bug box,"
advanced puzzles	stamp album, magnifying
art/hobby supplies	glass, camera, chemistry set,
sports uniforms	foreign language tapes
learning games	
music/art/videos	

Begin a scrapbook for certificates, report cards, school art and writings, photographs, autographs, souvenirs ...

Every Child Needs One

These are the possessions that have withstood the test of time—ones that will remain precious long after the last Barbie Dream House and Highway of Terror multi-looped car ramp have gone to that giant junk heap in the sky ...

riding toy/bike	wooden puzzles
stuffed animals/dolls	records/tapes
books	musical instruments
balls	Matchbox cars
building blocks	

And He Still Lives Today!

It was apparently Clement Clarke Moore who transformed the tall stately Saint Nicholas into a "fat jolly old elf" and the Americanization of the Dutch *San Nicolaas* or *Sinter Claes* became our beloved Santa Claus.

In 1863, Thomas Nast, a German-born illustrator who also created the Democratic donkey and the Republican elephant, drew an elfin Santa sitting in his North Pole workshop, studying a behavior book, and recording the names of "who's naughty and nice."

Haddon Sundblom, illustrating Coca-Cola ads in the 1920s, depicted our current image of Santa, enlarging him back to the imposing grandfather figure we all know and love today.

And in case there is any doubt, in the worldwide magical kingdom of Christmas love and sharing, "Yes, Virginia, there *is* a Santa Claus!"

Fun, Inexpensive Little Gifts for Small Fry

Something for the carpool, scout troop, soccer team, neighbors, school friends:

Advent calendar
Christmas stickers
funny soaps
printed gift enclosure cards/ bookplates
refrigerator magnets
reindeer antlers
12 days of Christmas candle (page 60)
arts and craft supplies: ink stamp, crazy erasers, Playdoh, crayons, template and ruler, sidewalk chalk …
personalized: pencils, cup, cocoa mug, toothbrush, visor, notepad, bookmark, hair ribbons, shoelaces, flashlights …
And for Older, Wiser Friends: comic books, baseball cards, posters, team souvenirs
Jewelry made from: puzzle pieces, laminated comics, film negatives, old jewelry pieces and watch faces, dominos
Gilded Baroque Picture Frame (page 124)

TALK ABOUT TOYS

- Consider toy safety above all—not just for the intended child, but also his younger siblings and pets.
- Select toys that you are capable of assembling. Be realistic about your "toy engineering" skills (or have the store do it!). Teenagers might earn extra Christmas money selling out their time and effort to doing this for harried young moms and dads.
- Encourage development of reasoning skills, imagination, and creativity … physical and mental exercise. Strengthen coordination—both fine and gross motor skills. Introduce a variety of learning experiences. Toys are one of a child's primary links to the world.
- Encourage talents and successes, minimize frustration and failure (like those stupid scissors even an adult can't cut with). Don't force a child without adequate fine motor coordination to become an artist, or a passive child to be unreasonably active and athletic. Offer opportunities to *choose* experiences.
- Don't buy so many toys that the child is overwhelmed (and underdeprived) and don't buy "grownup" toys (CD player, private telephone or television, microscope, chemistry set …) too early.
- If you see something you want, buy it—particularly if it is a popular item (doll, electric train, one-of-a-kind …). You'll be devastated if you go back and it's gone. If you're not positive this is a keeper, see if it can be returned or put on hold. Some of the most common toys run out at Christmas (anybody remember the Cabbage Patch frenzy of '83?).
- Put away some old toys before Christmas. They'll become new again some rainy day about February or March.

Teenagers

Do we never know what to give teenagers because they already have everything? Or is it because by this age they're so individualistic that it takes a little more work to come up with that one terrific gift idea? I prefer to think the answer falls principally in the latter quagmire.

Teenagers are an assorted lot of strong personalities (believe me, I'm treading in the quagmire even as we speak!). Take a close look at what and whom they're interested in, what they enjoy doing, and what makes them laugh. Celebrate what makes them themselves.

Consider musical, literary, and entertainment choices, clothing tastes, and "newly-growed" status items …

personal car keys	"date" calendar
makeup and beauty gook	tickets/subscriptions/travel
jewelry	promises/summer adventures
travel accessories	favorite college/team/music items,
"little black book"	clothing, posters …

Make a collage, shadowbox, or album of lifelong mementos and photographs. Decorate it with discarded and outgrown toys, favorite food labels, bumper stickers, newspaper headlines, best report card, and any other items that describe a uniquely unforgettable life story.

Guaranteed to Make You a Favorite Santa!

personalized or hand-painted "anything" (visor, toothbrush, comb and brush, bulletin board, sneakers, art box, footstool, name tape, address labels, denim jacket …)

"My Own Room" fun accessories (wall hangings, pillows, mobiles, toy storage, hope chest …)

painted toy box (paint on a car or train track, stove top, play village … for utmost entertainment opportunities)

"grownup" things (pocketbook, makeup, tools, tea set …)

miniatures and animal figures

containers (boxes, bags, and totes for: toys, art supplies, overnight gear, blocks, and other "kiddie litter")

bulletin board, chalkboard, easel

costumes and trendy clothing items

sports equipment and accessories

theater tickets/movie gift certificates

arts and crafts supplies

hobby kits (science, magic, models …)

magazine subscriptions (*National Geographic World, Ranger Rick, Seventeen* —a big hit with 13-year-olds!)

juvenile (the stupider the better) joke book

wall map of the "new" world, circus posters, team pennants …

Fit Part "A" into Part "B6" …

Assemble everything in advance of Christmas Eve, if at all possible. Nothing can ruin a perfectly good holiday like one's newly discovered incompetence understanding toy assembly instructions, the inability to fit A in B6 or find a missing whatchamacallit for the whatzit. You will also have a chance to pick up forgotten batteries or that $1/16"$ drill bit you needed to be a Master Constructor! A thin friend of mine uses the occasion of Christmas Eve to leisurely put out Santa Claus gifts, fill the stockings, enjoy a drink, a crackling fire, and an entire pound of M&M's with her Mr. Claus. Heaven!

Letters to Santa

When all else fails, why not resort to the trick Santa keeps up his furry red sleeve—the letter to Santa.

By the time they're old enough to talk, every child will be more than willing to dictate his personal request letter to Santa. When writing skills gain at least minimum proficiency, a laborious listing of hopes and best wishes for down-the-chimney delivery might just occupy a good quiet hour or two.

Letters to Santa, stealthily retrieved after they are taken out "to be mailed," are treasures to be saved over the years. What fun to bring them out in Christmases to come and chuckle over the fervent desires and literary expressions charmingly applied by the growing child.

For older family members, try this photocopied "Letter to Santa," distributed by hand or by mail well in advance of the holidays. Include a return envelope and completion deadline, conspicuously noted. Use as a handy reference for making gift-shopping practical and a whole lot easier … still endowing Christmas morning with some happy surprises.

Dear Reader:

Photocopy several copies of this list and distribute among family members well in advance of the holidays (perhaps in the first mail after Thanksgiving). Include a return envelope and completion deadline conspicuously noted above. Use this as a handy reference for making shopping a little easier, and Christmas morning will be full of happy surprises!

A FEW OF MY FAVORITE THINGS

Dear _____:

Happy holidays! Please complete the following and return to me at the North Pole via (_____address_____) by (___date___).

DEAR SANTA,

This year please bring me:

1._____

2._____

3._____

4._____

My sizes (this year) are:

Pants _____   Shirt/Blouse _____   Dress _____

Jacket _____   Shoes _____   Gloves _____

My favorite colors (this year) are: _____

_____

My favorite stores are: _____

_____

I like to collect: _____

_____

I absolutely do not need another: _____

_____

Signed: _____

Stocking Stuffers

Some of the "funnest" stuff of Christmas is found in the stockings. In the "old days," the stocking was the only receptacle of gifts from Santa, dating back to the legends of Saint Nicholas himself. Now we overdo it a little, with lots of BIG STUFF from the old fellow.

Here's hoping the tradition of stocking stuffing lives on forever, because this Santa loves picking out lots of neat little stuff for each little and big kid on my shopping list!

stickers and address labels
colored tape
socks or slippers
markers
mittens or gloves
spiffy Band-aids
personalized pencils
miniatures
toothbrush and travel case
small picture frame
art and craft supplies
five-year diary (with key!)
change purse (loaded!)
play makeup/jewelry
small flashlight
fun buttons/pins
miniature books/comics

subscription card
blowing bubbles
gift certificates
puppets
trading cards
batteries/toy accessories
tooth fairy pouch
fruits, nuts, candy, and money
coupon books from Mom and Dad
    can promise a day without
    chores, a trip to a movie or
    show, a playing partner for
    favorite games and activities,
    going out to lunch or break-
    fast with Dad, a self-created
    dinner menu …

Shopping with the Kids …

If taking each and every one of the kids anywhere near a store frightens, frazzles, or depresses you, try this: Go on a fact-finding mission—alone. Make a list (your own "catalog") of affordable gifts the children might want to give to each of their friends and family, including the store in which you found them. At home, let the children do their "shopping" from the list, then you can go back and pick it up. Sometimes two trips are worth the nightmare of one!

From Grandma and Grandpa

While many of you Grandmas have traded in your full cookie jars for a briefcase and you Grandpas are out there training for a marathon, your importance and relationship to a grandchild haven't changed. You are the link to family history.

Generation to generation, nothing can replace the treasures of our own past, both tangible and intangible. History and memory are the batteries that energize our culture and vitalize our collective soul. Give your grandchildren something lasting of their own heritage:

family mementos (include a card explaining history and significance)
an old family ornament
framed family "tree" (genealogy)
cassette recording of family stories (about the child's parent, past Christ-
    mas traditions and memories, re-animation of kinfolk now deceased,
    family history and funny anecdotes)
videocassette reproduction of "ancient" home movies

One of my favorite Christmas gifts ever is a little gold coin from my grandmother—an 1853 gold dollar that was originally found, newly-minted, in the toe of my great-grandmother's stocking. The monetary value is nothing to the value I place on this piece of my own family history.

Another exciting tradition particularly appropriate for grandparents is the giving of a "coming of age" gift. On the Christmas following a special birthday (10, 13, 16 …), you might present a grandchild with a significant gift of recognition: good quality dictionary or leather-bound Bible; adult watch; real jewelry; U.S. Savings Bond or stock certificate; engraved item; framed family coat of arms; trip to New York, the clan's native country or geographical region, Disneyland …

Don't Just Stand There ...

Take something to do while standing in the interminable lines of Christmas shoppers: a recipe book for future meal planning, needlework, a magazine, or even Harlequin's latest romance. Waiting can be traumatic when you're in a hurry and have a million things to do. Relax, pull out that paperback or last week's newspaper, and enjoy the twenty-minute gift of time from the department store. You will be amazed at how quickly you get to the head of the line!

LAST-MINUTE TIPS ON GIFT-SHOPPING

- Keep your gift list handy for year-round updates, jotting down notes and ideas.
- Narrow lists to three ideas with a #1 priority and two alternatives for each gift recipient.
- Take the list wherever you go out in shopping land, in case you happen into places that might have just what you're looking for.
- While shopping, take notes on things you see, possibilities for future purchase, batteries and other supplies required, inadequate information (does Alston already have a blue sweater with detachable angel wings?).
- List shopping centers and stores in order of convenience, according to location and time available to shop.
- Keep several basic, staple gifts available for last-minute emergencies and impulse giving.
- If you buy gifts during the year, wrap them immediately and record the purchase (hiding place included) in your notes.
- Keep all receipts and charge slips in one place in the event a return or an exchange is in order. If you shop early, be sure the store will honor returns months later.
- Have the children write or dictate a "Santa" list or letter.
- Take each child shopping (individually, if at all possible, with enough extra cash to get ice cream) to make a "Santa" survey *and* for picking out gifts for siblings, parents, friends ... thus teaching the meaning of giving, as well as receiving.
- Consider shopping by catalog—easy, fun, and it saves gas and hassle (unless you hate the prospect of being on the mailing list of 2,000 catalog companies next year).
- Try to buy during the year—it's easier on the budget and on you. Besides, you may regret not having picked up that "darling" ashtray from Ocean City!
- Allow plenty of time for personalization, monogramming, alterations ...
- DON'T WAIT UNTIL THE LAST MINUTE, if you can possibly help it. As I write this, it's actually December 23. And, because I don't always follow my own advice, I still have shopping to do. It's rainy, the streets and stores are massively crowded, everything good is already wrapped up under somebody else's tree, and I've spent too much time driving around looking for a parking space, finally tracking an individual emerging from the mall only eventually to sit and watch them sit and wait for some fellow passenger ... it's enough to kill even the most upbeat of spirits.
- When the going gets tough, return home immediately or take a break. If possible, don't ever shop when you've lost that refreshed, positive, and enthusiastic outlook we all need for generous giving.

FIVE

Presentation
Wrapping Gifts with Imagination

Presents endear absents …
—Charles Lamb

Even the most ordinary of gifts becomes extraordinary when wrapped in imaginative packaging. The very curiosity and anticipation aroused by an unusual package are often more thrilling than the actual gift inside. (Wouldn't you agree that a large portion of the excitement of Christmas is in the anticipation?) A spirit of promise and hope is well in keeping with the warmest meaning of the holidays. And if your insides match the outsides with a generosity of thoughtfulness, most certainly you will endear yourself to all the ones you love.

Personalize your packages. Use color, ribbons, decorations, and accessories. Trick the sneakiest package shakers and squeezers by disguising the gift in a misleading container (a tiny gift hidden inside a huge box, a huge gift hidden somewhere else—with clues wrapped up in a small box placed under the tree!). Add a jingle, squeak, deceptive texture, or weight to disguise your present. Liven up package opening with some clever surprises!

MATERIALS FOR WRAPPING

metallic paper	wallpaper leftovers
fabric	hand-painted paper/bags
tissue paper	trimmed/needleworked bags
foil	brightly-colored scarves
colored cellophane	cloth napkins
stamped newsprint	decorative boxes, bags, or gift wrap
comic strips	

Tricks of the Trade

• Pin fancy doilies onto a large piece of craft paper and spray paint to achieve a lacy effect.

Surprise Packaging—
Instead of Paper

Hand-paint a large burlap sack with Christmas greetings and decorations. Tie with raffia to enclose a large or bulky gift.

For another neat surprise gift, hide something small in a fabric bag and tie it onto the tree when no one is looking …

Gift bags, though not inexpensive, can be used over and over again … as can gift boxes.

Cookie tins also make good sturdy gift containers, especially for small breakables. After Christmas, use these to store fragile ornaments, rolled ribbon, cookie cutters …

Wrap exotic treasures in "angel cloth" — bright scarves tied with cord or ribbon.

Recycle used tissue paper and other gift papers to wrap ornaments and other decorations for storage. Roll used paper smoothly onto an old tube secured by a rubber band.

Make Your Own Gift Boxes

With your own clever decoration.

Use a heavyweight paper or cardboard. Determine the size of the box needed and measure the six sides (top, bottom, and four sides) as shown. Score the folds gently with a knife or straight-edge for a good sharp fold. See illustration. Be careful not to cut too deeply. Tuck tabs in and glue or tape together, if necessary, for strength. Paint, stencil, color, cover with fabric or paper …

Present posters in a postal tube painted, covered, trimmed …

Cover an old cigar box with pretty fabric and make a velvet cushion for the inside to cradle jewelry, perfume, money, or even a pair of socks …

Let a lovely or unusual container incite wonder and surprise!

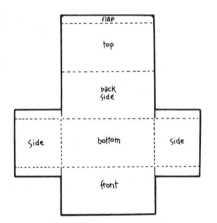

- Bags are the easiest gift wrap accessories. Buy white bakery bags. Decorate and tie with brightly colored yarn or ribbon. Simple.
- Wrap a huge gift in the largest-sized green plastic leaf bag you can find. Or use a large paper Christmas tablecloth. Tie with a tremendous bow.
- Stencil solid color paper for handmade gift wrap with a flair. This is the perfect decoration for packages to be mailed. No need for a bow. Cutout paper and fabric make excellent appliqués, as well.
- Use rubber cement instead of tape for tidily invisible folds.
- See "Greetings!" for printing ideas, and make your own gift wrap on recycled papers and bags.

Package Trimmings and Decorative Attachments

bows and ribbons	hair ribbons/neon shoelaces
yarn(s)	stickers-by-the-yard
small ornaments	printed slogan buttons
paper doilies	greenery and berries
decorated cookies	dried flowers/fruits
lace	stems of eucalyp-
candy canes and other candies	tus/wheat/lavender …
miniature stuffed animals	miniature musical instruments
strips of name tape	small baskets
(notions dept.)	silk flowers
Contact paper cutouts	miniature pine cones
colored or decorative tapes	potpourri or sachet

Your attachment could be a hint of what's inside (a chocolate tennis racket, tiny doll, personalized bookplate or bookmark …).

Little children will be mystified and delighted by a handwritten note from Santa describing the legendary significance of a very special gift. Make up a magical tale about the previous life of a new doll, the elfin creators of a new electric train set, the tiny angel who still lives in the hand-me-down dollhouse. Endow your gifts with pleasure and the treasure-trove of creative play potential.

Grownups, too, love extraordinary touches. Give a piece of jewelry magical powers or mysterious origins. Attach a witty poem about Santa's intentions for the super-electronic drill. Program a cryptic message into the new software.

Ribbons and Buttons and Bows

Attachments you can use to tie one on include: organdy, lace, French-wired ribbon, dried eucalyptus or pliable vine, strung cranberries or professionally dried fruit slices, sparkly star cord, gold or silver cord, natural jute, raffia, wired paper, curling ribbon, paper or cloth ribbons, hand-painted, satin, or grosgrain ribbons, plaid, polka-dotted, printed, or solid ribbons … mix two or more colors or textures …

Unusual Gift Containers—A Gift Inside a Gift

antique glass jars
decorated boxes
cookie jars/tins
Christmas stockings
plastic containers
personalized laundry bag

baskets
wooden sleigh
piñata (see page 235)
jewelry case/box
travel accessories case
homemade fortune cookies

see "A Festival of Feasting" for kitchen gift container ideas

Tie a new pair of blue jeans with a ribbon through the belt loops to close the top and ribbons pulled tight at the knees to close each leg. Fill with a fluffy pair of slippers, personalized T-shirt, funky vest, crazy socks, flannel boxers ...

To and From

Look for fresh and exciting ways to say "Especially to you from me!"
printed enclosure cards (design and/or print your own)
printed name tape (to label camp or college clothing)
initials cut from colored Contact paper, gift wrap, tape ... stick-on labels
    or stickers arranged in clever fashion
homemade initial or name stamps
gift wrap printed all over with recipient's name/nickname
cut-up greeting cards/collage
glitter glue
old-fashioned paper-cuts or new-fashioned graphics
small burlap or fabric squares painted with name and/or secret design
cross-stitched label/ornament with recipient's name
clay sculpted initials painted and varnished
craft wire molded with beads, feathers, string, and other "found" materi-
    als to suggest a particular individual
old photographs (possibly even embarrassing, like Dixie's yearbook pho-
    to!) framed and tied to the package

Or wrap each family member's gift(s) in a distinctively different paper and leave off name tags altogether. This confuses all shakers and squeezers until Christmas morning. Don't forget which color print or design is whose!

If a package contains something breakable or requires special handling instructions, don't trust *anything* to fate. Label with stick-ons that caution: "Glass," "Fragile," "This Side UP," "Do NOT Open 'Til December 25!"

Let the card on the outside hint what's inside. Dad always came up with crazy "From's," like our imaginary "Uncle Louis" (who is very practical), William Shakespeare and other literati (who present bookish gifts), and many more obscure and clownish givers who kept us guessing until the wrapping finally came off.

Guessing games can be fun on Christmas morning. Put clues as to the recipient into your package decoration and have everybody guess who it's for. The more humorous (all in good fun), the better.

Delivering Gifts …

can be a terrific family tradition. Stopping by friends' houses for a visit on Christmas Eve or before adds to the pleasure of giving and receiving.

SHIPPING GIFTS

Send Christmas presents in plenty of time to get there before December 25. Avoid long grouchy lines at the Post Office, typically filled right up to the 24th with those less organized than yourself. A warning "Do Not Open Before Christmas!" should delay all but the most curious until the big day.

Shipping Tips

- A heavy corrugated box serves as the outer mailing container, with the wrapped gift inside.
- Use popped corn, recycled excelsior (don't buy this stuff), shredded or balled newspapers … as filler to protect the gift inside its box. At least three inches of filler is suggested for the top and bottom of the box.
- Make out two address labels for each package, both including the "to and from" addresses. Tape one securely to the outside of the package and put the other conspicuously on the inside—just in case the outer label is somehow stripped off or obliterated.
- Insure anything breakable worth more than $10.
- Use heavy mailing paper and reinforced fiber filament tape for safe packaging. Don't use string. It gets caught in mail-processing machines.
- Wrap all food items airtight in plastic wrap or a zip bag. Cushion the bottom of the box with one of the above fillers and cover this with shredded tissue paper in one or more festive colors. Pack food items snugly inside and add with more tissue paper and filler.
- Label everything requiring special care: Fragile, Refrigeration Required, Glass, This Side Up, Perishable …
- If you use a delivery service, call ahead for specific shipping and packaging instructions required for your particular items.
- There are mailing/shipping shops now to do all this for you, if this is not your bag. But buyer beware, they're not cheap!

DELIVERING GIFTS BY FOOT, CAR, OR SLEIGH

When access through the chimney becomes messy, you may need a new approach to delivering gifts:

- Call ahead to announce your intention to "stop by for a few minutes …"
- Plan your delivery route in advance for efficient travel.
- Don't leave gifts in a mailbox or outside the door.
- If you want to sneak your surprise into the house, conceal it as best you can on arrival, ask a favor that will remove the host from the room, and quickly place your package among the pile of gifts under the tree.
- If you want to be EXCEPTIONALLY elf-like, call to be sure your

recipient is home (ask for a recipe or something) and steal up to the door, ring the bell, leave the gift, and RUN!

OPENING GIFTS AT CHRISTMAS

Gift-opening, that eagerly-anticipated moment of the holidays, should be a long leisurely process enjoyed by everyone (including Mom, who shouldn't be in the kitchen).

People want to enjoy their giving as well as their receiving, so gifts should be opened one at a time, with a proper pause for ooh-ing and ah-ing before the next package is delivered.

Small children will never stand for this. So plan Santa Claus and stocking-opening first, while the grownups eat breakfast and swill coffee to get themselves out of the 5:30 a.m. stupor.

Prepare a huge box to receive the torn paper and a basket for the bows. (Recycle as much as you can.) Appoint a "Santa Claus" to hand out the gifts (if Santa can't read, you might color-code each family member's package for easy identification and location).

Try to hand out gifts so that everybody opens one before you begin the next round. And open them slowly, patiently savoring the time of giving and receiving. Take pictures, take breaks, play Christmas music in the background, serve breakfast halfway through the pile ... and EN-JOY!

If you have a reunion of several adults and many, many children, you might consider exchanging some gifts among the grownups on Christmas Eve after the kids go to bed (you'll have to plan well in advance for pre-Christmas Eve toy assemblage), saving Santa and kiddie gifts (to and from) for Christmas morning.

As for expressing sincere and profuse thanks twenty-eight times in one morning, when I come up with a formula I'll let you know.

SIX

Decking the Halls
Bringing in the Christmas Spirit

Not necessarily "House Beautiful", but it's HOME.

One of the really terrific things about the holidays is that they give us an excuse to be creative, expressive, extravagant, and excessive—all in the spirit of the season.

Many folks who never even bother to change the centerpiece on their dining room table are moved by the spirit to transform their homes into veritable wonderlands of greenery, glimmer, gaiety, and warmth. Come December, pull out all your options and all of your imagination (but not *all* of your energy!) to dream up a decorating scheme that makes your Christmas HOME a merry place to be.

Encourage everyone — from Baby to Grandad — to participate in sprucing up for Santa's visit. The whole family should be involved in the selection of a favorite theme, color scheme, or even extent of gaudiness needed to convey your collective spirit.

Approach decorating with a well-organized plan—keep it simple and fun. Consider some of the SPECIAL THEMES mentioned in the following pages, or create an atmosphere all your own. Make generous use of NATURE'S HARVEST, the plentiful resources right outside your door. DECK THE HALLS WITH ... interesting and unusual arrangements and handmade items you have crafted and collected over the years.

Use your *Handbook* as a reference for ideas and techniques, as a reminder of the myriad possibilities for making the grand seasonal transformation. Flip through magazines and other books for more ideas, but don't succumb to frantic paranoia over all the highly stylized and unrealistic photographic perfection.

Again, DO YOUR OWN THING! and love every minute of it. Decorating can be such a high-spirited and creative experience and bring so much pleasure to you and everyone else who enjoys the cheerful atmosphere created by your very own hand(s).

Here's hoping inspiration hits you like a full-force winter wind!

Christmas Symbols and Characters

Consider the possibilities:
Angels
Bells
Birds
Candy Canes
Christmas Trees
Dove and Olive Branch
Drummer Boy
Elves
Gingerbread People
Gnomes
Madonna and Child
Mice
Nativity Figures
Nutcracker
Pear Trees
Reindeer
Rocking Horses
Santa Claus
Snow Men (and Women)
Snowflakes
Stars
Sugar Plum Fairy
Teddy Bears
Tin Soldiers
Wise Men
Wreaths

DECORATING IDEAS

Special Themes

Select a theme or an element and run away with it, using the same idea in as many ways and places as you can: the tree, stockings, centerpiece, door decorations, gift wrap, cards, figure displays ...

> 'Twas the night before Christmas
> and all through the house ...
> Everything had been garnished
> with a little red mouse.
> You could see a red mouse
> *everywhere* in the house!
> On the mantel, the table, the front
> door, the tree,
> My stocking ... and Mom even
> stuck one on ME!

Well, some people tend to overdo—a little! But the idea of picking a symbol, color scheme, or particular theme and using it as the basis for all (or most) of your decorating can cause quite an effect. An entire mood and atmosphere will arise from your efforts.

Carrying on like this can also lead you to become something of a collector—all year round, at every gift shop, yard sale, or flea market, your eyes are peeled for "just one more" little mouse, angel, elf, Santa ...

Or you might go completely overboard and establish a collection of Christmas symbols for each of your children, grandchildren, nieces and nephews ... Arrange them all together on a mantel for dramatic effect, or simply allow your little treasures to appear unexpectedly all over the house (like the little red Christmas mouse ...).

"Let it Snow!"

This can be great fun, especially for those of us living beyond the Arctic Circle who consider ourselves lucky to have a couple of icicles dangling from the daffodils on December 25. When we dream of a White Christmas—and wake up again to the same greenish-brown lawn—having a winter wonderland inside is our only vehicle to imaginary sleigh rides and snowmen. And white goes with everything—so this decorating scheme fits just about any interior.

Use cotton, polyester fiberfill, or lightweight fabric to create mounds of "snow" on tabletops and the mantel. Small mirrors sprayed with artificial snow make lovely skating rinks and you can frost your windows and even the tree with this spray stuff for a wintry effect.

Create a village scene with a collection of German wooden houses or ceramic English cottages, fill small sleighs with miniature gifts, arrange an assortment of bundled up caroling figures around a lamppost.

Hang crocheted cotton or shiny silver snowflakes from a chandelier or light fixture. Recycle that awful Styrofoam packaging material by threading it on fishing line, and run it up and down windowpanes to give the effect of a snowfall. Build a "snowman" in the den using Styrofoam "snowballs," toothpicks, and buttons. Or make a Styrofoam "snowball" wreath and decorate it with brightly colored knitted mittens and a scarf or muffler … Think Snow! and let your imagination go.

A Williamsburg Christmas

Very complementary to a colonial or traditional decor, this theme takes you and your family back to the days of 18th century Williamsburg and the very charming, very simple Christmas celebrated then and there.

Spend some time familiarizing yourselves with colonial times and the life of Williamsburg. Consider the resources colonials had to work with and leave out the twentieth century trappings if your goal is authenticity (minimal use of ribbons, electronic reindeer, and, sorry, electric tree lights).

Fruit, greenery, and other natural things were the primary decorating materials. Christmastime was also a celebration of the end of the harvest, and the bounty of the outdoors was prominently displayed: garlands and wreaths were fashioned from Virginia pine, waxy magnolia, soft red cedar, rosemary, and cherry laurel. Nuts, cones, seed pods, dried herbs, perennials, and wildflowers were available throughout the countryside.

The timelessly beautiful Williamsburg apple cone—featuring apples, citrus, pineapple, and other natural garnishment—was a standard decoration. Fruit also decorated garlands, wreaths, doorways, and mantels. Pewter and brass, silver épergnes, and candelabra were brought out for the celebration. Soft candlelight, pungent spices, sweet-smelling potpourri, and dried arrangements, as well as gingerbread, lent sensual warmth to the holidays.

Perhaps one of the most charming elements of a Williamsburg Christmas is its very simplicity. Decorating and gift-giving embraced qualities of resourcefulness and thoughtfulness. Manifold was the spirit of celebration. Holiday visits among friends and family quite likely were the only such time together in the entire year, so naturally, this was a season of relaxed renewal of family ties after the hard and satisfying harvest.

Bring out your wassail bowl and celebrate a colonial Christmas for a warm and gentle feeling of the good old days.

 Begin devising a plan for Christmas decorating, and repeat it (or most of it) every year, if you are comfortable with tradition. A few additions and subtractions will lend a little excitement and creativity to old family customs.

Mini-Wreaths

Make mini-wreaths for decoration, napkin rings, windows, and tree ornaments, as attachments for larger wreaths, to decorate candleholders ... using one or more of the following:

bay laurel leaves
birch twigs
clusters of cranberries
dried apple slices
dried flowers and herbs
dried red chili peppers
jingle bells
juniper branches
mini pine cones
slender vines

An Old-Fashioned Country Christmas

Antique-lovers and even "good reproduction" collectors can fill their homes with an assortment of old and old-looking items: cross-stitched samplers, old-fashioned tins filled with nuts and hard candies, knitted stockings, ornaments and wreaths made from recycled quilt scraps, a wooden rocking horse, hammered tin shapes, baskets filled with pine cones and greenery, hanging pomanders and spice bags, pottery, quilling, gingham, and gingerbread ...

Antique dolls and wooden trains can nestle near the tree, which is trimmed with popcorn and cranberry strings, hand-carved, hand-sewn, home-grown, or home-baked ornaments. Arrange country collectibles on a mantel with greenery and white candles, use small print fabrics "aged" with a soaking in dark tea, include natural pine cutouts, stenciled boxes, teddy bears and decoys, and all the other delightful country elements you can find—in the city or country, at home or abroad (study French and English country styles for variations on this theme).

Make or collect things that reflect hand-crafted originality and charm. Often, small children are the very best at this. Their innocent and uninhibited spirits are capable of reproducing that free primitive style so endearing to folk art lovers everywhere.

A Nature Lover's Christmas

Bring the forest inside, with all its Christmas green finery and naturally seasonal scent. The outdoors provide a wealth of free materials for use in holiday decorating. NATURE'S HARVEST, beginning on page 85, is your guide to greenery and the many more natural objects available, including instructions for making wreaths, garlands, swags, centerpieces, mantel arrangements ... and many other holiday accents from the bountiful gifts of nature.

Garnish greenery with cones, seeds, pods, dried herbs, grasses, and flowers for an environmentally perfect scenario. Animal lovers can bring in tiny bird and animal figures to recreate the great outdoors as atmospherically as possible. And don't forget the mistletoe!

The Twelve Days of Christmas

Imagine twelve, count 'em, twelve focal points throughout your living room, dining room, and whatever other places receive best exposure. Try gilded pears, wax or marble pears, real pears, jewelled or glass pears, silver, pewter, or brass pears. Put pears in bowls, on potted bare branches, on the tree, or hanging from the chandelier.

Arrange the "gifts" for each of the Twelve Days all together on a mantel or tabletop, or spread them about the room(s). You can make your own using one or more of the crafting techniques in this book, or collect Twelve Days decorative items and figures from small shops and catalogs over the years. In case you need a reminder, my true love gave:

A partridge in a pear tree
Two turtle doves
Three French hens
Four calling birds
Five golden rings
Six geese a-laying
Seven swans a-swimming
Eight maids a-milking
Nine ladies dancing
Ten lords a-leaping
Eleven drummers drumming
Twelve pipers piping

Color Themes

Fabric, spray paint, glitter, ribbons, shiny or patterned paper, ornaments, flowers ... can complement or appropriately overwhelm your everyday decor with a dramatic color or pattern scheme.

Wrap all your gifts under the tree with the same paper and bows. Tie the same color bows on several limbs of the tree. Use the specific color scheme for all your ornaments, centerpieces, decorative accents ... Put several colored glass balls in a silver bowl, make or buy table linens, the tree skirt, stockings, and possibly even the wreath using the same color or pattern of fabric.

Suitable Christmas colorations run the gamut from red and green (of course) to gold, white, silver, light blue, even pink, purple, or chartreuse (each according to taste!). Mix two or three colors, such as light blue and silver, gold and white, silver and gold ... for a dramatic effect. Use a standard print or pattern: candy cane stripes, a colorful plaid, silvery snowflakes, a mixture of calicos. Fabric stores often have many Christmas fabrics to choose from.

One word of caution: Be sure you love the color scheme. If you decorate as early as I do, you'll be seeing a lot of it for three to four weeks, year after year!

Personalized Themes

Anybody in your family a tennis buff? golfer? shell collector? Personalize your Christmas with clever adaptations of the family hobby: a wreath made of tennis balls, tree ornaments of painted golf balls, ribboned sand

Spray paint items to give color to your decorations: pine cones, sweet gum balls, magnolia leaves, tree limbs, baskets, dried vegetables, eucalyptus, dried flowers and grasses ... A little gold looks especially dramatic amongst nature's colors.

Waving the Old Red, White, and ... Green

Red Things:
apples
berries
candies
candles
cherries
cranberries
glass balls
grapes
hearts
jellybeans
poinsettias
pomegranates
red pepper
roses
strawberries
tulips
White Things:
baby's breath
bleached pine cones
bleached sand dollars
candles
chrysanthemums
cotton
garlic
glass balls
lilies
poinsettias
polyester fiberfill
popcorn
Green Things:
apples
artichokes
berries
candles
candy
Chinese cabbage
eucalyptus
glass balls
gourds
grapes
green peppers
greenery
jellybeans
limes
osage oranges
pears
poinsettias

About Mistletoe

Mistletoe is a parasitic plant that can be found hanging smugly from the bare branches of winter's treetops. Most holiday mistletoe is leafy green with soft white berries. These berries may be poisonous to human beings and should be kept well out of reach of children and pets.

Olde English tradition held that whichever woman might "accidentally" wander underneath the kissing ball must pay the penalty by allowing herself to be kissed. There was also the custom that with each kiss under the mistletoe, a berry must be plucked from the bunch. When all the berries were gone, there could be no more kissing. No cheating allowed!

Norse legend said that mistletoe not only commanded a kiss, but also brought luck and fertility. Tucking a sprig of it in invitations and cards will wish your friends a happy and bountiful New Year (and perhaps a new little tax deduction as well!).

dollars and starfish. Your personal involvement in a sport or hobby makes you the best source for dreaming up all kinds of possibilities. This kind of decorating is especially fun for Christmas travelers to vacation homes at the beach, lake, or golf and tennis resort. If you know someone with a second home, consider giving recreationally-correct decorations for their holiday pleasure.

Collectors can highlight their collectibles at Christmas as well. Use porcelain figures in a holiday scene. Lay an electric train village around the base of the tree. Surround carved birds or decoys with greenery and candles.

And what of you friends of the feathered and furry? An "Animal Christmas!" Make Santa caps for all your cats and canines, real and stuffed. Decorate teddy bears with bright red bows and put Christmas birds all over the house, in the tree, among the garlands, attached to your wreaths, and hanging from the chandelier.

Bring all your stuffed friends out of the bedroom (and don't forget Rubber Duckie from the tub), so they too can decorate, be decorated, and enjoy the holidays with the "grownups"! You might even feel generous enough to give them a special tree of their own, and stockings, too, of course. (Credit for this idea goes to my "godchildren" Wadsworth, Waldo, and Wendell. They know who they are!)

This isn't even the tip of the North Pole's biggest iceberg when it comes to personalizing your holidays. A world of ideas is right there where you live. And while some of these themes may sound a little unsophisticated and crazy, the odds are that you will have tons more fun with something like this than you ever have before.

An International Christmas

For those lucky enough to be world travelers, collecting Christmas decorations and ornaments from every port is a terrific way to make the trip last even longer than your leather luggage. Even if you only travel to the nearest flea market or international bazaar, you can pick up several items to carry out this theme.

The world is rich with Christmas traditions, and there are many unusual and interesting ways to decorate and celebrate faraway places. Do some research and craft or collect your own international decorations, saying "Merry Christmas" in many languages. As your imagination wanders, you will feel you have been there yourself.

If your family has a strong national heritage, discover Christmas as it was celebrated in the "old country." Trace your history and carry on some of the traditions of your ancestors, both in decorating and celebrating. What a memorable learning experience you all will share!

A Child's Christmas

The year we took Geoffrey, ripened to a full 11 months of age, up to North Carolina for his first Christmas, Mom sparked the childishness in all of us with this theme—in honor of the family's first grandchild. (Did it take much for a group whose collectively favored Broadway musical and life philosophy is still "Peter Pan"?)

Geoffrey couldn't appreciate as we did the dear display of "little people" things: tiny toy ornaments, bugles and bows, wooden soldiers, and old rag dolls in antiqued rockers. The tree lights were all white, so as not to distract from the colorful carved miniatures adorning the tree.

A small village scene was laid on the upstairs hall dresser with houses, churches, horse-drawn sleighs, people and animal figures, and matchboxes wrapped as gifts, nestled under a miniature tree. All around the house, bowls were filled with fresh fruits, nuts, and colorful candies, to the childish delight of all the "grownup" offspring.

There are so many bright and gaily-colored elements of childhood: clowns, Raggedy Ann and Andy, electric trains, teddy bears, rocking horses, reindeer, snowmen, drums and horns and bells and cymbals—all the symbols of our Christmases Past (I fear I've aged myself here), recreating the magic we knew when sliding down the banister on Christmas morning ourselves.

Memories we treasure always live again on December 25.

There—just a few suggestions to get the creative juices flowing. Bring your own imagination and style to Christmas—and have some fun decorating …

THE GREAT OUTDOORS

The outside of your house can and should be a showcase of spirit. I suppose you have seen at least one "masterpiece" of overzealousness. When we were little, we used to drive out to a house where the residents pulled no stops in displaying their holiday hysteria. It was a tradition full of laughter and excitement, year after year.

There, a neon Santa and eight tiny reindeer paused up on the housetop, two or three nativity scenes were scattered about the yard, plus a few angels, elves, and snowmen. Strings, strings, and more strings of large-bulb multi-colored lights boxed up and swirled haphazardly around the house, surrounding trees and bushes. Electric candy canes were lit to reflect at least two or three pink flamingos and clay chicks not native to Bethlehem but apparently presumed to have been there all the same!

Although we thrilled to this sight as children, it's not altogether necessary to duplicate such a scene in order to convince the neighbors of your enthusiasm. The sight of a cheerfully decorated housefront does, however, provoke many a lifted spirit. This can be your gift to the neighborhood.

See "Christmas—Here, There, and Everywhere," page 200, for international celebration ideas.

Make it Easy on Yourself

The simplest wreath you can "make" is the greenery wreath you buy, and add your own attachments—even if it's just a big fluffy bow!

At the very least, put an attractive wreath or decoration on your front door. If you have a streetside mailbox, coordinate your wreath with greenery and ribbons attached to the box (being careful not to obstruct the mail carrier's ability to deliver all your cards and party invitations). Consider putting another matching bow on a lamppost or at the bottom of each handrail of your front steps.

Hang garlands or wreaths in each window. Candy cane stripe the posts or columns. Follow the natural lines of small trees and bushes with tiny twinkling starlights.

For kids "from 1 to 92 ... ," do something extraordinary to attract Santa's attention on Christmas Eve. Have your favorite handyperson (you?) cut out a large plywood mittened hand, stocking, Christmas tree ... and paint a huge sign for the front yard: "Santa, please stop here!" "Merry Christmas to All!" or any other cheerful message you wish to share with the outer world.

An outdoor nativity scene, subtly lit and nestled among small trees and bushes, is inspirational.

If you are lucky enough to have lots of snow, use this natural element to make a Santa Snowman (and Ms. Santa, too), or a clever snow sculpture, using the family's combined creativity and glovepower. Line your driveway or walkway with luminaries.

Spread the spirit!

SAFETY FACTORS TO CONSIDER

- Be sure all tree lights and electrical displays have safe, unexposed wiring, with a maximum of three strings in a series to one outlet.
- Keep strings and cords away from the tree's source of moisture and out of the way of moving "traffic."
- Never burn tree lights overnight or when no one is home.
- Always extinguish candles before leaving a room.
- Consider putting the tree inside a playpen or on a high stool or table, so small youngsters can't pull the whole thing down on top of themselves.
- Never burn gift wrap in the fireplace. It burns too quickly and creates a dangerous heat level in the chimney. Save old scraps and pieces for future wrappings, craft projects, and child's play.
- Dried materials, Spanish moss, greenery treated with glycerine, little boys and girls in curls and flannel pajamas, and other flammable objects should be kept well away from fireplaces and burning candles.

 Another safety factor to remember: never burn gift wrap in the fireplace. It burns so quickly, a dangerous heat level is created in the chimney. Save old scraps and pieces for future wrapping needs, craft projects, and kids' play.

ABOUT DECORATING AND SMALL CHILDREN

If you have very small children, you naturally will have to make several concessions to safety in deference to aesthetics (not to mention broken treasures).

Only you know the extent to which your child can restrain himself from climbing onto the table to see for himself if porcelain angels can fly or just how high a shiny glass ball bounces. Decorate accordingly. Save your precious breakables for absolutely out-of-reach locations or for Christmas Future.

When our twins were two, we were so confident in their ability to handle the tree with decorum that we neglected to make special arrangements for its (and their) safety. Good old Zack, however, managed to pull the whole thing down on top of himself, not once but twice that year. He remained unharmed, if not a little shaken, but we lost a couple of handmade ornaments to the experience.

In similar situations, it would be wise to anchor the top of the tree with fishing line tied to a wall fixture or toggle bolt. Or you could try the previously mentioned playpen or circular gate "now you see it, now you can't touch it" trick.

If you encourage curiosity, however, exposure to a tree and other colorful decorations can be a source of pure joy to a toddler who tirelessly circles the lower branches, touching the ornaments and taking one or two off for closer inspection. As long as the child is cautioned to handle with care, allow him to touch, feel, explore, and enjoy the tree with all its plastic, fabric, wooden, and otherwise childproof treasures. Keep the breakables confined to higher branches.

And don't be surprised to see little ones dance and jump up and down in amazement at the first lighting of the tree. One of the best parts of Christmas is seeing those lights reflecting magically in Baby's eyes.

Let Me Do It, Mommy!

In order to give small children something to decorate and play with, keep a basket full of stuffed Christmas figures, bendable Santas, puppets, and plastic snowmen in the same room with the other decorations.

NATURALLY YOURS

Recall, at Christmas, the kinds of decorative materials used in the days before K-Mart and Christmas City became intimate with our credit cards. Natural elements add a richness to your displays that a month's wages worth of plastic holly, electric lights, and glass balls can't touch.

Nature's Harvest

Any Christmas-lover worth his salt in resourcefulness begins decorating with the supplies Nature gives us. Who can resist the God-given bounty right in our own backyards? The sheer gorgeousness of natural things, the pine-sweet scent, and a price tag that has withstood centuries of inflation are reason enough to fill our homes with as much from Nature as we can, as long as we are sure to give back as much in the way of gentle care and replenishment as we can.

Begin with the EVERGREEN: "A plant that bears its leaves all the year round." (*Science Dictionary of the Plant World*)

Evergreens

Evergreens have been used for centuries in celebration of winter festivals—historically significant as a symbol of life during an otherwise cold and barren winter. The pagan festival of Saturnalia in ancient Rome is the source of many of our present Christmas customs, one of which is this widespread use of plants in holiday decorating.

The Romans, well known for their excesses in times of celebration, lined the streets, filled their homes, and crowned their heads with various and sundry pieces of greenery.

Mistletoe and holly were considered sacred plants. The holly and ivy were thought to be sexual images: holly representing the male, ivy, the female. The two together supposedly represent the reproductive urge; and more generally, the battle of the sexes.

And we can all chuckle at the superstition that claimed whichever plant—holly or ivy—was brought into the house would determine who ruled the roost! As if you guys had a chance!

Boxwood
Cedar
Douglas Fir
Fir
Hemlock
Holly
Ivy
Juniper

Laurel
Magnolia
Pine
Privet
Rhododendron
Spruce
Yew

Preparation and Preservation of Natural Things

Select branches and leaves that are fresh and unblemished, with full growth, and of the desired length and shape. Use sharp cutting shears to make the cut at a 45° angle (this encourages replacement growth, so you're only pruning, not destroying). Breaking off stems with your fingers damages the plant. *Always* use clippers or shears, and cut sparingly, so as not to maim the evergreen. Plants are often at their best and most vibrant early in the morning, when the dew is still on the rose ...

When you get the greenery back to the house, mash the branch ends with a hammer or mallet. Soak ends in cool water overnight before using in an arrangement.

If you wish to preserve the greenery indefinitely, soak the stem ends in three parts hot water to one part glycerin (or antifreeze, which is basically the same thing and cheaper) for one to three weeks. Set in a cool dark place and don't let solution dry out. When absorption is complete, all of the leaves will feel oily and turn slightly brownish. This process should keep the foliage indefinitely in an arrangement without water (good for ivy, hydrangea, holly, hosta, mahonia, magnolia, beech ...).

Dipping the ends of ivy, pine, and cedar stems in melted paraffin or candle wax seals in moisture. Dry stems overnight on a sheet of newspaper. This procedure also keeps sap from leaking all over walls and furniture.

If you are using greenery in a centerpiece or display that holds water, be sure to keep the water constantly replenished to ensure lasting freshness. This, of course, includes the cut Christmas tree.

Other tips for prolonging cut greenery's freshness:

- Saturate floral foam in water before inserting greenery and keep moist.
- Put portable arrangements in the sink occasionally and spray.
- Push stems into a juicy apple or potato (78% of which is water) for a constant supply of moisture in arrangements. A hairpin or toothpick makes holes for inserting stems.

The thicker the leaf, the longer the absorption process. With magnolia, use a more concentrated glycerin or antifreeze solution (two parts water to one part glycerin). Glycerin is available at the drug store and performs an interesting range of functions, from sweetening cookie frostings to manufacturing dynamite.

- Add one of the following to water—approximately 1 teaspoon per gallon—to prolong plant and flower life: Floralife, Peter's Special (available at hardware, florist, and discount stores), salt, sugar, bleach, 7-Up, or one or two aspirin. The function of these additives is to slow the growth of bacteria which causes deterioration.

ACCESSORIES TO INDIVIDUALIZE AND HIGHLIGHT GREENERY ARRANGEMENTS

- Make an assortment of pine or balsa wood cutouts (Christmas shapes, birds, flowers …) attached to short pieces of dowel, for interesting accents. Drill a hole in the bottom of the cutout, insert the glued dowel and let dry. Paint or stain as desired. Insert in wreaths, potted plants, garlands …
- Weave cool-burning miniature white tree-lights (available in electric or battery-powered strands) throughout an arrangement or display for extra sparkle (wreaths, pine cones, dried flowers, a bowl of shiny glass balls …).
- Tape small stems of herbs and dried flowers to toothpicks for inserting into arrangements, wreaths …
- Or consider one of the many other accent choices on this page for drawing special attention to your natural greenery. As always, these are just to get you started. You may have some great idea all your own. Go with it.

USING FLORAL SUPPLIES

Florists and craft or hardware stores (which are usually less expensive) can provide you with all you need to create many natural displays. While you're shopping, investigate the many supplies and tools available, study ready-made arrangements, and look for unusual accents to use in your own unique designs.

Floral Tape: Green or brown floral tape is used for wrapping wire stems, attaching wooden picks to natural stems for inserting into base materials, taping branches together, and covering wiring.

Floral Foam: The "oasis," or dense foam block, is used as a base for greenery arrangement. An oasis holds moisture temporarily, can be cut with a sharp knife to fit any size container, or pierced with an awl or pin for stem insertion, and may be covered with chicken wire to make a sturdier foundation for heavy arrangements. Soak before using and keep moist, or your oasis will dry up and die.

Accessories for Arrangements

baby's breath
bells
berries
bird and animal figures
candy canes/peppermints
doily cones
dried corn husks
dried flowers/grasses
dried gourds
eucalyptus (green, brown, gilded …)
fabric sachets
fruits and nuts
glass balls
miniature toys/instruments
natural cotton bolls
origami
ornaments
osage oranges
paper fans
pierced tin cutouts
potpourri
Queen Anne's lace
ribbons and bows
seed pods
silk flowers
strawflowers
sweet gum balls
tin cookie cutters
vegetables
whole spices
wired pine cones
wood cutouts

When you decorate with natural things, the smells of Christmas mix with the scent of luscious baking things to fill your home with the fragrant sensations of this wonderful holiday.

Using a Hot-Melt Glue Gun

Hot-melt glue is polyethylene-based and sold in stick cartridges. Preheat the gun for five minutes, insert the glue cartridge, place the gun point on one of the surfaces to be joined, and press the trigger, allowing a bead of glue to be released. Immediately attach the two surfaces, as glue sets by cooling. Hold 30-60 seconds, applying slight pressure.

The glue gun has many uses in decorating and craft-making. It is an inexpensive, effective tool that adheres many objects together. Replacement cartridges of glue are available at most discount department stores and hardwares.

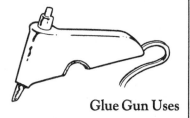

Glue Gun Uses

Making and repairing: ornaments, wreaths, candle attachments, placecard decorations, napkin rings, costume construction, broken toys, decorated baskets and boxes, ribbon barrettes, party favors, reindeer antlers, pine cone construction, nut crafts, dried flowers, kissing balls, jewelry making …

Wired Picks: One of the best inventions known to floral design, these wood picks can be wired to branches, pine cones, and stems, then inserted into an oasis, Styrofoam, or a straw wreath form. These may also be used to attach fruit to cones and arrangements, but the dye used on the wood is toxic, so the fruit must not be eaten after having been pierced.

Wire: Available in a variety of lengths and gauges, a spool of floral wire is typically green for minimal visibility among stems and leaves. The higher the gauge, the thinner and lighter the wire. Every household should have at least some floral wire, as it fulfills a multitude of needs, both practical and creative.

Floral Pins: U-shaped pins secure greenery, moss, grasses … to wreath forms, are approximately 2" in length, and act as staples when making attachments. You can bend short pieces of plain wire to make these yourself.

Glass "Frogs" and Metal Pin-Holders: Secure these arrangement bases to the bottom of shallow containers with a piece of floral clay and insert or impale stems evenly.

Floral Clay: A green clay for securing arrangement bases to the bottom of containers, this material also holds candles firmly in their holders, stabilizes small figures in a scene or an arrangement, and seals moisture leaks in containers, among other things.

"Plasti-tak" or "Stick-um": Another sticky subject useful for greenery arrangement, stabilizing objects, and safely attaching NBA posters to painted walls.

Chicken Wire: Best at about a 2" (5 cm) mesh. See page 93 for how-to's on molding and using chicken wire in decorating, crafts, and floral arrangements.

Glossy Wood Tone: Spray pine cones, nuts, gumballs, and other natural items with an added luster. Lay on newspaper, applying several light coats rather than one heavy one.

Rocks, Pebbles, Marbles, Sand, Shells: Any of these can be used to anchor arrangements in a bowl or vase, adding visual interest as well as neatness to the display. Add slowly, after stems are in place, to stand them securely in position. And don't pour these too dramatically into glass containers. The results could send slivers down your spine.

Hot-Melt Glue Gun: This is a wonderful tool for floral arranging and a sleighful of other things, too. Another "every household" necessity.

Staple Gun: For heavy-duty stapling, you can attach greenery and other objects to plywood.

Chenille Stems (pipe cleaners): These make good loops for hanging wreaths and other objects, because they're less likely to scratch woodwork and walls.

Sphagnum Moss, also Spanish moss, bun moss (green, velvety garden variety), lichen: Line a wire planter with this, or use as a planting medium or an arrangement naturalizer. If used as a planting medium, set plant and/or stems into the moss securely and keep moist and fresh with frequent mistings (preferably in the sink). When not in use, store moist (except Spanish moss) in a sealed plastic bag.

Attaching, Tying, Twisting, and "All-Togethers" of Natural Arrangements

Outdoor things—branches of greenery, flowers, and berries—are flexible and versatile materials for a number of arrangements and decorations. Use these over doorways, on stairways, in garlands and swags, as wreaths, and in baskets and bowls. Construct kissing balls and chandelier adornments. Make arcs, trim window sills, surround candles, cover mantels …

Practice using floral supplies and tools. Just knowing what they are and how to use them opens up the great big outdoors to you and your family—at Christmas and all year round.

MAKING A GARLAND

This is a traditional favorite for indoor and outdoor decoration.

Measure a ¼" thick rope the length you will need to make your garland or swag drape loosely across the fireplace, over the doorway, or around the front porch. You might dye the rope green to make an invisible support to your natural arrangement, or use green floral tape to cover.

With a continuous roll of floral wire, wrap evergreen stems—all pointed in the same direction—securely to the rope. Each cluster of greenery should hide the wiring of the previous stem. Prune to shape, if necessary.

For stairways and other roped garlands, run the greenery in one direction the full length of the rope. If you plan a center, over doorways or the fireplace, begin wiring in the middle of the measured rope, wiring greenery down each side in opposite directions. Attach a bow or other accents at the center and at other intervals, if desired.

MAKING A WREATH

When faced with the initial decision of whether to buy a straw, wire, or Styrofoam wreath form, consider the following properties of each:

Make it Easy on Yourself

Of course, the easiest (and perfectly acceptable) way to drape lengths of garland around your home is to buy them where you buy your tree (or from mail-order catalogs). Sold by the yard or foot, these come in pine, fir, cedar … so take your measurements with you.

Straw Forms: Probably the most versatile wreath form available, these are usually displayed at stores wrapped in green or black plastic, which can be removed if you prefer the straw background. For a greenery wreath, or one made with other dark materials, it's best to leave on the plastic for a background that doesn't fight with your attachments.

The straw form is sturdy, can withstand years of picking and piercing, is relatively inexpensive, and can be used approximately three million ways (only a few of which will be described here!). Wrap it with Spanish moss. Attach any and all kinds of greenery, dried herbs, fruit, toys, ribbons … Cover it with cloth or a multitude of bows. Use it flat on the table as an arrangement base … and so on and so on.

For attaching objects to a straw form, use: wired picks, U-pins, floral wire, monofilament (fishing line), a hot-melt glue gun …

Wire Forms: The wire form is best for wiring objects together to make a wreath, particularly those made of greenery and pine cones. This form usually has three sturdy rings onto which you wire various elements until the desired fullness is achieved.

Styrofoam Forms: The least practical, and even less environmentally correct, of the three available forms, Styrofoam is good only for light attachments, such as wrapped candies, bows, and cloth coverings. Wire picks leave holes that continue to grow, so Styro forms are not likely candidates for reuse.

Tie a high gauge wire (#22-26) to lightweight objects, or tape items to or impale them on toothpicks, to insert into the Styrofoam wreath form.

Plywood Base Form: This sturdy flat form takes odd attachments with a hot-melt glue gun or staple gun. You can cut one of these yourself and let your imagination run wild with paint, texture, Advent candles, a Christmas card collage, abstract symbolism …

Wreath Construction

❄ PREPARING ITEMS FOR ATTACHMENT

- Cut stems of greenery, dried flowers, eucalyptus … in short lengths of about 4-6" for making wreaths. Once the wreath is completed, prune back for a full uniform shape.
- Wire stems of greenery, herbs, dried flowers, bunches of berries, pine cones … with wired picks for insertion into straw forms.
- Tape lightweight stems to toothpicks using green floral tape in order to insert into straw or Styrofoam.

 Use small nails at regular intervals and floral wire (if necessary) to hang your garlands inside and outside the Christmas house.

- Wire greenery stems with a twist of short length of wire, leaving enough excess to wrap around wire wreath form. Overlap to hide wiring.
- Insert picks into straw and Styrofoam wreaths at an angle, each going in the same direction all around the form.
- Wire stems, candies, bows ... in the same direction, overlapping wiring with each successive attachment.
- When making a wreath, or any other greenery or floral arrangement, begin construction with the larger materials and stems. Fill in and shape with the smaller items. Add focal interest, texture, and color with accessories.

See page 87 for more on attaching fruits, nuts, vegetables ...

Step 1

EXPERIMENT WITH WREATHS, MAKE A ...

Magnolia Wreath

Drape your door with Southern hospitality ... and make a wreath using the evergreen magnolia's large shiny, waxy leaves.

1. Gather leaves that are unblemished, bright green, and uniform in size. The number you will need depends on the size wreath. Wash with cold water and cut off stems.
2. Using U-pins (floral pins), attach leaves around the inside of a straw wreath form, overlapping to cover the entire form (see illustration).
3. Attach leaves around the outside edge, going in the same direction and overlapping the edge.
4. For the final layer, spread sets of three leaves in a fan shape and attach the joint with U-pins (as shown). Add fruit, silk magnolia blossoms, red berries, or other accents, as desired.

Steps 2 and 3

Eucalyptus Wreath

This fragrant stem comes in many colors and can even be spray-painted when dried. Mix colors or use only one to make an attractive wreath.

1. Cut eucalyptus stems into 4-6" lengths, leaving a leaf at the top of each stem.
2. Wire three or four stems in a cluster to a wire pick.
3. Insert picks into a straw wreath form at an angle all around the form to desired fullness. Add baby's breath, dried flowers, herbs ... for additional color, texture, and accent.

Step 4

 Smaller wreath forms, given a little body and fullness with attachments, make good-looking candle rings for a dining table centerpiece.

Spanish Moss Wreath

Buy Spanish moss at the florist or craft supply store. If you gather your own, spray thoroughly with insecticide and dry before bringing inside.

1. Pull moss out in rope-like lengths and wrap loosely around a straw wreath form.
2. Use a roll of monofilament (fishing line) to wrap around the moss at intervals, not too tightly, and tie ends behind the wreath.
3. Attach colorful dried flowers, herbs, spices, and delicate velvet or satin ribbons to finish.
4. Spray with hairspray to hold.

Dried Apple Wreath

Select unblemished apples for this project. Cut whole apples horizontally in slices about $1/8$" thick, leaving the skin on. Soak slices in lemon juice with 1 teaspoon of salt stirred in. Pat dry with paper towels and lay flat on a wire screen that fits in your oven. Place screen directly on the oven rack and dry apples at low heat (120-150° F) for approximately four to six hours. Apples should be leathery but not brittle. Check occasionally, as ovens vary (mine seems to enjoy burning things). Cool slices and store in an airtight container until ready to use.

Spray liberally or brush with clear acrylic finish, front and back, let dry, and repeat, to seal. Dried apple slices can be wired to make a wreath, or glued with a hot-melt glue gun to a Styrofoam or plywood wreath form to cover.

Make mini-wreaths for ornaments, package decorations, or gifts. Or string dried fruit for swags and draped accents. This drying procedure also works using star fruit (carambola), or you can now find commercially-preserved (as opposed to pruny old dried-up for chewing) fruit for decorating: pomegranates, lemons, oranges, apples, carambola, figs, artichokes ...

Pine Cone Wreath

A wire base works best for pine cone wreaths, but you can also wire cones and insert into straw wreath forms with wire picks.

Gather some whole and some cut pine cones (see page 100 about cutting and wiring pine cones). Attach wired cones beginning on the outside rim of the form, using the largest cones one next to the other, each pointing in the same direction around the wreath. Do the same around the inner circle with uniform, smaller cones. Use medium-sized cones to fill in the center ring of the wreath form.

To fill gaps in a pine cone wreath, attach smaller cones, nuts, acorns, and pine cone "flowers" (page 100). Drill a small ($1/16$" bit) hole into nuts and acorns and push a high-gauge wire through to attach to wreath. Drizzle clear-drying glue or hot-melt glue around and in between the pine cones to hold secure, lest they wobble and wiggle and all fall down.

Spray completed wreath with glossy acrylic spray, Glossy Wood Tone, or a gold, silver, or colored spray paint.

Wire baskets and other pine cone construction forms are also available at craft shops and through mail-order concerns, often discovered in the backs of magazines.

Vine Wreath

Collect vines just after they have dropped their leaves—they will be still pliable, ripe, and ready for twining and twisting.

To make several wreaths at once, drive six stakes into the ground in a circular pattern the size of the wreaths desired. Weave vine in, out, and around, interweaving enough to make a good strong wreath. Tie at various intervals with a strong twine, jute, or craft wire, or perhaps a section of vine pliable enough to tie and knot. Tuck all free ends, except those charming curlicues, inside the wreath. Dry. Lift off the stakes and add accents.

To make a single wreath, loop the thickest vine into a circle the desired size. Wind smaller vines around this, twisting and tucking ends as you go. Tie off unruly ends with wire, jute, or another piece of pliable vine.

You can make vine arrangements in any shape by hammering nails in formation into a piece of plywood. Weave, as above, let dry, and lift off. Or wrap pliable vines around a greenery wreath, dwarf Alberta spruce ... or even your Christmas tree for a woodsy accent.

For more wreath ideas, see page 89.

ALTERNATIVE NATURAL ARRANGEMENTS AND CONSTRUCTIONS

- Decorate a straw fan, hearth broom, or basket with a cluster of wired greenery, flowers, grasses, and other accent materials.
- Tie sheaves of wheat, oat, or corn with wire and/or ribbon. Attach eucalyptus, pine cones, wood cutouts, miniature figures ...
- Shape wire mesh or chicken wire into various shapes (tree, star, wreath, teddy bear ...). Fill inside with damp sphagnum moss. Insert greenery to cover entire shape and prune to uniformity. Add accents and spray occasionally with mister to keep moist.
- To make a table arrangement, fill a bowl or container with soaked oasis and cover the entire container with chicken wire for added support. Insert larger branches and stems first, filling in with smaller materials until container is completely hidden. Add attachments with wired picks or wire.
- Line baskets, clay containers, and other non-moistureproof containers with basket liners, plastic saucers, foil, or plastic wrap before arranging moist plants or flowers inside. Plant an indoor garden in a large container by blending together a variety of greenery and grasses, bulbs and flowering plants, twisted wood stems, sphagnum, Spanish moss, pebbles ... Keep moist.

How to Shape Chicken Wire or Screen Wire Mesh

Buy chicken wire with a 2" (5 cm) mesh for greenery arrangements and craft armatures. The mesh can be shaped, rolled, twisted, and wired together for many uses.

Cut with sharp wire cutters. If you want a heavier mesh, use a lower gauge wire. You can also find green plastic-coated mesh for camouflage, rustproof, and scratchproof reliability.

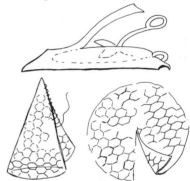

To make a chicken wire wreath: Cut a long mesh rectangle. Fold over to make a cylinder and thread seam together with wire. Bend carefully into a circle and thread ends together.

To make a chicken wire tree: Cut wire mesh into a circle whose radius is the approximate height of tree desired. Cut a radius to the center and fold mesh over to make a cone shape, threading together with thin wire. Trim or fold excess inside. This cone form might also be the beginning of a Christmas angel. Add wings, head, and halo ... and spray with gold paint for a heavenly sight.

Fold and bend wire into other shapes to craft your designs.

For inserting greenery: Fill center of wire form with damp sphagnum moss and insert greenery stems evenly into holes. Trim to shape. Mist to keep moist.

Look for the Unusual ... Green and Natural Things

bay laurel
bittersweet
catkins
Chinese lantern seedpods
clematis seed heads
contorted hazel
cotton lavender (santolina)
eleagonus
evergreens
hardy ferns
"Harry Lauder's walking stick"
hawthorn
ivy (plain and variegated)
lady apple
magnolia cones
olive branches
privet
pyracantha
rose of Sharon
rosemary
sage
sweet gum balls
winter jasmine

• Construct a dramatic arch for over fireplaces or large mirrors, using a plastic-covered oasis or homemade armature (wiring together the heaviest branches at their base and adding smaller branches wired to the center). Trim and mount arch on hooks or large nails.

Make Kissing Balls

Traditionally composed of a double-hoop circle with streamers attached at the bottom and the all-important mistletoe hung from the center, the "olde English" kissing ball is the elaborate first cousin to our own simple sprig of mistletoe hung over the doorway with care.

One way to make a kissing ball is with two wooden embroidery hoops (given up embroidery? recycle!). Glue together to make a ball shape, decorate with ribbons, trim, beads ... and tie a sprig of mistletoe in the center with ribbons through the top for hanging any and everywhere!

Another kissing ball consists of a large Styrofoam ball tied with ribbons for hanging, covered with inserted natural or manmade materials (sprigs of greenery, berries, small cones or seed pods ... taped to toothpicks or pieces of wire, or hot-melt glued directly onto the ball).

Or wire two pint plastic berry baskets together over a soaked oasis. Attach greenery through the holes with wired picks to cover. Prune greenery to shape and trim with ribbons and/or berries. Freshen occasionally by misting in the sink. Let drip-dry before rehanging.

And don't forget the mistletoe!

A Berry Merry Christmas

The green of the holly leaf and the red of its berry make this a perfect Christmas plant—dyed to match for the season by Mother Nature herself.

Other plants sporting berries, available at different times of the year in different parts of the country (or through catalogs, florists, wholesale suppliers ...), are: bayberry, bittersweet, canella, hawthorn, ligustrum, mistletoe, nandina, pink pepperberry, pittosporum, pyracantha, snowberry, tallowberry, viburnum ...

Pick berries early, as birds are even more attracted to them than we are. Careful handling reduces detachment and allows for bountiful use in decorating. Remove excess leaves and put stems in water until ready to use.

Cut berries won't last long (about three weeks), but dipping stem ends in melted paraffin and setting them on newspaper to dry overnight will increase longevity.

Blue and green ligustrum berries usually keep their color when dried, as do some others. Follow these simple steps to dry berries:

1. Cut stems at a 45° angle just before ripe.
2. Strip off all leaves.
3. Tie into small bunches with string or wire.

4. Hang in cool, dark, dry place, or stand in an empty jar to dry.

Keep children away from all berries picked outside. Some are poisonous, and who wants to take chances?

FLOWERS AT CHRISTMAS

The Poinsettia

Without a doubt, the best-known floral symbol of the season is the poinsettia. Seventeenth-century Mexican Franciscans are believed to have been the first to include poinsettias in the Christmas celebration. Our country's first foreign minister to Mexico, Dr. Joel R. Poinsett, is the American for whom the plant is named. In 1828, he sent cuttings of the flower as gifts to friends in the United States.

Potted poinsettias come small and large, usually in clay or plastic pots wrapped in that singularly unattractive foil wrap. Sorry, but I don't like it. Enhance the beauty of the flower by removing the crumply foil immediately and wrapping the pot in colorful Christmas fabric, gold or silver tissue paper, natural burlap … anything for a more tasteful look.

On the other hand, you could put the pot in a decorative basket, cachepot, terracotta pot, or some other more enchanting container for holiday purposes. Heavy gold or silver tissue paper can be twisted in rolls and wrapped in layers around the pot for a potentially exotic look as well.

Display poinsettias alone or grouped in attractive, multi-colored clusters. Hang them in baskets from the ceiling. For the intensely extravagant, there is always the arrangement of potted poinsettias on graduated steps in the formation of a grand Christmas tree. These plants also make wonderful teacher and neighbor gifts.

❄ SELECTION AND CARE OF POINSETTIAS

Choose plants with strong, leafy stems whose leaves don't drop when lightly shaken. Leaves should be full and grow all the way down the stem. A large, tight flower head also indicates a healthy poinsettia.

Display plants in indirect light, away from extreme cold or heat sources, such as vents, radiators, doors, and television tops. An indoor temperature between 60° and 70° F is best for most plants (saving energy and winter heating bills, too).

Keep soil moist, not wet. If the leaves turn yellow, you are watering too much. If they begin to drop off, you are not watering enough. Be sure to allow for proper drainage when repotting plants.

❄ PRESERVING YOUR POINSETTIA

Cut plant back after flowering, and repot in clean soil. Put in a sunny window away from drafts. Fertilize with Peter's Special and keep moist at all times.

Poinsettias are hothouse plants and need special treatment every day from October 1 to December 15 in order to bloom again at Christmas. Put the plant in a dark closet during this time for fourteen hours each day. Keep moist. The alternating light and dark is required for reflowering.

Christmas Cactus

Another "flower" that sometimes blooms during the holidays is the fickle, prickly Christmas cactus, which requires full sun, moderate temperatures (four to six weeks of blooming with a night temp of 50-65° F), and moist soil. Reddish-pink blooms appear on these indoor plants during the winter months and, perched on a sunny windowsill, add another colorful attraction to your holiday home.

Kalanchoes, Bittersweet, Camellias, Amaryllis, Paperwhite ...

Consider the many other winter bloomers that make wonderful holiday arrangements. Take advantage of the naturally flowering cold-weather varieties, as well as lovely stems, leaves, and seed heads found outdoors (or via the hothouse at the grocery, florist's, farmer's market, wholesale floral supplier, through mail-order catalogs ... .) at Christmastime:

alstroemeria	miniature crown-of-thorns
amaryllis	miniature rose
anthurium	ornamental cabbage
bird of paradise	paperwhite narcissus
camellia	red ginger "torch"
Chinese lantern	roses
crab apple	snowdrop (galanthus)
cyclamen	tulips
dendrobium orchid	

Proper Care Techniques for Cut Flowers

- Always recut the stem ends under running water when you arrive home with cut flowers.
- Fill a clean container with warm water (except for bulb flowers—tulip, iris, daffodil, gladiolus—which prefer cool water).
- Trim all leaves and petals that would be covered in water. These decay quickly and cause bacterial growth.
- Provide cut flowers with fresh water every day or so. Clean the vase with each water change.
- Avoid placing flowers in dry or heated areas (near radiators, vents, direct sunlight). Keep room temperature moderately cool.
- Add a little salt, sugar, liquid bleach, 7-Up ... to flower water to retard bacterial growth.
- Dye cut flowers by dipping stems cut at a 45° angle into a solution of household dye. White flowers will turn the shade of the dye, while colored blooms will blend to shades the way mixed paint colors do.
- Wire tiny flower vases or glass test tubes inside wreaths and garlands to hold water for small cut-flower accents.

Forcing Bulbs

About six weeks before you want a bloom, plant bulbs of paperwhite narcissus, amaryllis, iris, tulips . . . pointed end up in a shallow container on a thin layer of pebbles. Fill container, to just below where the shoots are beginning to appear, with sandy potting soil that is slightly acidic or simply with more pebbles. Top with Spanish moss or sphagnum, or plant grass seed around the bulbs for a nifty indoor garden look. Water thoroughly at potting time and then regularly when growth begins. Give forced bulbs warm sunlight and light fertilizer just before and during the flowering period. When flowers begin to die back, reduce watering gradually and discontinue watering when leaves have withered. (Just after flowering, the leaves are still feeding the bulb for next year's blooms.) Let dormant bulbs rest in a cool, dark, dry place until next year. Mark on your calendar to take them out again in late fall for a repeat performance.

Silk and Dried Flowers

For those who prefer the longevity and minimum care requirements of a dried or silk flower, there are several varieties of these available in various price and quality categories.

An artistically rendered silk flower is a thing of sheer inspiration. If the price tag of the really good ones puts you off, begin now collecting one or two stems at a time. A tall slender vase or Japanese dish needs only one stem to make a thoroughly dramatic statement. Add a bit of Spanish moss at the mouth of the vase to give body and accent the stem.

For Christmas decorating, look for branches of silken holly with berries, permanently bright and leafy poinsettias, deep red and white roses stemming from a huge crystal bowl. Mix in some secondary colors —creams and gentle pinks, pale green, blues, purples, and even yellows —to make striking combinations. The initial investment may be high, but the quality and durability will be enjoyed by many for years to come.

For a more earthy, natural look, dry your own flowers and grasses during the spring, summer, and fall for use in holiday decorations and during the rest of the year as well. Many different types of flowers can be dried successfully and easily in the privacy of your own home to achieve the soft color and appearance that tends to remind one of faded silk or antique brocade . . .

Pick flowers, herbs, and interesting stems for drying early in the blossoming stage—first thing in the morning on a dry day. One of the following methods may be used to dry flowers: air-drying, drying in an agent, or using a flower press.

Air-Drying: Hang towel-blotted flowers in a cool, dry, dark room, tying a few together in clusters with some wire or string. Grasses can be dried on a well-ventilated screen. In two to three weeks, depending on thickness, stems should feel crisp to the gentle touch. Spray with clear acrylic spray or hair spray and store carefully wrapped in tissue inside a cardboard box until ready to use. Warning: Mice are attracted to dried flowers.

Natural Materials for Drying and Decorating

allium
artemesia
artichoke
birch twigs
bittersweet
bracken fern
canella berries
daisies
eucalyptus
fennel
fig
flowering plum
globe amaranth
grapevine
hydrangea
lady crab apple
lavender
lotus or iris pods
love-in-a-mist
malaleuca
milkweed
okra pods
persimmon
pink pepperberry
pittosporum
pomegranate
pussywillow
pyracantha
Queen Anne's lace
quince
rabbit tobacco
red chili peppers
rose hips
rose of Sharon
rosemary
sage
sedum
seed heads and seed pods
silver honesty
statice
strawflowers
sweet Annie
tallowberries
tea rose
thyme
white/purple larkspur
yarrow

Take any and all precautions to safeguard against their infiltration (mousetraps?).

Drying in an Agent: Try one of the following.

1. A mixture of one part corn meal to one part borax (takes about two to three weeks).
2. Kitty litter (good for large flowers, dries in about two weeks).
3. Silica gel (commercially-prepared drying agent). This is the most expedient, efficient, and expensive material, but it can be reused/recycled indefinitely. Follow instructions on container.

Pour drying agent into an airtight container to a depth of 2". Cut flower stems to 1" from flower head and insert in agent, head up. Sprinkle more of the agent gently to cover flower completely and close container airtight. Let stand three to eight days, depending on flower size. Drying is complete when the flower feels crisp to the tender touch. Pour the agent off carefully, using a cotton swab or soft toothbrush to remove dusty particles.

To re-stem the flower head, insert a medium gauge wire of the desired length into the dried stem and wrap with green floral tape the full length of the wire. Attach silk or dried leaves to the "stem" as you tape, if desired. Dried flowers are very popular now in natural decorative pieces, wreaths, topiaries, floral arrangements ... Consider some of these possibilities:

- With a hot-melt glue gun, attach tiny dried buds to Styrofoam balls or cones for topiaries.
- Make candle wreaths on circles of heavy cardboard.
- Tie long stems of dried grasses, flowers, and herbs into a bundle with jute, and lay on top of a smoldering fire for a fine fragrance.
- Wire dried flowers and herbs to make swags for a mantelpiece, doorway, mirror ... or to tie back draperies, decorate the tree, weave through natural greenery ...
- Add to natural arrangements, gather in bouquets for tree and wreath decoration, arrange in vases ... light-colored dried flowers and herbs highlight and brighten the darker colors of an arrangement. Tape or wire short lengths to wire picks or toothpicks for insertion into wreaths and garlands.

Using a Flower Press: Make your own flower press, or buy one, and keep handy for yearly excursions into the fields or to give as gifts to your favorite nature lovers (include thorough instructions with the gift).

Making a Flower Press

2 (8" x 12") pieces of stiff cardboard, matboard, or thin plywood

2 (1 yd. each) lengths of ribbon blotting paper (available at craft and hobby stores)

Cut slits in the cardboard or drill holes in the wood, as pictured, for inserting the ribbon. Lay a sheet of blotting paper on one side of the inside of the press. Without overlapping, lay flowers of similar thickness on top of the paper. Cover with another sheet of blotting paper. Add more layers of flowers and paper, covering the final layer of flowers with a top sheet of blotting paper and the top half of the press.

Pull ribbons tightly to close, and put heavy books on top of the press, leaving untouched for at least 30 days.

Carefully remove flowers with tweezers and arrange on background of paper, fabric, wood, glass, or acrylic. In creating your design, begin with the larger flowers and fill in with several layers of the more delicate ones. A toothpick and clear-drying glue are best for attaching to various surfaces. Lay a sheet of glass or acrylic on top of arrangements meant to be preserved and frame.

Other uses for pressed flowers include decorating: placecards, notecards, stationery, calligraphed scrolls, lampshades, box lids, serving trays, coasters, framed wedding invitations or photographs, birth announcements, gift bags or packages ...

Topiaries

Training ivy to grow in a particular shape, or decisively pruning sprigs of boxwood, holly, and other greenery inserted into various forms can be the beginning of a beautiful mantelpiece. Wire frames for training ivy growth are available at floral supply houses. Plant ivy in the container and encourage the vines to grow up the stick, into and around the wire form, tucking pieces in to hold the shape. Keep moist with regular watering and occasional misting.

Or you can make a topiary form with a thick dowel stick inserted into a Styrofoam ball and "planted" in a pot of pebbles, shells, or marbles. Insert cut sprigs to desired fullness. Or glue dried buds and seed pods to a surface that has been rolled in glue and covered with a base layer of crushed herbs or lavender. Trim stray pieces to create a neat, uniform shape.

PINE CONES

Evergreens provide us with another windfall of seasonal accents, simply at the drop of a cone. Pines, hemlock, spruce, fir, magnolia, redwood, and more drop various sizes and shapes of cones that make wonderful Christmas decorations.

Collect cones in early fall, preferably cutting fresh, perfect ones from the tree with sharp metal clippers. Or pick up fallen cones, checking carefully for rotting spots and other imperfections.

When you get the cones back home, clean off some of the sticky "pitch" with turpentine and air for two to three days to dry them out. Or soak cones containing pitch in lukewarm water, then bake in the oven at a high temperature. The pitch forms a nice natural glaze as it bakes.

Queen Anne's Lace

Carefully remove the stems from Queen Anne's lace and press in a flower press until dried. Spray with hair spray, clear acrylic, or a colored spray paint. Tie with embroidery floss to hang on the tree, in windows, in a wreath or garland ...

Attaching Pine Cones

To wire pine cones for greenery attachment, use a #22 gauge floral or craft wire wrapped above the first row of scales from the cone bottom, leaving enough extra wire to twist together around the center and then to wire to an arrangement.

Pine Cone "Flowers"

Uses for Pine Cones

- Pile several nice cones into a large basket tied with a bright ribbon.
- Attach cones to garlands, wreaths, and other arrangements.
- Tie ribbons to cones and hang as tree ornaments, dangle from a light fixture, or over an open doorway.
- Use sharp wire cutters to cut cones into "flowers." Hold cone at the top and push clippers between the scales three rows from the bottom, as far into the center as they will go. Turn to the other side and continue to cut toward the middle at the same point, rotating the cone as you cut, until it breaks into two pieces. The inside will look like a single-petaled flower … and the top, like a zinnia. Both can be used to accessorize greenery, or wrapped wire "stems" can be attached to the cone "flowers" and covered with floral tape to secure and use in an arrangement. Spray paint for color variety.
- Glue pine cones together in gradually smaller circles to form a pine cone tree, using more glue to attach one tier to another. The hot-melt glue gun is also an excellent tool for adding small nuts, sweet gum balls, and other ornaments to this miniature "tree." Spray over all with Glossy Wood Tone for a lustrous finish. Or simply drape with shiny gold or silver cording and put a miniature star on top of your pine cone tree.
- A terrific and fun idea is to plant grass seed in a pine cone and watch it sprout. Drop loose soil into the cone's scales and sprinkle with seed. Place cones in shallow sand or sphagnum, and water sparingly, setting in a warm light place. Watch them sprout with winter greenery and then tie with bright red Christmas ribbons for a real conversation piece.
- See how to make a pine cone wreath on page 92.

If you're not into nature hunts, or don't happen to live near the pine forest, you will find mail order cones and cone-craft accessories from supply houses listed in the backs of magazines.

TWIGS, VINES, BRANCHES, STEMS, DRIFTWOOD

Branches and limbs bared by a fall's worth of raking look stunning in silhouette against the winter sky. Nudity is kind to old trees.

One of my favorite decorative accessories is a simple stand of twisted limbs in a vase, jug, or other interesting container. Seek in woods or shopping venues: corkscrew hazel (*corylus avellana contorta*), willow (*salix*) stems, red-barked dogwood (*cornus alba*) … Very dramatic stuff.

Another use for interestingly shaped branches and limbs is as a small "tree" for hanging special ornaments.

The "Bare" Tree

Place long curved branches of appropriate size in a container, securing at the bottom with floral clay, marbles, smooth pebbles, or a "frog." If the branches are large and unruly, fill a good-sized container with pebbles or sand to provide a deep, strong base. If this doesn't work, pour a base mixture of plaster of Paris and small stones into the container around the stems for a permanent foundation.

Attach candies, ribbons, small ornaments, bows, birds, dried flowers, painted eggs, children's handmade ornaments, sachet bags ... to tree limbs. The possibilities are endless.

You might also decorate a "bare" tree with little toys and trinkets for surprise gifts to Christmas guests—everyone is allowed to select a favorite treat.

For a sophisticated effect, spray paint bare limbs a stark white, adding sparkle with a string of tiny white lights for nighttime glitter. Crystal or silver ornaments also look smashing on this tree.

The nature lover would decorate his "bare" tree with drapings of Spanish moss, small vine baskets, birds and animal figures perched on each limb.

Driftwood resting on a table, shelf, or mantel makes an eye-catching base for miniature birds, animal figures, or a tiny nativity scene. Attach wooden figures by gluing thumbtacks onto their bottom and inserting into the soft wood.

Vines such as honeysuckle, wisteria, grape, and kudzu have produced an extremely popular twist on the traditional evergreen wreath. Bared and dried vines wrapped and twisted in a circle make rustic door and wall decorations, as well as unusual centerpieces on the dining table, where these might encircle a large candle, greenery, a miniature scene, an antique decoy, or form a nest for a whole flock of bird figures.

See page 93 for making wreaths and other wild and crazy decorations from pliable vine. Accent with baby's breath, eucalyptus, dried flowers and herbs, narrow strands of ribbon ...

Nuts, Pods, Seed Heads, Fungi, Osage Oranges ...

These bring texture and eye appeal to arrangements. Use thin wire or a hot-melt glue gun to secure their attachment. Buy seed pods already dried, or dry them yourself as you would flowers and stems. Hairspray keeps seed heads intact. Consider lotus or okra pods, milkweed pods, gumballs, cotton bolls, pussywillow, wheat sheaves, acorns, walnuts, chestnuts, pecans. All or some of these wired or glued together would make interesting swags or garlands.

Osage oranges are a terrestrial phenomenon more closely resembling miniature Martian heads than Florida's finest, but they make colorful additions to Williamsburg apple cones, cornucopias, and other decorative arrangements. Considerably less expensive than fresh fruit (they're free), osage oranges are inedible, relatively indestructible (until they rot), and provide a resourceful and unusual objet d'art to surprise any and all visitors yet unenlightened as to their existence. Collect osage oranges at their peak in mid-November to mid-December. Grown on the small *maclura palmifera* tree, of the mulberry family, this bright fruit is mostly available in the rich, moist, woodsy soil of the south and southwest.

Kathy's "Bear" Tree

A variation on the "Bare" Tree is the "Bear" Tree—an annual custom of my friend Kathy, who has a huge menagerie of stuffed bears. To placate these strong personalities (each of them speaks in his or her own voice) on Christmas Eve, she trims a tree exclusively in bears—small carved, clay, paper, papier-mâché, glass, porcelain, stuffed (and smiling) teddies ... Wendell, Bearyshnikov, Teddy Roosevelt Bear, et al., are unanimously delighted!

Pine Cone Firestarters

Dip dried pine cones into paraffin melted in a coffee can placed in hot (not boiling) water. Let dry on newspaper. Tie several of these in a small burlap bag or arrange in an interesting container with a card instructing their use as "kindling."

We Need a Little Christmas!

Then there was the year poor Missy, newly-graduated apartment dweller, was unable to relinquish the early returns from her first employment for an extravagance so grand as a Christmas tree. She had no lights, no stand, no ornaments … nothin'.

Sympathetic Sis to the rescue — we got some tiny red bows and quickly went about transforming her potted Norfolk Island pine into a merry! merry! masterpiece. We added a single tacky glass ball for the sake of sentiment, laughed, and set out to make eggnog.

The moral of this story is: you can make a merry Christmas out of just about *anything*. And houseplants that wilt and whisper for water all year long will adore the ornamentation of bows, tiny tree lights, shiny balls, small figures, and any other attention you can give them. Use the greenery and other accessories already in your home to your full Christmas advantage when time, funds, and/or energy limitations demand bright creativity and resourcefulness.

Resourcefulness. Let this be the catchword of the '90s … and beyond.

Other "Little Christmas" Ideas You Might Try

- String tiny white lights on a ficus or other "house tree."
- Cover ordinary clay pots with festive Christmas fabric or colorful tissue tied with a ribbon or raffia.
- Lay a manger scene under the shade of a Middle-Eastern-like palm or fern.
- Add natural greenery, berries, miniature pine cones, and other "found" objects to everyday decorative objects, such as candlesticks, coat hooks and racks, baskets, chandeliers, light fixtures …
- Use bright red ribbons and bows to brighten up these same items.
- "Gift wrap" a hall mirror, picture frame, or pillow with ribbon and a big bow.
- Fill a basket or baskets with shiny red apples, oranges, pears, lemons, limes, pine cones, greenery …
- Pull out all your candlesticks and arrange a cluster of Christmas candles on a table or mantel.

DECORATING WITH FOOD

Being a child of the "think of all the starving kids in China" generation, I admit to having a difficult time advocating the use of edibles for the luxury of pure aesthetics. But who can resist the shapes, fragrance, and color of fresh fruits and vegetables?

Drill holes in sweet gum balls and dried pods with a $1/16$" drill bit. String or wire to make a chain, spray with Glossy Wood Tone or colored paint, and hang on the tree, or in wreaths and garlands.

The farmer's market, grocery store, or your own garden can be the source of many colorful decorating supplies.

Select firm, fresh, slightly unripe items. Check for blemishes and choose attractive shapes and sizes.

Clean fruit and vegetables with a dry cloth and consider one of the following methods for highlighting color with a glossy shine:

1. Gloss fruits and vegetables not to be eaten with a clear liquid floor wax.
2. Put a shine on produce you plan to display now, eat later with a light vegetable oil and gentle buffing.

Depending on the heat and humidity levels in your home, fresh produce lasts several days at room temperature. Keep your eye on it and replace pieces that become soft or begin to mold or smell. Keep fruit bowls well ventilated by filling the bottom with a few unshelled walnuts. Allowing air to circulate around produce retards spot rotting, and cool temperatures (60-70° F) are best for preservation over time.

Drying Vegetables and Fruits for Ornamental Use

Effectively dried produce will last a long time in home arrangements.

Red peppers are easy to grow and dry colorfully in time for Christmas. Hang them by a thread or wire in a dry place out of direct sunlight until they are crisp and slightly shriveled. You can also air-dry onions, garlic, okra pods ...

Artichokes can also be dried for arrangements (if you can sacrifice these delicacies to decorative rather than culinary art!). Stuff tissue paper between leaves, expanding as desired. Set artichokes on bottom (after trimming the stem) in a flat baking dish filled to a 1" depth with silica gel. Place in a 125-150° F oven overnight or until dry. Petals may be forced open further during the drying process.

Pomegranates highlight the Christmas color scheme. Cut fruit in half, scooping out the center. Thread #16 gauge wire in approximately 10" lengths through each side of the half and hang to dry in a well-ventilated place.

Dried gourds are perhaps one of the best-known examples of dried fruits used for decorative purposes. Many cultures use these for musical instruments, or colorfully dye and paint them for ornamentation. Pick gourds for drying after the first frost. Wash and dip in Lysol liquid disinfectant. Rinse with cool water and pat dry. Drill tiny holes in the top and bottom and dry hanging or on a rack or screen with good circulation. The gourd will be completely dry when the seeds rattle when the gourd is shaken. Paint with clear acrylic spray.

A Few of My Favorite Things ...

If I were allowed only four things to turn my everyday house into a holiday charmer, I'd have:
a bolt of red ribbon, a bundle of berries, a few candles, and a branch or two of greenery

 Use softened fruits to make delicious banana nut breads, applesauce, cakes, and puddings.

Wiring Fruit and Vegetables for Decorative Use

Push #16 gauge wire through the center of the produce, or below center, as needed for display. Twist wire ends underneath or behind piece and wrap ends around a wired pick for attachment to straw, wire forms, ropes, hooks, or ... um, Styrofoam.

Wired picks inserted through the fruit center are also used for attaching produce to wire forms and garlands, but remember never to eat fruit or vegetables pierced by floral picks. The dye is toxic.

Commercially-dried fruits and vegetables are widely available—not inexpensive, but long-lasting.

Williamsburg Apple Cone

One of America's best-loved traditions, this centerpiece is made with cone-shaped wood forms in many colorful and creative designs. Fruits, vegetables, nuts, foliage, and whatever else strikes your fancy mix well with fresh greenery for a captivating colonial accent.

The wooden cone forms are available in craft and hobby shops, some floral and department stores, or may be ordered from:

Colonial Williamsburg
201 Fifth Avenue
P.O. Box CH
Williamsburg, VA 23187

Use magnolia leaves stemming as a skirt from the base. The largest items (apples, oranges, lemons ...) are attached to the lower pegs, while gradually smaller items (kumquats, grapes, boxwood, holly, nuts ...) fill the upper areas and any gaps between the fruits and vegetables.

Inserting cloves in each fruit makes good "scents," and nandina or holly berries tucked among the greenery adds a nice accent. Top the entire cone with a pineapple for the authentic Williamsburg look.

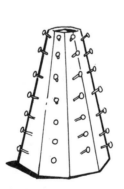

Undecorated cone

Williamsburg Apple Cone

 Yates apples are small, hard apples perfect for arrangements. Winesap is another good variety for decorating.

Other Decorative Uses for Fruits and Vegetables

- Fill a bowl or basket with apples, oranges, grapes, bananas, nuts in shell, pomegranates …
- Let grapes tumble from a silver épergne.
- Mix a Christmas cornucopia of greenery, fruits, and vegetables, spilling bountifully onto a table.
- Fill each tray of a glass or silver salver with fruits, cookies, candies, marzipan, nuts …
- Cover an interestingly shaped Styrofoam block base with fruit and nuts, or simply arrange items on a table on plastic protective strips in various unusual configurations: S curves, star, circle, spiral, diamond … Conceal plastic or Styrofoam with sphagnum or Spanish moss and fill in with greenery, candles, ribbon …
- Decorate a basket or bowl of bright shiny apples or pomegranates with Christmas green holly or ivy.
- Attach small apples and citrus fruits wired with floral picks to a Styrofoam cone form; fill the gaps with nuts and greenery.
- Attach wired fruits, vegetables, and wrapped treats to wreaths, swags, garlands, and other arrangements for color and texture.
- Tie polished fruits with ribbons at the stem and hang from a large chandelier, in a doorway, from a window frame, from hooks attached to ceiling beams …
- Insert long slender candles, small votives, or birthday candles in holes cut in fruit and arrange among greenery on a mantelpiece.
- String or wire cranberries and popcorn, gumdrops and marshmallows, dried fruits and vegetables … for the tree, swags, garlands, and ornaments. Create circles, star and heart shapes, drapes, and multiple rows for new twists on an old-fashioned tradition.
- Use gourds, fruits, and vegetables as flower vases. Scoop a small hole into the top of the produce, insert a moistened piece of oasis or a water-filled plastic pill bottle, and add fresh flowers and sprigs of greenery.
- Frost grapes (see page 175) and lay on a silver tray around a crystal vase of red and white tulips or roses.
- Roll apples in egg whites, then in granulated sugar for a frosty look.
- Stud apples and citrus fruits with cloves in interesting patterns and display in a bowl or all wired together on heavy gauge wire for hanging or draping. These also make a seasonal statement floating in mulled wine or hot cider in a punch bowl.

 See page 103 for instructions on oven-drying apples and star fruit for wreaths and other decorations.

A Reminder of What's Available

From the grocery or farmer's market … to your fruitful imagination:

apples
artichokes
asparagus
bananas
broccoli
Chinese cabbage
coconut
cranberries
garlic
grapefruit
grapes
kiwi
kumquats
lemons
limes
mangoes
okra
onions
oranges
papaya & pears
peppers
pineapple
plums
pomegranate
squash
star fruit (carambola)
zucchini
acorns & chestnuts
filberts & hazelnuts
macadamias
pecans & walnuts
candy canes
gumdrops
hard candies
Hershey Kisses
Lifesavers
lollipops
M&M's
marshmallows
peppermints
sugar cubes
sugar ice cream cones

SUGAR AND SPICE ... AND EVERYTHING NICE

Something sweet that's good to eat is also fun to look at. If you can keep the kids (and that means all of you!) from filching the decorations, bright and colorful candies and spices are swell holiday attractions.

- Use clear-drying glue or a hot-melt glue gun to attach round peppermints or decorative hard candies to a Styrofoam wreath or cone. Spray with clear acrylic spray for an inedible candy wreath or tree.
- Arrange peppermints or flat hard candies in patterns (just barely touching) on a cookie sheet. Melt together (just barely) in a 300° F oven for 3-5 minutes (watch carefully). Remove to freezer to harden and hang on the tree.
- Use thin wire or ornament hooks to hang colorful chocolate kisses from bared tree limbs, a houseplant, or the decorated tree.
- Decorate the house with colorfully frosted cookies, using them as wreath adornments, hanging displays, ornaments ...
- Fill miniature baskets or halved and painted eggshells with gumdrops and other tiny sweets. Hang or set out around the house (saving plenty of extras for refills).
- Wire a natural-colored or painted ice cream sugar cone with #22 gauge wire and hang, filled with sugary treats, nuts, or popcorn balls. Or cover a Styrofoam ball with fabric, tied with a ribbon, to create "fake" ice cream cones for the tree.
- Use candy canes all over: tie a bunch of big canes with ribbon, display canes and old-fashioned candy sticks in a glass canister decorated for the holidays, glue canes to a plastic pint container and spray with clear acrylic to fill with wrapped peppermints and kisses.
- Trim a miniature tabletop tree or pine cone tree with whole spices: anise, nutmeg, cinnamon sticks, blade mace, cardamom, gingerroot, allspice ...
- Gather up whole cloves in sheer fabric or net circles tied with ribbon for hanging or bunching into a basket.
- Plant "lollipop" cookies on sticks in clay pots, with kisses and gumdrops as your planting medium. Tie a sweet bow with licorice strings or ribbon around each stick for a terrific decoration or gift.
- Wrap large cinnamon sticks with ribbon and attach a net-wrapped bag of smaller spices, dried flowers, and tiny ornaments for decoration.

AC-SCENTS—THE SPICY SMELLS OF A CHRISTMAS HOUSE

Begin these projects by mid-November ...

Pomander Balls

Make some for yourself, more for friends.

6-8 apples/oranges/lemons
½ lb. whole cloves
¼ c. each: ground cinnamon, cloves, nutmeg, allspice
¼ c. powdered orris root (from the pharmacy)
4 drops of one of the following: essence of rose, clove, jasmine, sandalwood, lemon verbena, cinnamon ... (The essence is optional, but gives a stronger fragrance you can enjoy longer. Oils are available at cosmetic and health stores.)

Insert whole cloves closely together all around the fruit. This takes forever—so rent a good movie and involve the whole family. Take care not to tear the fruit's skin. Coat balls completely in the spice mixture and orris root. Hang by ribbon in a warm, dry place for approximately one week. A closet is excellent, and the fragrance remains in this small area for a decent length of time. Add oils after drying is complete, and renew fragrance with droplets of oil as needed.

Quick Pomanders

Make balls as above. Bake in a tin pan in warm (200° F) oven for approximately three hours. Cool. If desired, wrap pomander balls in fabric, lace, or netting, and tie with ribbon to hang all over the place.

Potpourri

... is available everywhere in every fragrance, all the time. Baskets and jars, boxes and bowls of potpourri will fill your home with a delightful sensuality. Even though the French word means "rotted pot," the stuff still smells divine, and a clever mix can be pretty to look at as well. Gather ingredients from the country and the garden, the grocery and the health food store: cones, dried spices, dried flowers and petals, dried citrus peel, beechnuts, seed pods, leaves, cedar shavings, crushed whole spices (crushing releases the oil), lichen ... Add ground spices (1 T. each of orris root powder, nutmeg, cinnamon, cloves, and ½ oz. powdered gum benzoin) and essential oils all mixed together in a paste according to your favorite "flavor." Crumble over and stir into mixture, then set aside to cure over 6-8 weeks in an airtight container in a dry, warm place. Shake occasionally to mix.

- Tie tiny baskets of potpourri to the tree.
- Fill a glass or crystal bowl with spices and petals for a fresh bath deodorizer.

Balsam Pillow Sachets

Pick new growth (the most fragrant) balsam needles at the tip of the branch. Dry on a wire mesh screen, allowing full circulation, for one week. Put dried needles in a jar with 2 T. salt per one cup needles.

Shake the jar occasionally (whenever you unload the dishwasher?) while drying approximately three weeks. For added fragrance, add 1 T. cedar bark and 1 t. oil of pine.

Stuff balsam in loose-weave fabric bags and decorate with lace, ribbon, raffia, dried flowers ... Add to the stuffing of a new pillow, put in closets and drawers, use to scent fabric ornaments or stuffed animals and dolls ...

Harriet Kirkpatrick's Pecan Shell and Spice Decoys

Materials:
plastic decoy (or other figure)
    available at sporting goods
    and hobby supply stores
crushed pecan shells
hardware cloth (large screening)
medium window screening
fine window screening
white glue or gesso
pieces of crushed cinnamon
    sticks and cloves
2 T. ground or instant coffee
2 whole allspice
cinnamon oil

Make three piles, mixing pecan shells and 1/3 of the cinnamon and clove pieces, sifting through each fineness of wire screening: sift through large screen first and reserve large pieces. Sift through medium screen and reserve pieces to another pile. Sift remaining shell through fine wire and reserve debris in third pile. Discard powder. Paint entire surface of decoy with white glue, except for the bill. Set duck in aluminum pie pan and pour shell/spice mixture from the first pile over the glued figure. Fill in gaps, first with the second pile, and finally with the third from the finest screening. Figure should be completely covered. Paint the duck's bill with glue and dip into some rich ground coffee. Glue allspice for eyes and trim with ribbon or dried flowers. Make several of these at one time for teachers, friends, and family gifts, and more for your own decorating. Drizzle with cinnamon oil when dry.

- Fill net or fabric bags with potpourri and tie with ribbon for tree, wreath, swag ... ornaments.
- Cover plastic forms with white glue or gesso, dip and roll in potpourri to cover. Tie with ribbon for color.

DECK THE HALLS WITH ...

The holidays bring with them a bounty of traditions and symbols. Customs originating in every corner of the world have given us many means with which to celebrate the season: Advent, the crèche, candles, stockings, wreaths ... and, of course, the Christmas tree. Each tradition has a meaning all its own, meanings attached to individual religions, lands, and families.

Consider each and every one of the Christmas symbols, customs, and traditions as you decorate. Utilize bought items, natural and found objects, and hand-crafting techniques to realize your own interpretations of the season, to create your own very special meanings, and to suit your own very original style.

Gather together *all* your resources and DECK THE HALLS!

Deck the Halls with ... Advent Wreaths and Calendars

❄ ADVENT WREATHS

Advent wreaths can be made from almost anything: greenery, Spanish moss, dried herbs and flowers, clay ... as long as you include the requisite four candles for each of the four Sundays of Advent, and the all-important white candle in the center for Christmas Day.

Let it be said that due to the surprising quickness with which Advent arrives after the already full Thanksgiving weekend, it is even permissible to use a plastic wreath for purposes of celebration ... when getting yourself together with something green and natural is beyond your immediate grasp (though it must be said here that I am opposed to the use of plastic except in the direst emergencies!).

Many families enjoy the custom of lighting the Advent candles in their homes, with scripture readings, songs and poetry, or Advent readings from church booklets. This is a ceremony rich in meaning and tradition and should be included in every Christmas celebration.

Another celebration of Advent is the daily opening of windows on specially-made calendars marking the 25 days of December in joyous anticipation of that all-important 25th.

 Scented oils and fragrances are available in many "flavors": pine, lemon, cinnamon, bayberry, musk, rose, mixed bouquet, apples and spice ... Putting a drop or two of oil on a light bulb creates atmosphere with the flick of a switch. The heat brings the scent to life. Add oils to dried items to accent the natural fragrance.

❄ ADVENT CALENDARS

Advent calendars are available at stationery, gift, and department stores, in styles as elaborate, religious, or secular as you choose. There are gilded paper calendars with nativity scenes behind each of the windows, as well as Snoopys and Disney characters, hiding gifts and greetings to be revealed each day.

Try making your own. You only need two sheets of paper or heavy cardboard. With a sharp mat knife, cut windows that fold open to reveal each of the 25 tiny pictures you have drawn or cut out from old cards or magazines.

Children love animals, Christmas symbols, pictures of gifts, candies, and favorite cartoon characters or silly faces. They don't seem to care all that much what is behind the window … just that another one is opened. And that means one day closer to Christmas!

Even more popular than pictures are tiny candies or gifts included for each of the 25 days, or perhaps just the four Sundays of Advent. Glue, wire, sew, or hook these little gifts to a wooden, cardboard, or fabric-covered calendar board or box cut in the shape of a Christmas tree, a star, a gingerbread house … use the best of your creative powers to thrill the little ones during the exciting countdown.

Deck the Halls with … Colorful Christmas Wreaths

Anybody who doesn't at least hang a wreath on the front door at Christmas is surely a direct descendant of Ebenezer Scrooge. And he was not known to have children, so there's *no* excuse!

The wreath has come to be one of the most visible outward signs of Christmas spirit on home and storefronts everywhere. It doesn't take much to make one; many of the best supplies are free—a few branches of evergreen, some pine cones, and an old twisted coat hanger

Several wreath-making ideas have already come your way. Here are a few more.

❄ BARE STRAW WREATHS

The traditional greenery wreath is certainly a lovely symbol of the season, but not all wreaths have to be green.

One of the favorites is the straw wreath form available at decorating and floral supply stores. The straw has that clean country look, providing a good neutral background for all kinds of shapes and colors but also allows the option of overwrapping it with ribbon or fabric or whatever. Its density invites plenty of good-natured poking fun, and holds up well under the ordeal. Craft pins, straight pins, wired picks, and craft wire attach all kinds of things to the straw wreath form, or you can leave several relatively nude, if doing so matches your color scheme, style, and idea of a good time.

Advent

Advent, the coming of Christ, is celebrated each of the four Sundays preceding Christmas and culminates with a special celebration on Christmas Day. Most often, a set of four purple candles is arranged in a greenery wreath, one candle lit each Sunday. These surround a large white candle in the center, which is finally lit on Christmas Day. Advent candles symbolize Christ and his light—"I am the light and the way."

The custom of Advent wreaths and calendars originated in Germany and Scandinavia. Candles surrounded by evergreens were suspended from the ceiling by bright red ribbons, a glowing decoration to reflect the true meaning of Christmas.

Make it Easy on Yourself

Using a straw wreath form and spiked candleholders, you can make an attractive Advent wreath in a jiffy. Insert candleholders into form, decorate with greenery, ribbon, berries, dried flowers … and place a large white candle on a circle of cardboard in the center.

❄ OTHER NON-GREENERY WREATH IDEAS

- Make a wreath with dried red peppers, dried onion and garlic, bay leaves …
- Twist strands and strands of tiny twinkling lights around a wreath form for sparkle in the dark.
- Make a wreath of whole spices and nuts.
- Wire several small pomander balls, clove-studded citrus, and cheery apple head Santas (see page 229) onto heavy #18 gauge wire and bend in a circle, tying the ends and finishing with a bow.
- Wire natural sponges in a wreath for the bath, over a mirror or even the "throne." Pleat a colorful new terry washcloth, stitching down the middle to fan out on either side, and attach some new red and green toothbrushes personalized for each family member at the seam.
- Wrap around to encircle other materials: eucalyptus, corn husks, dried pomegranates, bleached sand dollars and starfish, papier-mâché or clay objects, angelic soft-sculpture faces … for an unusual wreath whose very ring symbolizes the unity and eternity of Christ, His and our own love for one and all.

Deck the Halls with … Candles

Many of life's special occasions include the use of candles: Christmas, Hanukkah, birthdays, weddings. From ancient times to the present, candles have symbolized joy and hope, warmth, light, and life, particularly during the otherwise cold and gloomy days of winter.

Cluster candles in various lengths and widths, surround with greenery, wrap with ribbons or mini-wreaths, stand in interesting candlesticks and holders, insert in floral arrangements …

Available in many colors, sizes, and scents, candles gently illuminate your decorating, while pine, cranberry, cinnamon, sandalwood … scented candles fill the home with Christmas spice.

❄ THE USE AND CARE OF CANDLES

- Put candles in the freezer before using to slow burning and dripping. Dripping can also be minimized by dipping candles in the following solution:

2 oz. dextrin (available at the pharmacy)	2 oz. Epsom salts
	13 oz. water

 Some favorite "gifts" of small children are the tiniest, cheapest things on the dime store shelves: plastic jewelry, cars, planes, dinosaurs, insects, snakes, cowboys and Indians … the kinds of "precious" treasures coveted from gumball machines in the grocery store! Scrounge up a good collection of old party favors over the years. Children never seem to notice or mind recycling.

- Use floral or modeling clay to secure candles in various holders— you may want to paint the clay with food dye to match, if it will be visible.
- Paint solid white candles with melted candle wax or crayons melted in paraffin for a bit of pizzazz.
- Save leftover candle stubs to make new candles (see page 233) or to use as melted wax for other craft projects. Recycle!

❈ ACCENT CANDLES IN INNOVATIVE HOLDERS

- Create unusual candleholders with clay, using a candle to form the indentation needed to hold it securely. Dry, paint, decorate, varnish.
- Make mini-wreaths with vines, greenery, dried materials … to cover plain everyday candleholders.
- Glue heads of thumbtacks to a plain wood block for a candle base to be used in greenery arrangements. Or decorate the block itself.
- Using an ice pick or awl, make small holes in apples, oranges, or vegetables and insert long, slender candles to be lit at a dramatic moment during Christmas dinner.
- Recycle old candleholders by covering with papier-mâché, painting, gilding, utilizing concealed in full greenery arrangements …

❈ LUMINARIES ("LUMINARIOS")

These popular Mexican decorations light up the outside of the home with a spirited glow. Use:

10 or 15 lb. brown paper bags (or colorful gift bags)
sand
votive candles

Turn the tops of the bags down to make cuffs. Pour 3" of sand into the bottom of each bag and stabilize the candle by inserting it into the sand. Line the sidewalk, driveway, or curbside with luminaries during a party or on the nights before Christmas. The sand will put out the candles when they finish burning. If you're feeling super-inventive, pierce and/or stencil-cut designs on the upper half of the bags before filling with sand. The light will shine through, illuminating your design.

Candles in the Window

The tradition of placing candles in windows is said to have originated in Syria, the birthplace of Jesus Christ, where the flame would light the Christ Child's way on his journey. Today we continue the custom, using real or electric candles at each window to give our homes a warm Christmas glow.

Another tradition involving candles has flickered and died— don't try this at home. During the nineteenth century, *real* candles were used to light natural Christmas trees. Huge buckets of water were kept in the tree room in anticipation of the bursts of flames frequently igniting the drying trees. With the invention of electric tree lights, candles took safer positions in the decorating of Christmas homes.

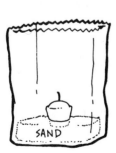

Dixie's Wire Mesh Baskets

Buy screen wire mesh (about #22 gauge) and cut in 10-12" squares with tin snips or sturdy scissors. Lay one square diagonally on top of another, molding mesh around a full (heavy) soda can or clear glass votive candleholder, fanning out about halfway up the can. Bend and twist to shape and tie underneath the spreading corners with raffia, natural jute, or a rubber band to hold shape. Spray-paint gold or silver. When paint is dry, add contrasting gold or silver ribbon, if desired. Use as a candleholder, candy basket, plant container ... May vary size to use.

Deck the Halls with ... Nativity Scenes and Crèches

A nativity scene, or crèche, lends inspirational presence to the holiday season. Scenes may be constructed from all kinds of materials: porcelain, carved wood, glass, bronze, paper, starched fabric, straw, papier-mâché ... The renderings of Christ's birth are as detailed and sophisticated, as crude and simple as the scene is interpreted by the many artists and craftsmen who have done so.

Small figures may be purchased in sets or collected individually over time to complete a scene—a simple Madonna and Child or an entire assembly of those assumed to have been in Bethlehem at the marvelous birth: Joseph, shepherds, wise men, angels, the drummer boy, and the many animals of field and stable.

International travelers will find nativity art a frequent offering of many a country's craftsmanship. Collecting pieces as you wander gives you valuable souvenirs, as well as wonderful reminders of your trip each Christmas as you put them on display.

Whether you buy nativity figures or make them yourself, the scene can be added to over the years to create a joyful tableau.

When laying out your scene, consider using greenery, straw, or hay to naturalize the crèche. Construct a wood or cardboard manger and stable to house your figures. See "Making Merry ... Craft Faces and Figures" for a variety of miniature construction techniques: liquid starch fabric molding, papier-mâché, coping saw wood cutouts, soft-sculpture, clay ...

Children also will enjoy recreating the nativity scene and may wish to make one of their own. Here is yet another way to take a bit of the commercialism out of Christmas and put some of the real meaning of the holiday back into your celebrations together.

Deck the Halls with ... Angels

Angels were the first bearers of the glad tidings—tidings of great joy to all men—and as such deserve a prominent position in the Christmas celebration. Collecting angel figures on travels and in little shops along the way will find you with delightful and lovely decorations. There are some truly marvelous figures available in the marketplace: some comical, some adorable, some primitive, and some gilded. Some are large and lacy and elegant, while others are almost too tiny to be seen. But what a heavenly gathering you might assemble with a year-round collection of angels!

My arty friend, Corinne, makes simply wonderful angel pins and stand-up sculpture from nothing more than snipped metal and paint, a pin backing or a wooden stand. The color, shape, and design are Corinne at her best ... true treasures.

And our young pal Anderson Currie, age four, after going through a

The word "crèche" is French for "cradle." St. Francis of Assisi is said to have made the first crèche for the people of his parish.

gallery with his mother looking at "real art" angels and other Christmas pieces, came home and decided to make his own. He directed Mom to cut out cardboard shapes from some old boxes (future recyclers of the world, hark!), designed a face and head shape, and went about painting an inspirational series of decorative angels to add to the Curries' real art collection—standing among greenery, perched against candlesticks, settled into the boughs of the tree ... Some of Anderson's angels are tall, some very small. Their robes are colorful, and some have even ascended to golden glitter status, but the charming aspect of the collection is that the faces—white circle eyes with dark black pupils, bold red "o's" for a mouth, and a small dot as the nose—are the universal feature that ties the series together in a beautiful chorus of innocence and awe. Exposure to the world of art can and does create creativity. Try to recapture the spiritual awe and free innocence of a four-year-old ... and see what you can come up with.

Again, go to the "Making Merry" BACK OF THE BOOK for tips on making little and large figures, and *get yourself some angels!*

For the mantel, the tree, the centerpiece, or even perched on your own shoulder, nothing is quite as glorious and uplifting as the glad tidings brought to us by the angels.

Deck the Halls with ... Stockings

The stocking could very well be the one decorative item that is totally yours and yours alone, recalling for you all Christmases past, waking those frosty mornings to find treasures left by Santa the eve before.

Select one for each family member—a durable, attractive, personalized stocking with the capacity to be stuffed full of fun and surprises, one that will be cherished and last through a lifetime of celebration.

Needleworked Stockings

Needlework shops offer many kits and patterns for needlepoint, cross-stitch, smocking, and embroidery in holiday motifs. There are also patterns for the old-fashioned handknit kinds, just like knitting a sweater. You can even use graph paper to create your own design to be reproduced as needlework.

Stitch an entire stocking or just handwork the cuff for attaching to a ready-made solid or print fabric stocking.

If you are making your own, simply draw a stocking pattern on newspaper, cut out your chosen fabric, and stitch together with a ½" seam. Clip corners and turn right side out. Stockings should be lined with a light cotton, satin, or contrasting print or solid. Cut lining from the same pattern as the stocking and stitch together with a ⁵⁄₈" seam, trim edges and insert. You don't need to turn the lining right side out, because the inside of the lining is the right side, right? Turn under the stocking top and slipstitch together.

Consider all these fabric possibilities for handmade stockings:

Kinds of Ribbon, String, Cord ... for Tying Things Up

... many widths, colors, and textures of:

covered cording (cut on bias)
curling
French-wired
gold/silver/color cording
grosgrain
lace
moiré
natural jute
paper
printed cotton
raffia
satin
sheer organdy
upholstery braid and cording
velverette
velvet
wired paper

Each family stocking should have the name or initials of its owner somewhere on the stocking to make it totally and absolutely his own. Even if you buy ready-made stockings, use a little embroidery thread, fabric marker, acrylic paint, appliqué, iron-on monogram … to personalize each one.

brocade	quilted cotton
burlap	quilted satin
chintz	satin
Christmas print	upholstery tapestry
corduroy	velvet/velveteen
moiré	wool
muslin	fake fur leopard print (?)
old quilt scraps	

❄ AND ALL THE TRIMMINGS

There are lots of materials for trimming or decorating stockings besides your own needlepoint, cross-stitch, or embroidery, which are also nice:

appliqués	old quilt scrap cutouts
buttons/beads	printed name tape
cotton crochet	ribbon
fabric	silky tassels
"faux" jewels	sponge or stamp printing
gold cord	tatting
hand-painted designs	tiny ornaments
lace	upholstery braid/trim

Carry out a theme you have adopted for all your Christmases with stitched-on, painted-on, or glued-on winter scenes; favorite animals; Christmas angels, nutcrackers, snowmen, reindeer, Santa, elves; old-fashioned toys; poinsettias …

Attach a felt pocket with a window big enough to frame a small photo of the stocking's owner, changing the photo from year to year to show Santa how much she has grown …

Sew lots of pockets onto the front, for small treats and surprises to be stuffed in on Christmas Eve …

 Give new needlework an antique appearance, by soaking in strong tea or coffee, then blocking to dry.

❄ SOCK STOCKING

Old argyles, knee socks, athletic socks, baby socks, or specially hand-knitted socks make fine authentic stockings for the fireplace. Sew on trim, initials, a monogram, or an embroidered design. If you find some big old knit socks with contrasting toes and heels, you will hang a fireside scene right out of "Twas the Night Before Christmas!"

❄ MADE BY ME, MYSELF

If you are the least bit artistic, a capable copy-cat, or even just a little free-spirited and funky, try using acrylic paints or fabric markers on a cloth stocking for a do-it-yourself holiday design. You could pick up a motif from upholstery or a favorite work of art, or just be wild with the paint and see what happens (modern art—a state of being!).

A child might just love to draw his own stocking design, and this will surely make a personalized treasure to appreciate for years to come. Hand-stitch around prominent portions of the design to throw them into relief for a quilted look.

❄ BLUE JEANS STOCKING

Who doesn't have an old pair of jeans—too short, too tight, torn seat? If the pants legs are salvageable, cut them off and make a blue jeans stocking. Cut a stocking shape from each leg using your newspaper pattern. Each side should be cut from the outside seam across the thigh to the inseam so the stocking will be big enough for maximum stuffing (the one time when hefty thighs are an advantage!).

With right sides together, stitch around the edge, making a ½" seam, clip corners and turn right side out. Topstitch around the edges for an authentic jeans look, line, and trim with a colorful red bandanna, silver studs, glittery appliqués, embroidery, lace, French fabric patches, acrylic paint-ons … just as they're doing with old denim jackets for a thousand bucks or so in the stores. (You can almost always steal someone else's ideas and make them your own, as long as you don't plan to sell … the best thing, however, is to branch out from the original idea with your own innovations.)

❄ STAND-UP STOCKINGS

Who says stockings have to be hung by the chimney with care? (well, besides Clement Clarke Moore). An unusual and interesting grouping of stand-up stockings—containers for Santa's surprises—can lend a clever touch to your decorating scheme.

Organize to Decorate

Bring order to the chaos of decorating:

1. Keep all supplies neatly stored together from one year to the next. It will be worth it!
2. Clear out non-essential everyday interior decorations (ashtrays, silk flower arrangements, centerpieces …) to make room for holiday accents.
3. Put out a few Christmas items at a time over a succession of days — Advent wreaths, greenery, candles, stockings … and limit yourself to leisurely good fun.

Got some old quilts that are in such bad shape you're ready to throw them away? WAIT! Salvage as much as you can by cutting out decent pieces and using them to make patchwork ornaments, throw pillows, stuffed toys, tablecloths, placemats, stockings …

Trim or cover an old pair of boots or galoshes (line with "odor-eaters" if necessary), or use several unique old boots—topped with fake fur, perhaps—one for each family member. You might even find some interesting ones at salvage stores, antique and flea markets.

Another trick is to drape moistened pre-starched fabric (see page 230) over an old boot or other form, sculpt to fit, remove when dry, and cover decoratively for a Santa receptacle.

Or make a boot form with chicken wire and papier-mâché over all.

Stand these unusual "stockings" near the fireplace or front door in anticipation of Santa's stuffings—or fill with greenery, apples, dried flowers.

❅ STOCKINGS DON'T HAVE TO BE SOCK-SHAPED

How about inverted "puppets," with an opening at the top instead of the bottom, for stuffing? Create characters with fabric and trim.

Or you could make each family member's favorite animal, Christmas character, or individualized elf … all crafted in the same style.

Soft-sculptured animals or dolls that sit, stand, or hang around just waiting for the Christmas Eve goodies can be endowed with a large mouth, pocket, pouch, apron, or bag to hold lots of good "stuff." Consider angels with full skirts; Mrs. Claus with a basket; little boys with lots of pockets; little girls with backpacks; Santa, elves, or trolls with over-the-shoulder bags …

❅ PET'S STOCKING

Don't forget the furry creatures in your life. They need a stocking, too, as Santa usually likes to leave a rawhide bone, catnip, rubber ball, or old slipper for their merry Christmas (actually, it's Rudolph who lobbies for all this, and you know Santa will do just about anything for Rudolph). A favorite pup might like his stocking in the shape of a bone. Or how about a carpet-covered stand-up stocking for kitty, to serve as a scratching post after Christmas?

Deck the Halls with … Ribbons and Bows

Once you learn how to make your own big fluffy bows, you will have Christmas decorating all wrapped up.

Aside from adorning gifts, ribbons and bows tie up greenery, dried grasses and flowers, fruits and other foodstuffs, pomander balls, spice bags … Large bows, small bows, simple ties, twisted ribbons, trailing ribbons, woven ribbons … all can be used freely and creatively in decorating.

- Decorate garlands and swags with bows and trailing ribbons.
- Tie tree limbs with bows. Or trail multiple streamers from an enormous bow at treetop.
- Make ribbon chains, using grosgrain, satin, or shiny curling ribbons.
- Wrap ribbon around wreaths, banisters, lampposts … for a candy cane look.

- Tie bows around candlesticks, sconces, a basket or pitcher handle, chair backs …
- Attach small bows to a stand of bare branches, the chandelier, houseplants …
- Hang polished apples, a pomander, or other dangling items by strands of glistening ribbons from a doorway, window frame, or sturdy light fixture.
- "Gift wrap" your dining room table by tying it up with a bow as the centerpiece.
- Tie sheer and shimmering organdy bows on silver and crystal ornaments to catch the glimmer of the tree lights.

Step 1

❆ HOW TO TIE (WIRE) YOUR OWN BOWS

More than any other aspect of holiday decorating, people seem most intimidated by the art of tying a bow. Relax! *You* are in charge, not the ribbon. If you goof up, just untie it, iron it, and start again. If you can't conquer your tying inhibitions, practice on some old ribbon several times until you work up the confidence to try it on the good stuff.

If you absolutely positively can't do it—okay, go ahead and fork out the exorbitant cost of a ready-made bow, but don't say I never tried to teach you how to make 'em yourself!

For each bow, you will need:

Step 2

3½ yds. of 3" wide ribbon
#22-24 gauge craft wire (approx. 1 yd. per bow)

a chenille stem (pipe cleaner) to attach bow to wreath

The type of ribbon you use can make a tremendous difference in how the bow will look. Ribbon wired around the edge is easiest to work with and holds its shape best through bad weather, humidity, and time. Taffeta ribbon has a good stiff body and is the same on both sides, which makes it easy to twist and loop without having to match a pattern. Velverette (velvet on one side, satin on the other) and printed cotton make attractive bows, but you do need to keep twisting and turning to keep the right side up. The only "ribbon" that is totally weatherproof is plastic, and, well, use your own good taste in compromising aesthetics with the elements!

Step 3

1. Begin by leaving a streamer approximately 12-15" long, as desired. Make your first loop according to the size of the bow you need, pinching the ribbon together at the bottom of the loop. Leaving a 3" length for twisting off the end, wrap the wire tightly around the first pinched gathering, which you are holding between your thumb and forefinger.

Steps 4 & 5

 The width of ribbon varies according to the size bow you want. A spool of craft wire is a wonderful investment for multiple bow-making and many other home projects.

2. Make an identical size loop on the opposite side, again gathering and pinching in the center, and again wrapping around that pinched center *in the same place*, overlapping the previous wiring. Pull wire tight.

3. Continue to make 6 to 7 loops, one and then an opposite, fluffing each loop to make a full bow, overlapping wire tightly with each loop at the gathers. If your ribbon is two-sided, twist the ribbon to keep the preferred side on top.

4. For the final round, pull a shorter loop around to the front and center of the bow, wrapping wire around the *center base of the loop* and then back around to the 3" length of wire from Step 1. Twist this end with the excess wire as tightly as possible. (The whole trick is to keep the wire tight, wrapped in one continuous central wiring.) Cut off any wire in excess of 3" and trim ribbon streamer to match the length of the original streamer.

5. Thread chenille stem under the central wiring and pull through, looping and twisting with the 3" length of wire for hanging.

See, it's not that difficult. Read the instructions again carefully. Study the diagram as you practice. Maybe you will become good enough to make and sell your own bows! You'll make a fortune!

Deck the Halls with ... Needlework

Fabric and fibers bring bright color and texture to the holidays. Fill your home with pillows, samplers, stockings, ornaments, soft-sculpture, guest towels, tree skirts, bell pulls ... the possibilities are as endless as the kits and materials available to ye of the nimble thimble.

Hang Christmas needlework in a bag near your TV all year long, to be picked up whenever you're watching "Brady Bunch" reruns, Challenge of the Gladiators, or one of those old Ronald Reagan film retrospectives. Take it with you to Little League baseball games and on long car trips. See THE BACK OF THE BOOK for needlework tips and techniques, and more ideas to "Make Merry!" with fabric and thread.

❄ PILLOWS TO SEW AND THROW

Embellish hand-worked pillows with Christmas figures, designs, and quotes or greetings to decorate sofas, chairs, and loveseats.

To make several quickie pillows, cut newspaper patterns of various shapes: squares, circles, Christmas trees, stars, angels ... Cut from a fabric that suits your decor and trim if desired with eyelet, lace, ribbon, ruffles, braid, fringe, tassels ... Incorporate buttons, cord, embroidery, and

 For a pretty finish to ribbon streamers, fold the ends in half and cut ribbon diagonally upwards toward the center.

appliqué to make designs. Hand-paint flowers, greenery, illustrations, or graphics in vibrant acrylics or soft watercolors.

Trim and decorate pillows with likenesses of your children, grandchildren, or pets! What a fun gift to make and give.

❄ MINIATURE DOORKNOB HANGERS

I'm crazy about these—little pillows that serve no purpose at all but to hang around looking stuffed and self-satisfied (like me after Christmas dinner!). They do, however, impart bits of wisdom in clever one-liners ... "I work so hard, I'm always finished!" kills me. For the holidays, stitch a Christmas greeting or phrase with small illustrations suitable to your theme or decor:

DECK THEM HALLS!

HO!HO!HO!

'Tis the season to be jolly!

Not a creature was stirring ... (for the kitchen)

My First Noel (for Baby's door)

Have a berry merry Christmas!

❄ FABRIC STUFF

Use leftover fabric scraps to cut out little figures, wreaths, and other Christmas shapes to sew and stuff as ornaments, mobile objects, or a crib-hanger. Bright colors and prints will open a baby's little eyes to the wonderful promise of Christmases to come ...

❄ SANTA CLAUS IS COMING TO TOWN

Make Santa caps of red fabric and trim with white fake fur or cotton batting. Stuffed animals and real live pets (always willing to participate in holiday hilarity) should each have a Santa cap to wear, as well as should the kids, you, your spouse, and probably Mr. Coffee, too.

You might want to whip up a huge canvas bag to decorate as Santa's bag—to hang by the tree, the fireplace, or on the hatrack ... in case you have some surprises to pack before the 25th. Or fill smaller drawstring bags with candies and nuts, small gifts and whatevers, for special deliveries and to have on hand for friends who happen by over the holidays.

The children might love playing Santa's helper in a cute elf costume with green tights, a hand-stitched brocade vest, turtleneck shirt, and feather cap.

Deck the Halls with ... Dancing and Prancing Things

Suspend something from your ceiling and walls and add dimension to your decorating: silver balls hanging from chandeliers, pomanders tied with ribbon across a doorway, a Moravian star hanging in the foyer ...

Limiting yourself to standing and sitting decorations can be ... well,

Start a Poetry Collection

Collect poems and phrases from favorite old Christmas cards and keep on file for needlework, designing your own greetings, calligraphy projects ...

How to Hang it All

Use hanging things as a centerpiece, dangling a decoration from the chandelier centered over the dining table. A dramatic effect is created by reflecting hanging objects in mirror tiles strategically placed on the table underneath.

Attach things to walls using: various-sized picture hooks (sized according to weight of object to be hung), wall mount tape, sticky putty, Plasti-tak, small nails (make an "x" with tape before nailing into plaster). Toggle bolts are necessary for heavy items. Consult your friendly hardware store clerk.

For hanging and dangling decorations, use craft wire, monofilament thread, heavy sewing thread, ribbon, yarn, string, ornament hangers, and red licorice whips!

limiting. There are only so many end tables, shelves, dining tables, and empty corners to work with.

Hanging decorations offer many advantages: out of the reach of children or grandchildren (usually), don't take up much living and working space, "highly" visible and eye-catching (watch your head!), as well as a multitude of possibilities:

- Framed needlework, samplers, Christmas card collage, calligraphed favorite verse or carol, photo history of visits to Santa …
- Ribboned pomanders and netted spice bags …
- Painted wooden spoons (great Santa faces)
- Clay or sugar cookie cutouts
- Gingerbread people or shapes
- Strings of paper dolls (trimmed and dressed with wrapping paper)
- Mini-wreaths (vine, greenery, dried herbs, stuffed fabric …)
- Greeting card cutouts (spray with clear acrylic and glue on a shiny paper backing)
- Tiny mirrors reflecting holiday liveliness hung on ribbons of varying lengths
- Collection of brass handbells tied with ribbon
- Favorite ornaments (special series, 12 days of Christmas, Santas, angels, silver snowflakes …)
- Ribboned cinnamon sticks
- Hand-painted eggs
- Painted or natural pine cones
- Gilded or bleached natural seashells
- MISTLETOE!

❄ PAPER SNOWFLAKES

Remember these from elementary school art class? Using aluminum foil, gift wrap, tissue paper, construction paper … cut paper into circles. Fold in half, then again in thirds, fourths, or more. Trim around the top, squaring or rounding off, and cut notches of different shapes into the sides, using small manicure scissors. Open up for a one-of-a-kind snowflake. Hang in windows, from light fixtures, on the tree, over doorways … These also make pretty package decorations, particularly for mailing.

❄ THE SUN, MOON, AND STARS

Gilded or silvery celestial orbs, crescents, and five-pointed stars are gorgeous Christmas decorations. Make or buy them, tie with shimmering organdy, and hang any and everywhere.

Or make shiny string balls: Dip string of medium thickness into white glue and wrap around an inflated balloon, carefully overlapping each end. Dry thoroughly, pop! and remove the balloon, and tie with ribbon or spiralled craft wire to hang. Use round balloons in various sizes for an interplanetary effect … spray paint or glitter for color and glitz.

❄ WIRE ART

A fairly low gauge craft wire in copper, bronze, silver, or green can be twisted and tied to make witty little hanging things for tree ornaments, mobiles, or all kinds of breezy dancers suspended from above. Mix wire colors and gauges, add beads, feathers, buttons, sequins ... and use small twists of thin wire to tie one piece to another. This is fun for all ages. Look at the designs of Matisse or Picasso or Calder before starting, and take off with your own re-visions. Fun friend gifts, dangling earrings or pendants, napkin rings, package decorations ... too.

❄ MOBILES

Balancing is the most important technique in composing a mobile. Beginning at the top, hang dangling things from mobile wires (available at craft stores) using monofilament thread. Adjust the length of string to balance each side of the mobile and work your way downward, adding new wires and hooks to keep balance.

Create a fun mobile using one of these:

painted ping-pong balls
cutout greeting cards (glue shiny
   paper on backs)
toy airplanes and lightweight cards
angels

tree ornaments or multi-colored
   glass balls
painted clothespin figures
tiny stuffed animals
miniature string balls

Allow hanging forms on the mobile to move freely; don't crowd things together so they are constantly bumping into one another. If this happens, you have accidentally made a wind chime.

Deck the Halls with ... Miniatures, Figures, and Scenes

The world of miniatures can be quite fascinating, a hobby for the entire family. Use all your resources and imagination to create tiny replicas for decorating your Christmas home. You may never want to put them away.

Miniature replicas of a New England village buried in snow and decorated for the holidays have been favorite displays over the years—from Maine to California. No matter where we live, this Currier and Ives rendering is our picture of Christmas in America.

With the popular renaissance of American folk art, the tiny wooden village pieces are readily available for Christmas and year-round decorating. Lay out the village on piles of polyester fiberfill or cotton batting, with a round mirror pond and tiny trees (available at model train accessory and hobby shops). Take a sentimental journey to Christmas as we always hope it will be—peaceful and lovely, snowy and serene.

Decorate and accessorize your village or other miniature scene with the following and all the other ideas that will come to you as you work:

cars, carriages, and sleds made from small matchboxes, or real antique-
   style Matchbox cars, trucks, and buses

Make a Christmas Shadowbox

Many sizes of shadowboxes are available at craft stores. Fill each individual compartment with special Christmas mementos: a tiny knit stocking, standing ornaments, spray snow, nativity figures, wrapped candy canes, popcorn, plastic cranberries, tinsel, icicles ... all kinds of things for beauty and sentiment. Cover the front with glass (yes, popcorn will survive under glass; mine has for twenty years!). A great birthday or graduation gift too, filled with life memorabilia and souvenirs ...

Setting the Scene

Display your miniature scene around the tree or on a salt relief board, or consider some of these other possibilities:

inside a fish bowl, rose bowl, or brandy snifter
in a shadowbox, for standing or hanging on a wall
in a cutout eggshell
in a dollhouse
in a Lucite box
amidst the tracks of an electric train set
under a glass dome

To make a realistic miniature display board, consider using the same method we all used to make salt maps for geography class:

1 c. salt
2 c. cornstarch
3 c. cold water
4 c. baking soda

Mix all ingredients together and boil in a large saucepan until mixture reaches the consistency of mashed potatoes. Spread onto plywood or heavy cardboard with a spatula, shaping and building up relief to form hills, mountains, snowdrifts … A new product, colored glue, makes shiny bright rivers and streams.

black electrical tape for a paved road made icy with a little "snow" sprayed on top
small tree twigs and bits of evergreen inserted in clay base sprayed with "snow" or threads of fiberfill
painted wood building blocks to resemble homes, storefronts, churches
tiny animals from dime store plastic sets
miniature dolls, dollhouse figures, or homemade "little people"
inverted toothpaste caps painted with rust nail polish for flowerpots and tree-stands
tied bundles of small sticks for firelogs (red, yellow, and orange cellophane simulates flames)
miniature pine cones painted green to become huge evergreens next to a mirrored pond
small mosaic tiles as cobblestones or stepstones
corrugated metal edging (garden stores) or cut and glued balsa wood fences and bridges
dyed bits of natural sponge for hedges
matchboxes wrapped as gaily-colored packages for a sleigh
salt mixed with a drop of black acrylic paint and sprinkled over white glue to simulate gravel
mailboxes, milk carts, streetlamps … cut from tin
Decorate a miniature Christmas tree with:
candle-wicking knots on string for popcorn chains
gilded tiny pine cones for ornaments
glued-on sequins and beads
gold or silver cord, or craft beading garlands
cut strips of tinsel
tiny white pompoms as snowballs
Spray all lightly with artificial snow!
Besides the village scene, consider miniaturizing your own version of:

The Nativity	Victorian dollhouse
Santa's workshop	Angels on a cloud
A country Christmas	Gingerbread village
Nutcracker scene	Electric train set
Animals' Christmas	Dickens' Christmas Carol
12 Days of Christmas	The Night Before Christmas
Sleighride	Santa's sleigh (and eight tiny rein-
International Christmas	deer)

Miniature accessories and materials are available at craft, hobby, and dollhouse specialty shops. Collecting and making pieces for miniature display is a project to bring years and years of pleasure and fun. Patiently create a family keepsake to enjoy together every Christmas season.

To insert a miniature scene in an eggshell, carefully cut out one side with small scissors, drip melted wax into the bottom, and insert figures in hot wax to stand, securing until wax cools.

Deck the Halls with … Clever Christmas Containers

A clever container for greenery, candies, gifts, flowers, miniatures … is a key ingredient for making an eye-catching arrangement. Entire conversations have begun over the use of something "cute" or unusual, sophisticated or outrageous, as a decorative accessory. The very best ones, as a matter of fact, are old things recycled into something new.

❄ CONTAINERS FOR INTERESTING DISPLAY

Sitting in your house right now, perhaps very quietly, perhaps on the endangered species/yard sale list, is something wonderful and unexpected, just waiting to be asked to participate in Christmas decorating. Is it:

- an old leather boot? Cover it with fabric, or leave natural (don't forget the "odor-eaters"!) and fill with something seasonal.
- a metal watering can? Paint, stencil, or tie with a bow.
- a stack of clay pots? Cover with fabric, paint, decoupage, lacquer … to use in groupings or scattered about with fun contents—anything growing, shiny, edible, or surprising.
- a vacant fishbowl? Fill with glass balls, a miniature scene, polyester fiberfill surrounding silver snowflakes glued to the sides …
- a small burlap bag? Paint or stencil … dip in liquid starch, fill with balled newspapers to shape, dry, and fill with pine cone firestarters (see page 102), or line with colored tissue and use to serve popcorn and pretzels when entertaining.
- a shallow large basket? Hang on a wall or door. Put sphagnum or Spanish moss in the bottom half as a nest for birds, a woodland setting for tiny elves or animals … or plant with an indoor garden.

❄ AND THE SOMETHINGS TO PUT INSIDE …

… fruit, greenery, nuts, pine cones, popcorn, colored water or liqueurs, small packages, papier-mâché or clay shapes, flowers, pomanders and cloved fruit, potpourri, sachets and spice bags, branches with or without ornamentation, miniature figures and scenes, toys, stuffed animals, glass balls, candies, candles, ornaments, crystal snowflakes, silk flowers, Christmas cards … ad infinitum …

KIDSDECORATING

Many of the projects and ideas suggested in DECK THE HALLS are suited to the whole family. Look for "Children, crafts for" in the Index for some of the best. It's fun to do things together, but even kids need to learn and experience the pleasure of doing and making things by themselves. See KIDSCRAFTS in THE BACK OF THE BOOK for guidelines to introducing them to their own hands and imaginations.

Other Display Containers

antique bottles and jars
big "Santa's bag"
brandy snifters
brass boxes
ceramic bowls, jugs
coil-rope basket
copper molds, colanders
cornucopias
cut glass bowls, pitchers
decorative boxes
Lucite containers
old-fashioned tins
painted cans or buckets
pewter bowls, pitchers
pine cone basket
ribboned basket
silver bowls, pitchers
stenciled peach basket
stockings
wine bottles

Show it Off!

Parents, find it in your heart to display at least one handmade Christmas decoration — from even the littlest angel — somewhere prominently in your Christmas house. You don't have to sacrifice your own aesthetics: give children their own little tree, let them decorate their rooms, and let the den or playroom be the domain of all the enormous "art projects" brought home from preschool.

'Specially Fun for Kids

Tape a huge piece of paper (from a roll) to a wall and color, paint, or collage a Christmas mural — nativity scene, Christmas village, Santa's workshop …

Use construction paper cutouts mounted on cardboard to make a Rudolph face. Cut a hole where the nose should be and blow up a red balloon through the hole … so the red-nosed reindeer can light Santa's way.

Wax milk cartons and juice cans covered with construction paper are excellent materials for a miniature Christmas village scene. See "Miniatures" (page 227) for accessory ideas.

Make a holiday banner with felt cutouts on a large background piece of felt to hang on the bedroom door. Hang on a dowel tied with string.

Compose a collage or mobile with old card cutouts, magazines, and gift wrap scraps.

String popcorn and/or cranberries on filament thread to hang on the tree or drape through garlands. Or use #18-20 gauge wire and string cranberries into stars, bells, trees, and other shapes.

Cover a plastic gallon milk jug with papier-mâché. Paint skin color and varnish. Glue on craft eyes, felt cutouts, and cotton to make a Santa face. Make a cap from felt.

Using gumdrops and miniature marshmallows, make a gumdrop tree on a thorny tree limb brought from outside. Tiny bows add extra color.

❋ STARCHY STRING ORNAMENTS

thick cotton string	colored cellophane
liquid starch	white glue

Soak thick string in liquid starch. Arrange string in shapes on top of the colored cellophane. Drizzle white glue all around each shape and lay another sheet of cellophane on top. Let glue dry. Cut out around the outside of the string shapes. Punch holes through the tops and string to hang on the tree, from a mobile, in front of windows, from a chandelier …

❋ MS. CAUGHMAN'S GILDED BAROQUE PICTURE FRAMES

(These are a hit with my friend Dede's elementary art students and their parents!)

"found objects" for texture: pasta shapes, rice, cereal, buttons, coins, small toys, lace, doilies, ribbon, acorns, seed pods, dried and silk flowers and leaves, broken jewelry pieces, popped corn …	heavy cardboard or pre-cut mat board white glue old paint brush spray paint (gold, silver, colors)

Cut cardboard with a mat knife to make a broad frame and opening (4 x 6, 5 x 7, 8 x 10 …) for the picture, or use a pre-cut mat board. Brush liberally over the entire surface with white glue and arrange various objects to cover frame in an "artistic" manner (teach such concepts as symmetry, balance, line, form …). You can build up frame with cut cardboard pieces glued and stacked at the corners, make double borders … there are no limits to the possibilities. Let glue dry overnight and spray paint. Make cardboard backing and wire to hang, or attach cardboard support to stand. Paint a picture or take a photograph to go inside. Fabulous for decorating and as gifts … at *very* little expense.

❋ POMPOM RUDOLPH

2" diameter pompom (light brown)	3" diameter felt circle (red or green)
1" diameter pompom (beige)	small pompom (red)
	brown felt scraps
	white glue

Glue brown pompom to felt circle. Glue beige pompom to center of brown pompom, and small pompom to the tip of the beige one (head, snout, red nose!). Cut antlers and ears from the felt scraps and glue to the top of the head against the felt circle. Use a toothpick to glue on eyes. With a needle, run a strand of thread through the top of felt (or holepunch carefully and tie a narrow ribbon through) for hanging.

❋ SNOW BALL

baby food jar and lid	tiny plastic figures
felt	decorative accessories
2 t. plaster of Paris	½ t. tapioca

Mix plaster of Paris with 1 teaspoon of water to form a thick paste. Drop a small mound onto the center of the inside of the lid. Just before plaster sets, press in figure(s) and decorations to stand upright (waterproof Santa and tree, reindeer, nativity, snowman …). Let plaster harden. Fill jar with clean water. Use the tapioca for snow. Sift tapioca through a medium strainer to remove larger pieces, then again through a fine strainer to remove all powder. Pour remaining tapioca into the jar of water. Cover lid top with felt and screw lid on tightly. Invert. Shake and let it snow!

❋ BASKET OF CHRISTMAS EGGS

Use wax crayons or melted paraffin wax to paint Christmas designs on boiled eggs. Dip into egg dye and the crayon color will remain vivid against the dyed background. Decorate a green plastic berry basket with red and white ribbons and fill with Easter grass or Spanish moss to display eggs.

OH! CHRISTMAS TREE!

Trumpet blast! The crowning glory, that magical creation that makes us jump up and down when we are toddlers and brings a glistening of joy to our eyes as adults is, of course, the *Christmas Tree!*

No other seasonal decoration is nearly as grand, as wonderful, as everlasting in our memory as The Tree.

The Living Christmas Tree

If you live in cooler climates, consider a living Christmas tree. Pack the earth ball containing the roots in a bucket with sawdust, peat, potting soil, or other mulch. Keep soil continuously moist and plant outdoors as soon as possible after Christmas.

Living trees should not be kept indoors much longer than 10 days. Avoid proximity to heat sources, dramatic temperature changes, and dehydration. You might acclimate the plant to outdoor temperatures by giving it a day or two in the garage instead of going straight from a toasty indoors to the freezing outside.

Plant in a reasonably sunny location (your own yard, or as a donation to a local park, school, or church), digging a hole twice as wide and 6" deeper than the root ball. Break up soil around the hole, amend with organic material or packaged soil amendment, build a mound in the center of the hole on which to rest the root ball (allowing roots to spread out), loosen burlap and fold back into the soil (this will rot, adding more organic matter to the soil), and fill hole to original level, patting down to pack. Cover with 2-3" additional mulch, soak with water, and support tree with stakes if necessary.

Ask your nursery for specific care instructions for these types of live Christmas trees:

Canada hemlock
Eastern red cedar
Eastern white pine
Juniper
Leyland cypress
Loblolly pine
Noble fir
Virginia pine
White cedar

I used to worry that with the cutting down of each live Christmas tree, we were surely denuding the forests of America at a rapid clip. Fortunately, further research proved my fears to be groundless. Despite the millions of trees cut each year, the supply increases rather than diminishes. Tree farms are regularly replanted and cutting the old trees allows more space and light for the younger trees to develop and thrive. What a real life metaphor!

A History of Trimming

Early tree trimmings, evolving toward those of Victorian England, were predominantly foods, tiny toys, flowers, and lighted candles (with buckets of water on constant standby), homemade popcorn and berry strings, paper chains, tinsel, marzipan, gilded nuts, handmade printed paper figures, and paper flowers.

- Tinsel originated in Nuremberg, Germany (1878).
- Candy canes were made to represent the shepherd's crook.
- Glassblowers in Lauscha, Germany, made blown glass ornaments and put the town on the world map because of them, until a border dispute placed Lauscha inside East Germany, cutting off trade with the U.S. and Britain. With the falling of the Wall, these lovely blown glass treasures have once again become available in Christmas shops everywhere.
- Ralph E. Morris of New England Telephone Co. invented tree lights in 1895.
- In 1927, General Electric introduced parallel wiring. (Remember the old series wiring—if you lost one light, you lost them all? Am I dating myself, again?)

Tree ornaments and ornamentation continue to be popular today—and some of the best-loved are the ones saved from Grandad's tree.

Selecting Your Christmas Tree(s)

Select a tree for its size, shape, color, and height. The needles should be pliable and firmly attached (when you shake the branches and lots of needles fall off, move on to another one). The sappy stickiness of the trunk is another sign of freshness.

Favorite tree varieties are Fraser fir, Douglas fir, spruce, cedar, and hemlock—all of which have relatively short needles, and the Scotch and white pines, which have clusters of longer needles.

For specifics on craftsmanship, use of tools, materials, and methods for various craft media, refer to THE BACK OF THE BOOK.

When You Bring the Tree Home

Cut at least 2" off the trunk to unclog the sap and fit the trunk into your tree stand. Place the tree outside in a bucket of water until ready to bring inside to decorate, and maintain an adequate water supply for the tree until the day you take it down (check every day and water as needed).

Trimming the Tree

Once the tree is up in the stand, well watered, and surrounded by a pretty tree skirt, let the festivities begin!

Trim to music—your own harmonious voices or Elvis's Christmas album. Pop popcorn. Serve cookies or fruit, eggnog or cranberry punch. Make this the fun and festive occasion it deserves to be.

WARNING! How many years did it take us to learn to put the tree in the stand and drape the lights *before* calling everybody in for the actual trimming? The preliminaries can be grueling, even traumatic if the trunk doesn't fit the stand, 30 limbs need to be pruned, or two out of three strands of lights are tangled and don't work. You might even save the trimming for the next day, when everybody has gotten over it.

Trimming Tips

- Keep the tree skirt and floor dry by first laying a piece of cut plastic, an old shower curtain, or a large leaf bag on the floor beneath the stand. Then wrap more plastic (old dry cleaning bags?) lightly over the water source, topped with the tree skirt.
- Use only safety-tested lights with the approved UL label and never more than three strands in a series from one outlet.
- Most strands of lights have 35, 50, or 100 bulbs. Use this chart for determining how many bulbs you need for your size of tree:
  6-foot tree—120-160 miniature bulbs
  7-foot tree—160-200 miniature bulbs
  8-foot tree—200-240 miniature bulbs
- Place lights near the tips of the branches so they outline the natural shape of the tree.
- If there is a family argument about whether to use white or multi-colored bulbs, string the tree with both, plugged into separate plugs. Then you can take turns being happy ... and maybe even eventually all plug in at once! (Credit Kathy K., the peacemaker, with this idea.)
- Put glass balls deep into the tree, with the largest ones around the bottom, the smaller at the top—again to enhance the tree's form and dramatize the color theme.

 Save the 2" trunk that you cut from the bottom of your tree for next year's Yule Log (see page 196) and carry on the old Scandinavian tradition. Have each family member touch it for good luck.

The Origin of the Christmas Tree

The first known written description of a Christmas tree dates back to 1605, in Strasbourg. Germany was the original site of many Christmas customs, perhaps due to the fervor of German religious leader Martin Luther.

It is said that Luther, walking through the forest one cold night, saw a large tree illuminated by the stars. The inspirational sighting moved him to take a small fir home with him, attach lighted candles, and share with his family the beauty he saw and imagined to be like that on the night the angels appeared to the shepherds of Bethlehem.

Prince Albert, who was also German and a historically-prominent Christmas lover, brought the Christmas tree to England when he married Queen Victoria. The palace tree was decorated with "fancy cakes, gilt gingerbread and eggs filled with sweet meats ... toys and dolls ... suspended by variously colored ribbons from the branches ... and an angel with outstretched wings ..."

The 19th century world was watching Victoria and Albert, and soon Christmas trees were everywhere.

The first public recognition of the Christmas tree in America was in 1856 when President Franklin Pierce put up the first decorated tree in the White House. In 1923, Calvin Coolidge lit the first outdoor tree in our nation's capital, and in 1980, that tree remained unlit in honor of the American hostages held in Iran.

Tree Alternatives

If there is no room for a large tree, or even a tree at all, consider hanging a well-constructed grouping of evergreen branches wired cleverly to a coat-hanger from a ceiling hook and decorate as you would a tree. If you have a small balcony or terrace outside sliding glass doors, an outdoor tree — Alberta spruce, for instance — could be decorated for you and your guests to enjoy. Use natural decorations and outdoor lights ... and add a few trimmings for bird friends as well.

- Follow this sequence of trimming: lights first, followed by garlands, tree trim (bows, Queen Anne's lace or dried hydrangea, Spanish moss), ornaments (put series ornaments on first, spread around or clustered together, and then the one-of-a-kind trimmers), and finally THE ANGEL on top (or whatever favorite treetopper you have).

Before trimming, you might lay your ornaments out in categories (pack them up accordingly when taking the tree down): glass balls, porcelain figures, carved figures, Sesame Street characters ... so you can distribute them evenly around the tree without an overabundance of red balls in a small grouping to the left of Kermit the Frog. If little children will be a part of your Christmas, keep the breakables at the top of the tree. Little hearts will shatter just as yours will if something accidentally gets broken. Consider putting the tree in a playpen or surrounded by a large circular collapsible gate for safety's sake. See page 84 for other Christmas safety tips.

Themes and Special Effects

Center your decorating efforts around the tree. Continue your overall theme with the ornaments, if you have a special theme in mind, or consider distinctive trims for a spectacular effect:

Color themes: one, two, or three color dominant trims, using bows, lights, balls, flowers ...

A Child's Christmas: candies, miniature toys and musical instruments, teddy bears, soldiers, rocking horses, paper chains, Raggedy Ann and Andy ...

A Cookie Tree: baked and decorated cookies for trimming now, eating later, or to give to visitors stopping by ...

Old-Fashioned Country Christmas: popcorn and cranberry strings, stuffed calico or tin cookie cutter ornaments, painted wooden ornaments, fruit and candy canes, ribboned cinnamon sticks, corn husk figures, old lace ...

Naturalist's Christmas: ribboned pine cones, holly berries, baby's breath, dried flowers, miniature twisted vine hearts and baskets, birds and birds' nests, clusters of Spanish moss ... don't let electric lights spoil this natural tree.

International or Family Heritage Tree: see "Christmas — Here, There, and Everywhere" (page 195) for ornament ideas and traditions, or research family origins of celebration.

Animals and Birds: Pick a specific animal (or variety of animals) or bird, and find as many different kinds of ornaments representing these wildlife (carved, porcelain, straw, paper, papier-mâché, origami ...) versions of forest creatures, farm animals, zoo animals, teddy bears, reindeer, rabbits ...

Winter Wonderland: Use white and silver, tinsel icicles, silver foil, crystal, crochet and lace, silvery mirrors ... Cover branches with "snow" ...

Gnomes, Fairies, Elves, Trolls, and Santas: Another collectibles tree, see what a wide assortment of fantasy characters you can find or create with various arts and craft media.

The Twelve Days of Christmas: Need I say more? For a list of the twelve gifts, see page 81.

Origami Tree: Learn the art of paper-folding for an original, dramatic, highly colorful tree.

Other Collectibles: Join in the fun and discovery of collecting a special item for tree decoration. You can make, buy, and receive as gifts all varieties of birds, angels, Santas, bells, elves, rocking horses, bears, hand-carved figures, snowflakes ...

Dedicate your tree to any one of these special themes or a clever creation of your own. Or simply collect your own favorite ornaments to enjoy year after year.

For a *really* natural Christmas, cluster two or three (or more) "just plain trees" of various shapes and sizes in a large empty space. They really are beautiful just as themselves.

Loving Touches

Ornament ideas have appeared all through this book, in one form or another. Many of the craft techniques discussed in THE BACK OF THE BOOK mention ornament possibilities as well.

As a matter of fact, there are *so* many ways to make tree ornaments that when you have accumulated too many, put up a second tree! Here is just a brief reminder of some of the loving touches you can add to your evergreen:

- Wrap candies in silver or colored foil, or colorful tissue paper fringed at the ends. Hang by ribbon, monofilament, or thin craft wire ...
- Wire and spray-paint sugar ice cream cones and fill with nuts and candies, greenery, dried flowers ...
- Frost and decorate cookie cutouts with holes in the top for hanging ...
- Paint and trim: wooden clothespins, wood turnings, spools, ping-pong balls, empty eggshells, seashells, wooden drapery rings, molded wax shapes, white pine wood cutouts, clay, tin cutouts, miniature pillows ...
- Stitch in time: cross-stitch, English smocked fabric balls and other shapes, stuffed fabric, stocking faces, scrap quilt figures, candle-wicking on muslin, crocheted snowflakes, miniature knitted stockings, needlepoint ...
- Tie ribbons to: cinnamon sticks, clusters of dried flowers or seed heads, wheat sheaves, holly sprigs, apples and citrus fruit, tiny filled baskets, gilded Thanksgiving wishbone, bleached sand dollars, pine cones, pomanders, gilded nuts ...
- Use white and colorful papers to make: folded origami, snowflake cutouts, folded doily fans, cones, and baskets, strings of cutout paper dolls, decoupage, "gift-wrapped" matchboxes and wood blocks ...
- Spray old, small toys silver or gold and hang by ribbons.
- Cover Styrofoam balls with bay leaves using bronze craft pins.
- Gild eucalyptus or dried hydrangea, artichokes, Queen Anne's lace ... and other found objects for rich accents.

Catch the glimmer of tree lights by using lots of reflective materials:

Make Fabric Bows

A yard of colorful fabric (44-45" wide) can make a host of pretty bows for your tree or to decorate a wreath. Spray starch fabric or dip in liquid starch, and let dry. Press smooth. Use *sharp* scissors to cut 3" wide strips about 23" long. Tie onto tree branches.

gilded and silvered objects, mirrors, crystal and cut glass, shimmering ribbons . . .

Always sign and date your handmade ornaments. Who knows where they will be 100 years from now? You may be the great-great-great-grandparent who provides the Christmas legacy to the young of 2076! Paint or use a permanent marker to ink your initials and the year, inconspicuously, somewhere on the ornament.

Screw eye hooks into the top of wooden ornaments for hanging.

Hang tree ornaments with: wire ornament hooks, craft wire (lengths in a corkscrew shape made by wrapping the wire around a pencil), monofilament, embroidery floss, narrow ribbon or cord, gold or silver braid, yarn, string, licorice whips . . .

Keepsakes

What seems like years ago, I cross-stitched ornaments framed in a wooden drapery ring for each of my children. Their name and the year are stitched somewhere on the ornament, which was usually made from a pattern of their choosing (counted cross-stitch books abound with miniature Christmas patterns—co-op these with friends). Linley might choose the pink angel, Zack a candy cane totin' mouse, Geoffrey a frosty snowman on skis. As youngsters, they loved having their own set of special ornaments to hang on the tree, and I hope someday they will enjoy the collection as part of their own family tree.

Choose a style of ornament you enjoy making: cutout tin or wood, clay, papier-mâché, soft-sculpture, quilted . . . and make a new one each year. Or make a different kind each year, remembering to put the recipient's name and date on the ornament. Don't feel bad if you can't make one every year. I am still planning to get to the 1982 renditions—someday!

Family Treasures

Some ornaments are so precious, so unusual, that you hate to pack them away eleven months of the year. If you have some special collectibles, why not display them all year round?

Buy or build a shadow box or wall cabinet. Insert dowel pegs into the backboard and hang your ornaments with silken cord. This way you can showcase special crystal, hand-carved, silver, porcelain, and other unusual and valuable Christmas treasures. Include a small printed card with each ornament, describing its significance, place of origin, date of purchase, who made it . . . and any other facts of interest for posterity.

 Put a large bow at the treetop with matching ribbon streamers trailing all the way to the base of the tree.

Christmas ornaments lovingly collected and hung on the tree year after year are some of life's greatest treasures, so full of sentiment and recollection are they—of a memorable holiday, a trip to some new and exotic place, gift from a dear friend or loved one, symbol of an event or element of your family life ... If the house caught fire, I would save the ornaments and family photographs first. I hope your collection of memories means as much to you.

Updating the Traditional (Tired Old ...) Glass Ball

❊ PAINTED GLASS BALLS

glass balls	distilled water
rubbing alcohol	oil and enamel paints
gesso/Kilz	polyurethane

Carefully remove metal caps from ornaments and clean each ball with rubbing alcohol and a soft rag. Dry with paper towels or tissue. Insert a dowel stick or popsicle stick inside the ball opening and push into a block of Styrofoam to stabilize for painting.

Mix equal parts of gesso and distilled water, or spray on Kilz primer, applying one coat to each ball to cover evenly. Let dry completely overnight. Paint on designs with enamel or oil paint. You can repeat a design from your tree skirt, stockings, upholstery, favorite china pattern, Christmas card ...

Let painted ball dry and finish by dipping into polyurethane. Dry on dowels at least 24 hours. Replace metal caps and hang.

❊ BRAIDED GLASS BALLS

upholstery braid, fringe, trim	clear-drying white glue or hot-melt glue

Wrap old glass balls with braid, cord, fringe ... leaving space to reveal the original color at intervals, or covering the entire ball. Use the method above to stabilize ball on dowel while you work. You can also glue beads, ornamental jewels, glitter ... onto glass balls for a new look to an old tradition.

❊ STUFFED-SATIN COOKIE CUTOUTS

satin fabric scraps	needle and thread
lace, buttons, other trim	polyester fiberfill

You can make stuffed ornaments with almost any fabric, but satin looks especially glowing against the shining tree lights. Sew miniature stockings with elaborate trims, brown satin gingerbread people accented with buttons and white rickrack, quilted satin flowers and holly, colorful satin packages wrapped with cord or ribbon, angels, or other cookie-cutter shapes. You might even make little people to resemble each family member.

Cinnamon Ornaments

¾ c. ground cinnamon
1 T. ground allspice
2 T. ground cloves
1 T. ground nutmeg
1 c. applesauce

Mix all ingredients well and roll out to ¼" thickness on an ungreased cookie sheet. Cut shapes with a knife or cookie cutter and peel away excess dough. Insert crescent shaped pieces of copper wire into tops of "cookies" for hanging. Put in a dry warm place to dry for about a week. Tie with narrow satin ribbon to hang. Store in airtight container during the "off season."

More Tree-Trimmers

artificial snow
drapings of Spanish moss
gilded hydrangea stems tied with
    ribbon or wire
hanging pine cones
lacy garlands
miniature dried artichokes
    (natural or gilded)
ribboned dried fruits and
    vegetables
sheaves of dried grasses and
    flowers tied with raffia
straw birds' nests with birds (and
    a couple of eggs?)

❄ SNIPPED TIN AND WIRE SCULPTURE

Sheet tin, aluminum flashing, bronze, brass, and copper can be cut with tin snips, hammered, poked, bent, wired together ... with any number of other objects (beads, feathers, sequins ...) to make fabulous fun ornaments.

You can even paint the sheet metal in solid colors, sponge, or stencil it. Make a multi-dimensional tree, shiny stars and crescent moons, bird and animal shapes ... and hang with craft wire.

Talking to Myself about Tree Decorating

"That *House Beautiful* tree with only fat red ribbons and pine wood cutouts looked so good ... "

"Sure, but it's too professional looking. Not personal enough for a *real* tree."

"It's so clean and attractive. Think how easy it would be to decorate."

"But what about my collection of ornaments? I can't spend Christmas without the Gorham snowflakes, the needlepointed Santa, the ceramic angels "

"Think about aesthetics for a moment here "

"But what about good old-fashioned sentiment?"

"If it's good enough for *House Beautiful* ... "

"The kids would die if we didn't hang their fluorescent dough ornaments with the great green globs of glitter ... (pause) Well, maybe it's worth a thought ... "

Solution? How about two trees?!

The Children's Tree

One of my very favorite Christmas TV specials (and I can quote entire dialogues from just about every one!) is the Charlie Brown Christmas special, when Charlie Brown picks out the most pathetic-looking tree on the lot for the school Christmas pageant.

The tree is pathetic—but sweet. And there is a message in Charlie's simple charity: the tree nobody else wanted became magically beautiful in a loving environment.

While the sorcery of animation can transform a sickly plant into something glorious a heckuva lot better than we mortals can, don't you think you might do something with that sad little tree in the corner of the lot, quietly waiting for some generous soul to bring it home?

 A "Chrismon" tree is decorated with carved wood ornaments representing the symbols of Christianity: fish, cross, manger, lamb, star ... "Chrismon" means "Christ-monogram."

There is a place in our Christmas for the Charlie Brown tree—as the Children's Tree. Find a small, inexpensive, lonely (and charmingly pitiful) tree and take it home. You might even find a bargain, as well as establish a new tradition, waiting to do this on Christmas Eve. Give the plant plenty of TLC and let this tree be the one the children secretly decorate all by themselves, to surprise Santa.

They may want to keep it up in their room, next to the big family tree, or even outside—to decorate for the birds. The experience of taking something small and simple and making it into something inspirational on their very own will be an uplifting one for your angelic little innocents.

I'm for bringing as many pure and simple joys into the season as possible. Aren't you?

A "Hand-some" Angel

Kids' Ornaments—Easy and Fun

❄ HAND-SOME ANGELS

white poster paint	glitter glue
stiff blue paper	clear Contact paper
markers	gold cord
white glue	

Dip little hands in white poster paint and transfer print of each hand to the blue paper in a fan pattern. Cut around the handprints to make the angel wings. Cut angel head and body from additional paper, as shown in illustration, and glue wings to body. Let the children draw in the face, hair, and dress features. Glitter can be added for a sparkly halo. Put entire angel, wings and all, between two sheets of clear Contact paper and cut around outer edge to laminate. Punch a hole in the top and hang with gold cord.

❄ FELT LOLLIPOPS, CHRISTMAS TREES …

• Using different colors of felt, cut shapes of lollipops, trees, reindeer, angels … in duplicate. Glue bottom piece of felt, put a popsicle stick on top and glue the top piece over all, like making a popsicle stick sandwich! Decorate with cord, glitter, additional felt pieces … Hole punch and tie on a cord for hanging.

• Glue beads on pine cones to be ornaments, and tie ribbon or yarn around the top petals for hanging.

• Twist red and white pipe cleaners into a candy cane shape.

• Draw tree shapes on white paper and let children decorate with crayons or markers. Cover with clear Contact paper, punch a hole in the top, and thread with ribbon to hang.

• Cut out gingerbread men from brown paper and glue on sequins for eyes and buttons.

• Glue popsicle sticks into star, snowflake, and tree shapes.

For the Birds

Mix 2 lbs. melted ground suet, ½ c. peanut butter, 2 c. cornmeal, and bird seed ... Chill overnight. Serve to the birds in paper baking cups lining miniature baskets or a mesh orange bag tied to a tree. A cranberry or cherry on top would be a colorful and appetizing garnish!

TAKING DOWN THE TREE ... AND EVERYTHING ELSE

It's a sad job but everybody's got to do it. Take your time, grab a few bites of the dismantled gingerbread house, and be thinking in terms of next year as you bring down the Christmas house this year.

Pack ornaments carefully, categorized in groups for easier decorating next year. Great containers for storing ornaments are those huge popcorn tins. Save used tissue paper and gift wrap for layering and protecting delicate ornaments. Put the heaviest ones in first, the most fragile on the top layer.

Untie bows you want to keep, iron them and neatly roll tight to store. It's tough to keep a fluffy bow looking good from year to year.

Make a list of all the decorations you have and keep this in your Christmas file. You will be glad to have this handy reference when yearly adding to your decoration collection. Also note where everything is stored. Just this year, for the life of me, I couldn't find the Skating Santa drinking glasses ... until I finally started putting things in storage again, and there they were.

Lay the tree on an old sheet or a piece of plastic to carry out of the house, relatively needle-free (although the vacuum smells nice for days after vacuuming up stray evergreen needles). Put the untrimmed tree outside for a few more days of pleasure, and trim it again for the birds' Christmas. Then take the old tree to a recycling center for future mulch and other good things.

Take a few minutes to write down your thoughts about the Christmas just past. See "The Twelve Lists ... #12" for evaluation and future-planning tips.

Read through all the Christmas cards you received but were too busy to notice. Update your card address list, answer correspondence, and save your favorite cards for future projects.

It's bad luck to keep the tree up past Epiphany (January 6)!

SEVEN

All Decked Out
Festive Attire for Everyone

Mama in her kerchief and I in my cap …
—Clement Clarke Moore

Was it Carol Burnett in her role as the cleaning woman who attached the paper stick-on bow to her threadbare coat one Christmas? Very festive. Very chic.

Nobody can say, "I haven't got a thing to wear!" at Christmas. *Anyone* with a little spunk and imagination can make even the most glamourously-clad model in *Vogue* look dull by comparison.

Christmas is a time to let it all hang out with fashion. While red slacks and a green sweater might look ridiculous in March, they are considered sartorial splendor in December. If some festive attire seems tacky, well—tacky is *in* if it shows your Christmas spirit to its best advantage!

MR. CLAUS: THE WEARIN' OF THE GREEN … AND RED!

If you own a tux, you are set for the duration (and "endure"-ation) of dressing up for the truly elegant Christmas events. Perhaps all you need is a new pair of cufflinks or a flagrant bow tie (when "de rigeur"!).

Make sure your shoes are polished and that your waist hasn't gone to waste, or last-minute zip-ups could be tragic.

Renting a tuxedo and other formal wear is another option, although if you go out often and can make the initial investment, buying your own is the way to go. The suit will pay for itself very quickly.

For less formal events, you guys can make selections from your collection of everyday suits, ties, sport coats, or sweaters, but you may be inclined toward more gaily-coordinated wrappings, like:

red and green plaid bow tie
Christmas patterned ties and bright red socks
red sweater vest or Nordic ski sweater
seasonally-colored argyles
green slacks with red embroidered reindeer (erghh!)

Dressing Up …

Wear something festive as often as possible during the holidays. I promise it will lift your spirits and those of everyone who greets you on the street—anything red, green, or antlered will do!

One of These Years ...

I'm going to put together an authentic pair of Mr. and Ms. Santa outfits. The intention becomes more and more a part of my fantasy life with each busy year, but maybe someday ...

I would love to dress up for a last-minute Christmas Eve excursion to the mall, arrive at a dinner party so outrageously attired, surprise the kids (oh, Mom!) at school, or otherwise make jolly theatrical use of such a getup. (Fat chance I'd get away with the school idea, now that everybody's so cool ... maybe I'll have to wait for innocent little grandchildren to pull that trick!)

Costumes are great fun, and surely a Santa disguise would get a lot of wear over several years of healthy flamboyance.

If a red and white Santa suit and big black boots don't strike your fancy, what about an elf costume? Santa's helpers wear just about anything you could stitch up ... with leotards and a requisite elfin cap.

And who says "dress-up" is just for Halloween? Costumes can be a blast whenever the spirit moves you. Make a cute and crazy one in October—wear it to a masked ball or to trick-or-treat with the "other" kids. Wash off the pumpkin punch and M&M's stains, press, and hang in readiness for December madness. Imagine what a great Christmas card this would make —with the entire family so colorfully and spiritedly attired!

MS. CLAUS: ALL THAT GLITTERS ...

As the festive female, decorate yourself as you would your tree—tastefully and enchantingly, according to your own personal style, yet with an eye for the shape and surroundings!

For more formal affairs, you will no doubt want the most outstanding dress, shoes, and jewelry on the dance floor. Coordinate carefully with all the flair (and studied elegance of the latest fashion magazines) you can muster. And don't forget the shimmering stockings!

Prepare everything well enough in advance to know that all parts of the ensemble fit, have been cleaned, pressed, and suitably altered (watch out for gingerbread binges!).

An outfit you already have can become something new with the latest in a belt, jewelry, or other accessories. Consider using one or all of these before resorting to the expense of a totally new outfit.

Buy and collect basics—traditional timeless pieces like satiny skirts and silk slacks, sheer blouses, the eternal "little black dress" ... Coordinate new purchases with old, so that accessories will mix and match for at least a few seasons. Then, if you can, buy something really trendy, and/or outlandish, like a silver sequined camisole or red feather boa, to make yourself a seasonal standout.

Other holiday haute couture might include these trimming techniques:

Lace thin satin ribbons through a cable-knit sweater with bows tied at the ends.

Wear a silver, crystal, or other unusual Christmas ornament on a ribbon, cord, or chain, as a necklace.

Mix bright Christmas colors, in separates, for red and green "fun" dressing.

Add Christmas socks, hosiery, mufflers, caps, vests, sweaters ... to hype the holidays.

Make a crocheted lace collar to dress up a plain pullover sweater or dress.

Tie a fabric belt made of seasonally-colored (lime and fuschia, for example?) satin, silk, chiffon, or velveteen around the waist of a simple dress, skirt, or slacks and blouse.

Use a metallic belt "slide" or attention-getting brooch for added interest.

Replace plain buttons with jewel-tone button covers, rhinestones, pearl clusters ...

Put a sprig of mistletoe or silk holly at the throat of a crisp white blouse.

Being creative with clothing for kids is lots of fun, but start planning these projects early and be finished in plenty of time to give your little masterpieces plenty of wear-time ... An appliquéd Santa just isn't darling in January.

AND THE RANDOM ASSORTMENT OF ELVES ...

"Deck the kids!" (That's *decorate*, not deck, as in clobber!)

Youngsters are usually not shy about looking outlandishly festive (particularly on the heels of Halloween) and often actually enjoy it tremendously.

There will be parties, church functions, big family gatherings, a Christmas production or ballet, family portrait, and many other excuses to dress up the little ones over the holidays.

Don't be surprised or visibly disappointed, however, if your five-year-old refuses to wear the bright green reindeer sweater ... or when Carson insists on wearing her Minnie Mouse slippers with the lacy tights and red velvet pinafore. Fight these sparklers of independence only as long as you can, and then sigh, put on your most gracious sense of humor, and consider that "someday we'll laugh about ... " this stubborn blight on the family portrait!

Available today are so many outfits made especially for the holidays, both elegant and casual. Because these receive so little wear, you might find some real bargains at secondhand shops and children's clothing sales. When you're through with them, pass them down or offer them at a fair price for someone else to enjoy.

Creative Clothing Craft

Draw a Christmas picture, design, or greeting on a piece of white paper using specially-made fabric crayons. Transfer your drawing onto a T-shirt, nightgown, or other partially synthetic garment, using a hot iron and following the directions on the box. Be sure to reverse lettering, as all transfers reproduce SDRAWKCAB.

"Deck" the Kids With ...

- Jumpers, overalls, vests, sweatshirts, and dresses that are appliquéd, quilted, cross-stitched, or smocked in seasonal style.
- Matching dress and doll outfits, with the "twin" toy inserted in a prominent pocket. This is also fun to do with overalls.
- Year-round outfits "seasoned" by adding a detachable holiday touch, such as a smocked collar, detachable appliqué, bevy of bows, pinafore or apron ...
- Bows sewn on socks to match hair ribbons.
- Hand-painted Christmas designs on various articles of clothing (works especially well on denim, sweatshirts, cotton diaper covers, T-shirts ...).
- Bow or bow-tie made from a sprig of holly pinned to a plain white blouse or shirt.
- Hand-painted holiday hair ribbons or barrettes, or baby bibs with appropriate holiday quotes: "All I want for Christmas is my two front teeth ..." "My First Noel," "I'm a Chris-mess!" Stitch on Baby's name in seasonal colors and the year's date for safekeeping.
- Reindeer antlers made from brown terrycloth, stuffed, and sewn or glued onto red or green headbands, sweatbands, or baseball caps. You will actually need one of these for every member of the family.
- And don't forget face-painting: water-based paints can decorate rosy cheeks with Christmas trees, reindeer, angels (when appropriate!), hearts, snowmen ... lots of fun for Christmas parties and special events.

Christmas morning may be the time you choose to trim your family with colors of the season. Consider making or buying festively matching pajamas or robes, and perhaps even slippers to go with them. What a great photo around the tree!

EIGHT

Eat, Drink, and Be Merry
Entertaining with Ease

A little nonsense now and then
Is relished by the wisest men!
—Mary Michael

At Christmastime, our families seem to grow bigger and bigger as we want to reach out and pull in all of our most favorite people to share together in the spirit.

Probably the most frustrating aspect of *my* Christmas is not having the time, energy, or resources to give each of my special friends, big and small, a gift to say just how crazy I am about each one of them. It is impossible to extend gift-giving beyond certain limits, but there *is* a way to give something to those exceptional people in our lives:

AND THAT'S ENTERTAINMENT!

Some people actually enjoy devoting hours and hours of each holiday season to throwing a huge party for all their friends and acquaintances. Others celebrate the season simply—visiting and being visited at informal get-togethers.

Each of these types of entertainment, and all manners in between, can be gracious and gratifying.

The single most important ingredient to successful entertaining is that the event be a joy and delight both to the guests and to the hosts. With careful planning, a positive attitude, and the ability to assert your wildest imagination (plus a willingness to laugh in the face of adversity), entertaining can bring about some of the best and brightest fun of the holidays.

Get up your nerve and try it this year. You may find holiday entertaining a heart-lifting habit hard to break.

List #6 of "The Twelve Lists of Christmas" includes a sample form for an entertaining file. The more often you entertain, the better you will know what information helps you to best organize for each successive and successful event.

CONSIDER YOUR RESOURCES

Begin with this checklist to see if you're up to entertaining over the holidays:

1. How many people can you handle within your available space and facilities?
2. What kind of party best accommodates your budget (sit-down dinner, potluck, buffet, cocktail party, dessert)?
3. How much holiday time are you willing to give to party organization and follow-through?
4. Is your spouse (or roommate) up to it?

Are you still ready to go? Great! Start getting your act together and I will hold your hand as you consider what you have in the way of ...

Facilities

A man's (person's) home is his (her) castle. No matter how small, how "lived-in" (euphemism for "worn-out"!), and how unadaptable you think your house is ... it's home, and with a welcome mat out front and an equally generous portion of warmth and hospitality inside, everyone you bring in should feel at home as well.

Some of the best parties end up in the kitchen anyway, so prepare to open the whole house. Use the kids' rooms as storage for extraneous debris (*more* of it!) and lock the doors! Let the master bedroom become an expanded coat closet and the den a bar, with food and more drink stations (according to the number attending) located strategically in between.

In other words, don't let the size of your living room dictate the number of people you can comfortably entertain (and remember that not everybody will be able to come, so be a tad generous in making up your guest list, without throwing caution to the wind).

The Table(s)

If you are having a sit-down meal, consider stretching the dining room table with card tables or rent folding tables. Even a ping-pong table makes an elegant setting if you cover it with a nice cloth. Just don't let cozy turn into crowded. There is little worse than dueling elbows at a formal dinner.

Serving buffet-style can solve seating problems and give guests the freedom to eat when and where they wish (and feel less conspicuous about how *much* they eat!). A large table or sideboard laden with pick-me-ups, allowing traffic to flow easily and quickly, can provide one of the most efficient ways of serving, while freeing up the hosts to roam and enjoy their guests ... and vice versa.

Chairs and Sofas and Pillows

As with folding tables, folding chairs are also rentable, but remember that people don't seem to sit much at parties, so don't crowd the space with lots of seating. Just keep a few chairs available as needed.

For more casual affairs, it's fun to scatter fat, cushiony pillows about the room where people can unwind on the floor. But if several guests begin curling up with their heads on the pillows, it's time to bring out the coffee, turn up the music, and cue the belly dancer to jump out of that giant fruitcake!

Design a traffic pattern ahead of time that allows easy access to food, drink, and the powder room. Then arrange small seating groups elsewhere in the room, or rooms, available.

Eating Utensils, Serving Dishes, Linens, Candelabra ...

Once again, for a large party, it is possible to rent equipment, or borrow from a generous friend (Mom!).

If elegance is the ultimate objective, you will want to use your best china, crystal, silver, and linen, while you can certainly get away with paper and plastic for a more casual gathering. The stores are loaded with lively Christmas accessories in wonderful colors and designs. These by themselves add spirit to your table setting.

Adopt a mood with your menu and supplies—elegantly formal to cozily casual—and stick with it throughout your planning and execution.

Once the basic facilities and equipment have been taken care of, evaluate your options and decide on the date, time, and basic theme of your entertainment (for theme suggestions, see pages 145).

And now, get out pencil and paper (or your new Entertainment file), and begin recording the modus operandi for your brilliant career as a five-star entertainer.

ENTERTAINMENT LISTS

#1 The Guest List

Guessing who's coming to dinner can be one of the toughest parts of entertaining. Sometimes, it's almost best to put down everybody you can think of and then get together with your co-host and have a cross-out contest. Chances are, you will reach an amicable group close to the desired number and, if not, just serve plenty of good cheer and pray! (Or throw the same party on two consecutive nights, to get everybody in, as well as maximize the value of your best efforts—rentals, fresh flowers ...).

We often tend to take our best friends for granted, lavishing our most creative talents to impress mere acquaintances. Since it is said that "Entertainment is a gift we give to our friends ..." throw yourself wholeheartedly into their receiving the best pleasure you can give.

When Sending Invitations ...

• Have invitations printed or make them yourself, using techniques in "Greetings!" Chapter 3. Ready-made holiday invitations are also available. Select one that best sets the mood for your event.

• Besides the who, what, when, and where, list type of dress, meal, special entertainment, or other guest instructions needed to carry out the party theme and get the "ball" rolling.

• Include "RSVP by (date)" if you need an accurate head count, or if you distrust the postal service.

• Mail at least three weeks in advance and try to see that invitations don't arrive on a weekend when life is so thoroughly confusing they might become lost or—heaven forbid—forgotten!

• Written invitations aren't necessary for small gatherings. Telephone or make a casual "request of your company" with a note on your Christmas card.

Don't forget to invite a few more than you can accommodate—the Christmas season stretches everyone's social calendar, so there will be some regrets.

Make up your guest list with the first and last names of each invitee so you and your co-host will both know who is coming and become familiar with each guest (at least their names). If either of you is including persons unknown to the other, familiarize each other with these guests ahead of time so when you actually meet, you will have a better idea how to make each one feel welcome and comfortable.

Add addresses to the list and keep a copy by the phone to check off acceptances and regrets. Make an extra copy to keep in your permanent entertainment file for future reference.

#2 Menu and Shopping List

Plan foods that are easy to prepare ahead and that match the mood of the party. The number you are serving, the method of serving, and your budget should determine food choices. See "A Festival of Feasting" for some of my favorite party foods.

Make out a file card with your menu and separate recipe cards for each item included. Once you have all your recipes ready, you can make an organized shopping list of supplies and groceries.

If you plan to have an open bar, make a separate list of liquor needs, referring to a good bartender's guide for amounts and varieties needed, according to the size and length of your party. Allow one pound of ice per person.

#3 Equipment and Supplies

Plan how you will serve your menu and what utensils you will need. Make a list of equipment to be rented, bought, or borrowed to facilitate the overall plan.

Rent	Buy	Borrow
20 folding chairs	cocktail napkins	Mom's silver
folding table	Christmas music	Mom's china
karaoke for carol	frilled toothpicks	Mom's linen
sing		napkins
wine glasses		Mom

Keep these lists safely in your file, so you can easily organize the return of the rented and borrowed items without losing a security deposit or risking the wrath of a generous mother or friend.

#4 Decorating Needs

How will you decorate the table? Will you use any decorations in addition to your usual Christmas collection (fresh flowers, foliage, mistletoe, place-setting decorations …)?

Does the party theme suggest a few clever attractions? Decide how you will arrange the table (draw a diagram) and then list what you will need to accomplish the magic of transforming that ping-pong table into a glittering display of food and flora.

#5 Music and Entertainment

Some of the most successful parties are the ones packing a few extra punches (and I don't mean the fruity kind): live chamber music, a harpist or violinist, videotaped large-screen presentation of old Bing Crosby Christmas specials …

Bring ingenuity to your gathering with imaginative games, contests, musical selections, a special theme … Make up your overall plan and a list of props needed to bring this production to life:

1. Hire a live musician (perhaps even several months in advance).
2. Buy six prizes for _____ game.
3. Hide a mystery gift somewhere in the house for a treasure hunt.

#6 The "To-Do" List

This is the accumulation of all your data on one big list. Keep your category and planning cards on file, and keep this list at your desk, in your wallet, or under your pillow—with a pen nearby as you cheerfully check things off, and in restrained paranoia, add new "I almost forgot!" items.

PLACE SETTING DECORATIONS AND GIFTS

Let your table setting say, "I'm really glad you're here." A small decoration at every setting can also become a surprise gift for each guest at the end of the meal:

- Fill miniature baskets with candies. Gild or spray paint and line with a small square of tissue or fabric. Tie handle with a bow so it can be used as a tree ornament upon arriving in its new home.
- Surround votive candles with a mini-wreath base at each place.
- Set a small brass box at each place setting and fill one with a special surprise to be discovered by one lucky guest at meal's end. Or look for frankincense and myrrh at international bazaars, and give this traditional gift.
- Decorate each place setting with one of these:
  small plant or single flower in miniature vase
  tiny gift-wrapped packages
  miniature wreaths (napkin rings to go?)
  brass bell or miniature French horn tied with red ribbon
  matching ornaments or Christmas figures
  ribbon tied around wine and water goblets
  decorative nameplates or place cards
  ribboned scroll of a poem, a New Year's prediction, or a favorite carol done in calligraphy on parchment

For More Fun at a Dinner Party

Arrange a basket centerpiece filled with tiny gift-wrapped ornaments, sachets, potpourri, jewelry ... or put a clue in each package as to the whereabouts of a mystery gift, hidden somewhere in the house. The first to find the gift takes it home!

For a small dinner party, let the place setting decoration provide the entertainment. By each place, put a Christmas game card in a small basket, scroll, or envelope:
  Christmas carol charades
  Guess what gift I am? (20 questions, with crazy gifts)
  Holiday trivia (hostess asks the questions, guests write answers on the card—best score wins a bottle of New Year's Eve champagne!)

Other Entertaining Tips

- Whether hiring a teenager home from college, a maid, a butler, or a professional caterer, give any "hired help" a *written* list of instructions and discuss together in advance of the party.
- If you cannot get your guest list down to a manageable size, throw the same party on two consecutive nights. The house will be clean, decorations and flowers fresh, rental equipment gets double use over a weekend ... Double your recipes, double your fun!
- A clever outdoor decoration identifying your house will notify all

new-coming guests that "This must be the place!"

- Soft candlelight is dramatic and romantic—and hides a multitude of sins. Don't go to a lot of trouble meticulously cleaning every nook and cranny of the house *before* the party. You'll have enough of that when it's over!

- Be ready with all preparations as much in advance of party day as possible. Save only last-minute "necessaries" for then, and take it easy, soak in the tub, get a manicure or massage—and store up maximum energy for maximum fun *as the event is taking place.*

- When serving buffet style: Use large "dependable" plates (or for a more casual meal, baskets for each guest are great, with napkins and utensils already inserted), serve drinks after guests have been seated so they don't have to juggle so much at once, provide each diner with one large napkin and another small one tucked inside (one for the lap, the other for chin-mopping …), and try not to serve soupy-drippysaucyfloppy foods that tend to mix and run together in a messy, unappetizing manner.

- Use scooped fruits and vegetables as serving containers: scalloped melons, scooped cabbage, hollow citrus …

- Fill the house with the aroma of "Spicy Christmas Scent-sation" (see page 169).

- As party day draws near, begin to clear extraneous debris from your refrigerator so there will be plenty of room to store party food. Or use extra coolers and ice chests to keep foods fresh.

- Devise a guest list that creates a clever mixture of interesting and diverse friends and acquaintances. A skillful host knows how to make *each* individual feel fascinating and festive, the most treasured guest of all … .

AN ASSORTMENT OF COMMON AND UNCOMMONLY GOOD PARTY IDEAS

The Great Big Everybody-Is-My-Best-Friend Party

Ever been hit by a mad impulse to surround yourself with practically everybody you know, pulling them all together for a cozy good time?

A large party can be a terrific way to consolidate entertainment obligations when you are unable to entertain frequently, or so that you might introduce one group of friends to another. With the proper facilities, equipment, planning, and enthusiasm (plus a willingness to cheerfully devote precious holiday time to carrying out the grand production), a big party can be no more difficult than a small, intimate gathering.

 When planning a centerpiece at the dining table, be sure the arrangement doesn't extend above eye level of the shortest guest!

Keeping Spirits Light

Heavy drinking during the holidays seems to be going the way of the dinosaur, thank heavens! If you are serving alcohol to guests, be aware of your responsibilities regarding their safety and the safety of innocents who might be in their path.

- Serve plenty of food with alcohol.
- Keep cocktail hour short.
- Use lots of ice and less liquor when mixing drinks. You're not being stingy … just a good friend.
- Make sure everybody knows exactly what's in the punch.
- Have water available for safe thirst-quenching.
- Know that carbonated beverages enhance, rather than dilute alcohol absorption.
- Have plenty of non-alcoholic drinks available.
- Offer low-alcohol wines, alcohol-free (unfermented) or non-alcoholic (less than 0.5 percent alcohol) beers.
- Quietly call a cab or offer to get a ride for a guest too unsteady to drive.
- YOU may be liable in case of an accident involving one of your guests, should you serve someone who is noticeably intoxicated, knowing they eventually will be getting behind the wheel. Take care.

Smaller Parties and Get-Togethers

The elaborate detail and expense that go into planning a big dinner party can be minimized with a more casual or intimate (smaller) gathering over the holidays.

To sip and sup fireside with a few close friends (or acquaintances you would like to know better) gazing at the glittering tree and humming along with Bing's "White Christmas" ... what could be more relaxing than this?

Casual and comfortable is the theme. Carry it out with warm colors, crackling fire, and an atmosphere likened to an après-ski party at the lodge. Here's your chance to use your starter set of Christmas china, those funny Santa mugs, or the highball glasses with scantily-clad Santa's "helpers"!

A Coffee

Very casual and just the thing for a medium-sized group or just two or three favorite people. Organize a small shopping expedition to launch at your house, a gift-wrapping party, baking exchange, or even a group party-planning party (giving parties with other couples or individuals is a GREAT idea!). Serve coffee, tea, Bloody Marys, fruit juice, and/or soft drinks, and some delicious pastries, fresh fruit ...

A Brunch

Fun way to start the day and not as likely to interfere with other social commitments. Invite the bridge club, neighbors, your children's teachers, or the support staff at your office (and anyone else, for that matter). This is a heavier meal than you would serve at a coffee, a cross between breakfast and lunch.

A Luncheon

Basically the same as brunch. This meal might include the same menu, but would generally be served a little later, say from noon or one until mid-afternoon. Celebrate a post-shopping spree, ornament exchange, or one last calm sit-down lunch before school lets out for the holidays!

 Confidence and two generous dollops of real enthusiasm are all you need to throw a terrific party (and perhaps napkins, a couple of drinks, and several "nuts" to round out your most gracious efforts)!

A Cocktail Party

The duration and size of a cocktail party will determine the quantity and heaviness of hors d'oeuvres. Complement the amount of drinking with an adequate amount of eating. Keep food available in several locations and consider hiring someone as bartender along with someone else to replenish the food trays so you will be free to mingle with your guests and enjoy your own party.

A Dessert

This could range from a casual late night coffee to a very elegant event. Invite couples, or "just the girls." If the guest list is large, set up a table with several different sweets, and then have wine, alcohol-free punch, and coffee stations throughout the house. Serve mostly pick-up desserts and perhaps one or two sugar-free items (like cheese straws and nuts), but don't be surprised if people fail to eat as much as they drink. Keeping the party time to two hours or less cuts down on the less positive situations potentially resulting from this.

If you limit this to a smaller group, advise each guest to dress formally and create an atmosphere conducive to elegance. Serve an array of liqueurs or champagne and one or two very elaborate confections on your best china dessert plates. You might try a sophisticated ice sculpture as the centerpiece. Light the silver candelabra and listen to "The Messiah," or light the dessert itself for a glowing effect at your table.

A Wine and Cheese Party

Less formal than a dessert, this would be fun before dinner — as cocktails and hors d'oeuvres, or afterwards, with fruit — as a dessert. Consider inviting a wine expert to come and discuss various wines and serving techniques ... or research for yourself at the library, and drink to your newly-acquired good taste! Simply enjoy a jug of wine and hunk of cheese and crisp bread while sitting around the fire ... serve in "courses" as an expert explains the differences between French and California (Virginia, Georgia?) vineyards ... or serve a variety of selections in your good crystal with an assortment of labeled fine cheeses and crackers.

There is nothing sobering about a wine and cheese party! The pleasure and conversation that flows from the wine makes this kind of hospitality an easy way to "make merry." Just don't overdo it. You will know when it's time to pop in the cork.

Serving Wine and Cheese

- Offer several kinds of wine on a table or buffet, listing name and country on a card with other interesting data regarding each of the wines. Guests choose their favorite.
- Display cheese in the same way, with appropriate cheese placed near compatible wines. Soft, creamy dessert cheeses complement the lighter, fruitier wines, while the stronger hard cheeses are best with full-bodied, drier wines.
- Select three or four wines and serve one taste at a time, with a bit of cheese between each tasting. One bottle of wine serves 8-10 for tasting.
- White wine should be chilled (two hours in the fridge) but not too cold.
- Open red wines an hour before serving to allow them to breathe.
- Serve cheese at room temperature, garnished with slices of fruit, frosted grapes (see page 174) ...
- Many people love a fresh loaf of crusty bread (one mini-loaf per guest is adequate) or an assortment of fine crackers served with wine and cheese.
- Make or buy attractive cheese markers to stick in cheeses, labeled with the cheese's name: Camembert, Brie, Bel Paese ...

Reading about wine and cheese will help you make the proper serving selections. See "A Festival of Feasting" for many ways to dress up a cheese tray.

Make it Easy on Yourself

You want to have a few friends and family over but have no intention of using precious holiday time getting hassled over details, dips, and dinner. It's simply not your style.

So ... have a fast-food smorgasbord. All in good fun. Play up your wit at having thought of it by carrying simplicity to its limit: paper plates, paper cups, plastic utensils, canned drinks ... Swing by several fast-food joints at the last minute and pick up samples of the "specialty of the house!" Spread out a tableful of fried chicken, sliced pizza, tacos, onion rings, Chinese egg rolls, chicken wings ... and let everybody dig in. Couldn't be easier ... and you'll be surprised how much fun, too. Finish off the meal with a fancy dessert from the neighborhood bakery or ice cream shop.

A Progressive Dinner Party

We do this on New Year's Eve and it has become a sparkling tradition ... with a waiting list of new "members"! Each home should provide a pleasant ambiance—a blend of hospitality, decoration, and delicious dining. More than one family can show off their Christmas home, yet no one host is overwhelmed by the responsibilities of entertaining. You can even pool financial resources and work out a budget, so all's fair in love and warmth.

Start at one home for cocktails and an appetizer, move to another for the main course and salad (and/or soup), and settle on a third for dessert, champagne, coffee ... and twisting to the oldies. You could increase the stops by the number of courses served, but unless the homes are fairly close together, traveling becomes tiresome and takes up valuable party time. Rent a bus or van if you like and travel together, caroling as you go.

An Open House

Set aside a few hours one afternoon or evening for friends to drop by: to help decorate the tree, sing carols, exchange gifts, taste your baked goodies, drink hot buttered rum ...

You can phone your invitations, include a note on Christmas cards, or invite friends you meet at the supermarket and other word-of-mouth places. Casual, fun, friendly, and easy. Well, relatively.

A Tree-Trimming

A wonderful old-fashioned family gathering. Friends and relatives can bring an ornament or you provide the materials for each guest to make a special trimming for your tree right on the spot.

String cranberries and popcorn. Play carols or sing your own, accompanied by a friendly piano player or children's "orchestra" (pots, pans, wooden sticks, kazoos, bells ...). Bring out a tray of baked goods, fresh fruits, cheeses, popcorn in large baskets, cocoa, hot cider, or other warm and tingling drinks.

This event could go on all day, or gather everyone together at once, trim the tree, and then hold a magical tree-lighting ceremony with special poems, songs, stories, and sharing ...

An International Smorgasbord

Prepare or ask each guest to bring a favorite dish representing holiday traditions of another country, and cover the buffet table with sumptuous tastes of international cuisine. Research traditions and recipes in cookbooks and the library ... for a mind-, as well as tummy-, expanding experience! Carry out the international theme with decorations, costumes, music, entertainment, and a few surprises (a lucky almond hidden in the Swedish pudding ...).

A Toy Assembly Party

Invite a few young couples over for snacks, brew, and good company while getting something *very important* accomplished! Be sure to include at least one guest with competent mechanical skills and provide all the tools needed to maintain optimum efficiency as Santa's helpers. Your friends will thank you when Christmas Eve comes and all this is DONE!

CREATIVE USE OF TABLE LINENS FOR FESTIVE FEASTING

I often think the food in *Southern Living* and *House and Garden* magazines looks *extra* specially enticing because of the elegant surroundings—the table setting. Everything is stunningly coordinated—the plates even match the blueberries and cream! It's enough to make the average paper-plate perpetrator feel absolutely inadequate!

Let's face it—our own china may not match every main course, but we can still decorate to make an attractive table using different accessories to highlight our "cuisine artistry."

Tablecloths

- A lace or crocheted tablecloth looks exceptionally seasonal over a red or green solid tablecloth.
- Trim a ready-made cloth with ribbon, braid, contrasting ruffle, or lace. Sew appliqués on the skirt border. Use fabric paint to draw on holly, snowflakes, silvery moons and golden stars, poinsettias ... motifs transferred from your Christmas china ...
- Paint or trim napkins to match your tablecloth.
- A long-term project that will make a lovely heirloom is a muslin cloth decorated with the old-fashioned artistry of candlewicking, cotton crochet trim, or embroidery. See craft stores for materials and instructions.
- See THE BACK OF THE BOOK regarding techniques for printing fabrics.

Placemats

- Weave placemats with holiday bright ribbons ... or trim a solid or print mat with a contrasting ribbon border stitched on by hand or machine.
- Paint or stencil linen, muslin, or quilted mats and matching napkins.
- Cross-stitch or embroider Christmas designs and consider making a placemat for each family member with individual names stitched on as well.
- For each special child, make placemat faces or Christmas shapes from fabric, using trim and embroidery for detail and design.

Costumes and Dress-Up Parties

Though it seems like a major pain in the neck to have to put together a costume, I know few people who don't actually enjoy it once they stand before the mirror admiring a great get-up.

Dressing up is great fun, whether it's in costume or formalwear. You get to be somebody or something else, for a change. Because you are a participant before you even arrive, the party is in full swing the minute you get there. Spirits ... be free!

It's all in how you present it. Be enthusiastic and inspirational, and give each guest plenty of time to plan and prepare the costume of a lifetime by mailing out invitations extra early.

Invite guests to dress exclusively as Santa and give prizes for the nearest likeness, most original, most outrageous (red fur bikini and black leather boots?). Or open the floor to all Christmas figures: angels, shepherds, elves, reindeer, Scrooge, even a plug-in decorated Christmas tree!

Gather those with the wildest, craziest senses of humor and you will have a hilarious assortment of characters and conversation to ensure a lively gathering.

For the truly adventurous, pack this whole weird gang into a pickup truck and go caroling at the local mall, shopping for a tree, or carousing at a downtown dance palace. Make a public statement of your collective Christmas spirit!

Be sure to videotape the event and take plenty of photos, as this will be one party you will all want to remember (who could forget?).

- Sew a fabric napkin ring onto the placemat and insert a prettily folded napkin.
- Paint Lucite or mirrored placemats with enamel paints. The design on Lucite will show up well over a solid cloth.
- Make table runners using a stunning Christmas plaid, moiré, or chintz.
- For simply fun placemats, get each family member to make his own: paste holiday card cutouts, photographs, or magazine pictures onto paper in a collage—covering each side with clear Contact paper, or have each mat laminated at the print shop.

Napkin Rings

Wrap up a colorful napkin by each place setting. Possibilities for these are endless, and they can turn into hostess gifts as well.

- For simple napkin rings, decorate cardboard tubing cut into 2" sections with a sharp X-acto knife. Cover with fabric, foil, gift wrap, ribbon, papier-mâché …
- Glue needlework to the outside of a cardboard or plain old napkin ring (recycled!), fold over inside, and hide the seam with glued-on ribbon.
- Hand-paint plain wood rings. Stain wood after painting for an antiqued finish.
- Make mini-wreaths around napkins with woven vines, berried juniper, birch twigs, wired miniature pine cones, cranberries and/or popcorn strings …
- Using fabric, lambswool, and trim, make a Santa, an angel, or a Rudolph ring. Or sculpt something from commercial clay or dough clay.
- Tie a pleated napkin in the center with a gold or silver cord, silken braid tied with a tassel …
- Hammer odd silver forks and spoons around a pipe to make unique napkin rings.
- Use wired garlands or heavy craft wire and beads to fashion an unusual wire sculpture napkin ring (or square …).
- Stitch a quilted pouch onto a placemat to hold napkin and silver.
- Wire jingle bells together in a ring.
- Colorful napkins—printed, solid, hand-painted, trimmed—will look even better folded in an unusual way on the table. Pick up a book at the library or bookstore, illustrating folding techniques.
- Tie silverware together with a candy cane, finished off with a big Christmas bow.

When serving buffet-style, fold a smaller napkin inside a larger one, inserting flatware inside. The large napkin is to spread across the lap, preventing stains on holiday finery, and the smaller napkin is for delicately dabbing crumbs and cream sauce from sullied lips!

CHILDREN'S PARTIES

Entertaining is not for adults only. Kids are probably the largest single group of Christmas-lovers—and who can blame them? The magic, the cheer, the excitement and anticipation of Christmas are overwhelming.

Kids deserve a chance to celebrate, too, and the more involved they become in the planning, the more you all will enjoy it. Those over the age of six or seven can decide for themselves whom they would like to invite (the whole class?), what they want to serve (red and green Kool-Aid?), and what games and entertainment should be included for the pleasure of their company (an audience with the REAL Santa?).

Try one of these suggestions, and give of your time, energy, and sainted charity to all the youngsters in your life.

Writing Letters to Santa Party

Provide paper, crayons, and/or pencils to each guest. Naturally, you'll need stamps (Christmas seals or flavored "stamps" on page 46 will do) and a big Santa mailbag—or maybe a surprise visit from an elf just passing by who would be happy to make a personal delivery to the North Pole. Be sure to deliver the letters — on the sly — to every Santa responsible for the guests on your list.

Make Your Own Christmas Cards and Gift Wrap Party

Gather materials for print-making, coloring, painting, pasting … let each child create his special design for the holidays.

Christmas Bake-Off

This is for small, small groups (too many cooks spoil the gingerbread), but can be fun for little culinary artists who like to stir, pour, measure, roll out, and decorate. Make cookies to eat or hang on the tree. You could roll out the shapes and simply let the children decorate to their heart's delight. Use a toothpick to initial each unbaked cookie for easy identification when it comes out poppin' fresh (and heavily laden with sprinkles, no doubt) from the oven.

Secrets Workshop

Flip through Chapter 4, "Giving," and THE BACK OF THE BOOK for ideas. Provide elf hats for each guest and supervise in the making of holiday surprises for brother, sister, Mom, and Dad. Be sure each gift is wrapped (by the elves themselves) and swear all to secrecy until Christmas morning.

For Kids Only …

Inviting several little friends with or without their parents is a generous gift at Christmas. You know the tree may get knocked down, a couple of porcelain figures may be sacrificed to the occasion (or stash them safely away for the time being), and also that your nerves will most certainly be frazzled when the last muddy snow boot walks out the door. But giving a good time to the children (and perhaps a couple of free hours to their mothers) is one of the highest forms of generosity the season has to offer.

It's usually pretty much fun, too.

Someday We'll Laugh About ...

the time we invited 20 kids over to decorate gingerbread cookies.

The first mistake was planning the party between four and six in the afternoon. What I thought would be the best time (considering naps, school, and work schedules) so that the little darlings could take their cookies home for dessert AFTER supper (HA!), turned out to be a truly bad idea. Here I was, marooned with my own three overexcited children for the entire day in the world's slowest countdown to lift-off ... "*When* is it going to be 4:00?"

Trying to keep the house reasonably straight for company became futile, and I reminded myself it would be a wreck again by 6:00 anyway, so what the heck. We made the dough, all four of us, in what had to be one of the world's best arguments against a committee. I *tried* to be light-hearted and jolly, but accumulating tension and the fact that we still hadn't packed the first thing to go out of town the next day kept the true spirit of the occasion tentative at best.

Then — another colossal mistake—we all piled in the car to get a few additional supplies (when I could have made do with what I had). This opened the floor for highly audible temper tantrums for "Please! Just *one* pack of gum!" (I was feeling highly principled that day).

Well, everybody finally came and everybody had a wonderful time (including me) and the cleanup wasn't half bad (consisting mostly of finishing up the raw

(continued ...)

Teddy Bear Tea

Give your favorite little angels one more opportunity to wear their Christmas suits and dresses, *and* to dress up teddy bear (pig, duck?) in something spiffy and seasonal. Concoct an elegant little setting, with apple juice "tea" in cups and saucers, delicate sandwiches, and square-cut sugar cookies "gift-wrapped" with decorative frosting. Be sure teddy gets a plate, too. And take lots of pictures.

Caroling Party

Pop popcorn, warm cocoa, and spread the spirit throughout the neighborhood. Let kids dress up as crazy Christmas characters for door-to-door dazzling delivery of holiday tunes. Back home, read a special Christmas story by the fire while warming frosty toes and toasting marshmallows skewered on slender sticks found along the way.

Secret Santa Sleigh (Hay?) Ride

Have several families gather to collect old toys ("gently used") still in good condition, or invite each guest to bring one new toy, and take some kids to an orphanage or a children's shelter for a special Christmas party. Sharing the joy and giving of Christmas will be one of a child's finest moments during the holidays, and you will get a heartful yourself, guaranteed.

The Birds' Christmas

Trim a tree in the yard, at the school, or at a park, or somewhere conspicuous in the neighborhood with peanut-buttered pine cones rolled in birdseed, cranberry and popcorn strings, birdseed bells, sliced fruit, scalloped orange baskets filled with sunflower seeds, stale bread cookie cutter shapes ...

My Best Friend Party

Invite the parents and siblings of each of your children's *best friend* to a supper, breakfast, dessert, hayride ... You will all get to know each other better, and besides, turnabout's fair play. How many times have your kids been asked to entertain the children of *your* friends?!

THE SCHOOL CHRISTMAS PARTY

Each holiday, *somebody* has to be in charge of the first grade Christmas party. And every year it's a struggle coming up with something new and different to entertain in style (though the kids are rarely picky when food and fun are involved).

Thinking up something new and clever can be difficult, especially when you have a hundred other sugarplums dancing in your head. Maybe a few of these suggestions will get the creative juices flowing:

❄ REFRESHMENTS

any recipes from "KidsKitchen" (see page 187)
decorate-your-own cookie or cupcake
marshmallow snowmen
candied or flavored popcorn
popcorn balls in an ice cream sugar cone
Santa (or other) shape cake
M&M Elf Mix (M&M's, corn nuts, Bugles, peanuts, Cheerios …)
inverted sugar cone frosted green with red cinnamon candies (icky
    sweet, but thrillingly attractive!)

❄ DRINKS

red or green Kool-Aid
cranberry juice/7-Up punch
cocoa with candy cane stirrers
hot apple cider with cinnamon sticks
lime sherbet/ginger ale punch
boxed juice packs decorated with gift wrap and a bow

❄ FAVORS

small ornaments
miniature baskets filled with candies
printed balloons
personalized plastic cup/toothbrush/refrigerator magnet … decorated
    and plastic-wrapped gingerbread boys and girls
a make-and-eat necklace: lace Fruit Loops, Cheerios, Lifesavers … on a
    red licorice whip
pencils with clever eraser tops
Decorate a tree or bare limb with gift-wrapped surprises and allow each
    child to take one at the end of the party. Or provide a Santa's grab
    bag of wrapped surprises from the dime store.

Games and Entertainment

SANTA Bingo: Give each child a card and use M&M's or other candies for the chips. Call out the letter and number and have a small prize for the first to call "SANTA!"

Guess how many jellybeans: Put a predetermined number of jellybeans in a jar wrapped with ribbon. Let each child write his guess on a slip of paper containing his name. The one with the closest guess wins the jellybeans!

Make dot-to-dots, crossword puzzles, coloring sheets, or some other fun/educational handout for each child to do.

Construct a Christmas bean bag game: Sew a bean bag to look like a

(continued …)

dough myself and even "forcing" down a few gingerbread arms and legs buried under raisins, sprinkles, and cinnamon candies).

After it was all over, I really didn't feel half bad myself — about this generous gift of pleasure to the smaller fry in my life.

Candy Cane Rudolph

Glue small craft eyes to front hook of a wrapped candy cane with a small red pompom for the nose. Twist a brown chenille stem around the curve for antlers and tie a red bow around the "neck"!

Especially for the Teens in Your Life

If memory serves, and if everybody's teenagers are like mine, teenagers have very definite ideas about what they do and do not want to do in the way of entertainment. Besides "lots of food" and an ice-bucket of legal thirst quencher, "don't come downstairs — *ever!*" seems to be the only other requirement. I *do* remember that hayrides were a pretty acceptable, even highly-anticipated activity. A little romance at Christmas never hurt anybody!

gift. Make a cardboard box to resemble a chimney, and let each child try to throw the bean bag "down" the chimney. A stocking hung on the outside holds packs of gum for the winners.

Make-your-own refreshments: a gingerbread house using graham crackers, squeeze frosting, gumdrops, candies ... a gumdrop tree ... decorated cookies ... marshmallow-popcorn "Snowballs" decorated as Frosty the Snowman ...

Show a movie or series of Christmas specials.

Read, tell, act out, or put on a puppet show of a favorite Christmas story.

Sing carols and teach the kids a few fun Christmas songs they might not already know (go for some of the crazier ones not likely learned in music appreciation class!).

Exercise to a children's Christmas record (the Chipmunks, Sesame Street, *A Very Special Christmas* ...)

Bring along a Santa to take each child on his knee, and have a Polaroid picture made to take home.

Make a piñata (see page 235): Tie the piñata just above eye level of the participants. Provide a narrow stick or baseball bat for swinging. Blindfold the stick-holder and tell everyone else to stand back. Allow three swings and change "batters" until the candy and prizes spill out and the scramble begins. Not recommended for large groups!

Swinging at a piñata

NINE

A Festival of Feasting
Take-it-Easy Recipes

Christmas itself may be called into question
If carried so far, it creates indigestion.
—Ralph Bergengren

Holiday eating. It begins when we sneak candy from the kids'
Halloween bags, gobble our way through Thanksgiving dinner,
and obliterate our waistlines all December long. Then there's January 1,
when we resolve to begin redefining our figures—tomorrow.

Who can deny that holiday food is as delicious for its sentiment as it
is for its taste? So many of our memories and traditions are caught up in
eating special foods that taste good at special times of the year. Who
could love a plum pudding in July?

There is a love of festive food that we all share. What holiday, more
than Christmas, provides a table so heavily laden with sentimental favorites? When we think December, we think gingerbread, pecan pie, buttery
sugar cookies, roasted chestnuts, glazed turkey, oyster dressing, candy
canes, stollen, pfeffernuss, hot spiced tea or buttered rum ... even, um,
fruitcake. Just about all of us are willing to sacrifice our figures to the
holiday feeding frenzy. And preparing something mouth-watering as well
as irresistibly gorgeous can be a delectable Christmastime experience.

The world is fat with cookbooks and I'm not about to contribute
another. What I will contribute to *The Christmas Lover's Handbook* are a
few choice recipes of mine, my family, and friends, and some fun ideas
for garnishing and serving such holiday favorites as Christmas morning

Want to be Catered To?

If you absolutely can't stand to
cook (you consider having to put
a frozen dinner in the microwave
cruel and unusual punishment),
don't have the time, or wish a
table laden with scrumptious fare
happened simply by "laying a finger aside of your nose," consider
laying a finger on your phone and
calling in the caterers! They can
bake, simmer, and stew, and keep
you out of hot water with the
rest of your family!

While holiday eating is special and spectacular, neither your
stomach nor your schedule can take a constant flow of gourmet
delights. Plan several easy meals for busy days. Make ahead and
freeze more than one dinner's worth of a certain dish (soups, stews,
spaghetti sauce ...). Keep a place in your file for quick and easy menus. You
will be glad you did—all year long.

M&M's and Sugarplums ...

do not sweet little children make. Christmas morning may find their little faces dripping with the oranges, M&M's, and sugarplums they found in their stockings, but make a decent attempt to revive good nutrition and keep stomachs full until the Christmas feast begins. Minimize tears, tantrums, and trauma with a healthy start to a merry Christmas Day.

breakfast, seasonal party drinks and hors d'ouevres, the critical ingredients of a fine holiday feast, sugar and spice, and even a few ideas to make holiday mealtime a bit gentler on the cook ... along with some good clean fun for the littlest chefs in the family.

All this and more—with a large serving of EASY. (I strategically avoid recipes with any more than five ingredients!) My motto is "Get a Life! Get Out of the Kitchen!" (But hey, I still love to EAT!)

DURING THE BUSY HOLIDAYS ...

Avoid fast-food burnout and have a simply delicious meal at home.

Sandwiches and Quickie Suppers

❄ CROISSANT OR BAGEL SANDWICHES

Slice a croissant or bagel in half and fill with one of these or any other combination. Heat and eat, with a mug of hot canned soup.

> roast beef slices/Brie/toasted almonds
> turkey slices/jack cheese/sliced green olives
> ham slices/sharp cheddar/apple cubes

❄ PITA POCKET SANDWICHES

> chopped vegetables/any cheese/bean sprouts/salad dressing
> tuna/mayonnaise/celery chunks/Swiss cheese
> sliced avocado/bacon strips/tomato slices/ranch dressing

❄ GREAT ONE-DISH DINNERS TO CHOP AND STIR-FRY

> round steak/pepper/onion/mushrooms/chopped ginger
> chicken/broccoli/onion/waterchestnuts/mushrooms/pineapple chunks
> sausage slices/zucchini or summer squash/onion/tomato
> ham cubes/green pepper/pineapple/celery/sweet and sour sauce

❄ OTHER QUICK-AND-EASY SUPPER IDEAS

favorite soup, cornucopias of Lebanon bologna or salami filled with spiced cheese or flavored cream cheese, crackers, fruit

dump salad: leftover meat cubes, cold cooked vegetables, croutons, olives, garbanzo beans ... on a bed of lettuce

taco salad: browned beef with taco seasoning, tomatoes, onions, grated cheese, olives, avocados or guacamole, crumbled tortilla chips, salsa, sour cream ... on a bed of lettuce

cooked roast beef, turkey, or ham ready-sliced by the butcher for sandwich and quick supper supplies

Organize a Christmas casserole co-op with two or three other families. Take turns preparing enough lasagna, chili, vegetable soup, tuna casserole, goulash ... for everybody, and exchange. You cook like mad one day and get to take two or three days off!

Serve peanut butter and jelly one night. Nobody will die!

CHRISTMAS MORNING BREAKFAST

Plan something extraordinary for this special meal.

One universal imperative is that Christmas morning breakfast be planned and prepared ahead of time, if at all possible. There is so much impatience and excitement, starting before daybreak, and the designee of morning meal preparation (usually Mom) tends to miss out on some of the fun.

Christmas breakfast itself could become a special tradition in your house when you devise a menu everybody likes (especially the cook!). A favorite coffeecake, breakfast casserole, bread and fruit ... served year after year will add another warm memory to your celebration. Or consider turning breakfast into brunch and serve only two meals on Christmas Day.

Try some of these make-ahead offerings for breakfast around the tree. Some make wonderful brunch entrées, as well; others, accompaniments to a cozy holiday teatime.

❄ SAUSAGE STRATA

6 slices of bread (crusts removed)	¾ c. light cream
1½ lbs. sausage	½ t. salt
1 t. spiced mustard	dash of pepper
1 c. Swiss cheese, grated	dash of nutmeg
4 eggs, lightly beaten	1 t. Worcestershire sauce
1½ c. milk	

Arrange bread in bottom of greased 13" x 9" casserole. Brown sausage and drain off fat. Stir in mustard. Spoon sausage evenly over bread and sprinkle with cheese. Combine remaining ingredients and pour over all. Bake at 350° F for 25-30 minutes (30-35 minutes if refrigerated). May prepare one or two days in advance or cook ahead and freeze. Serves 6-8.

Helen Covington

❄ GINNY'S EASY QUICHE

8-12 strips of bacon, cooked and crumbled (substitute cooked spinach, asparagus, tiny shrimp, cooked sausage ...)	4 eggs
	1 pint half and half
	1 T. flour
	1 t. salt
1 unbaked 9" deep-dish pie crust	1½ T. melted butter
8 oz. grated Swiss cheese	

Crumble bacon (or substitute) into bottom of pie shell. Top with grated cheese. Combine remaining ingredients in blender or food processor and blend well. Pour into pie crust and bake at 375° F for about 35 minutes, or until knife inserted in center (don't puncture bottom crust) comes out clean. Let stand a few minutes before cutting.

Ginny Fick

Eggs: Red & Green Plate Special

How to Hard-Cook an Egg: Cover eggs in a pan with cold water. Bring to a boil and simmer 12-15 minutes. Immediately after cooking, run cold water over eggs to ease removal of the shell. The fresher the egg, the more difficult it is to peel.

Dyeing Hard-Cooked Eggs: Dye hard-cooked eggs as you would an Easter egg, using red and green colors and holiday designs. Put a colored egg into each stocking with a snack box of cereal and a juice box—a fun and easy way to start Christmas morning off right.

Egg Magic: Mix 3 T. powdered alum (from the drug store) with one cup of vinegar. Paint a message or name on the shell of a fresh egg with the mixture and let dry completely. Boil the egg. When it's peeled, your message should appear on the peeled egg!

Toasts with the Most

Christmas Toast or French Toast: Cut toasted bread or French toast with cookie cutters. Put a dollop of grape, raspberry, or strawberry jam in the center and sprinkle over all with confectioner's sugar.

Orange Toast: Mix ½ c. sugar, ¼ c. orange juice, and ½ t. grated orange rind. Spread on buttered bread and toast lightly.

Cinnamon Toast: Keep a shaker full of ¼ c. sugar, 1½ T. cinnamon, and a dash of nutmeg. Sprinkle on buttered bread and toast lightly.

❄ WILD RICE CASSEROLE

6 oz. pkg. wild rice mix
1 lb. bulk pork sausage
1 lb. ground chuck
1 onion, chopped
8 oz. can sliced mushrooms, drained
8 oz. can water chestnuts, drained
3 T. soy sauce
1 (2¾ oz.) pkg. sliced almonds

Prepare rice according to package directions. Set aside. Sauté onion in large pan and add sausage and beef to brown. Drain and add rice, mushrooms, water chestnuts, and soy sauce. Stir well to mix. Refrigerate in greased 2-quart casserole overnight or freeze. Let stand at room temperature 30 minutes before baking. Sprinkle the almonds on top and bake uncovered at 325° F for one hour. Bake unrefrigerated casserole only 25 minutes, or until heated through. Serves 8-10.

Zella McKnight

❄ THREE CHEESES AND SOME EGGS

6 eggs
1 c. milk
2 t. sugar
1 t. salt
1 lb. Monterey Jack, grated
3 oz. cream cheese
8 oz. cottage cheese
5 T. butter, cubed
1 t. baking powder

Mix eggs, milk, sugar, and salt in a large bowl. Add remaining ingredients and blend well. Pour into 13" x 9" baking dish and bake 30 minutes at 350° F. Serves 8-10.

❄ "WHO'S COUNTING FAT GRAMS?" ROLLS AND HAM

1½ c. scalded milk
½ c. butter
½ c. sugar
½ c. lard
2 pkgs. dry yeast
1/3 c. very warm water
1 t. salt
6-7 c. flour
1 egg
melted butter

Scald milk and add butter, sugar, and lard. Remove from heat and cool. Dissolve yeast in 1/3 c. very warm water and add with salt to milk mixture. Gradually stir in 3 c. flour. Add egg. Work in 3-4 more cups of flour with clean hands. Let rise in greased bowl to double original size (about 1½ hrs.). Break off golf ball size pieces of dough and flatten each into a disk. Dip half of disk in melted butter and fold in half. Arrange on jelly roll or round cake pan and let rise one hour. Brush tops with melted butter and bake 15-18 minutes in 350° F oven. Makes 3-4 dozen rolls. These freeze well, after baking, stored in a zipped plastic bag.

Split baked rolls and add whipped honey butter or sweet mustard, if desired.

Remove excess fat and lightly fry packaged country ham in a skillet (add no oil, but sprinkle a few drops of water into the pan) 3-4 minutes per side. Put it all together and YUMMMMM ...

Dixie Purvis

❄ ENGLISH SCONES FOR SANTA'S HELPERS

2 c. flour
1 t. salt
5 t. sugar
3 t. baking powder

4 T. butter
2 eggs, beaten
½ c. cream

Sift first four ingredients. Mix in butter. Blend cream into beaten eggs and add to flour mixture, stirring with a spoon until well blended. Spread out ½" thick on a lightly floured surface. Cut into shapes with cookie cutters or scalloped biscuit cutter and brush with egg white. Bake at 350° F 12-15 minutes until golden. Serve piping hot with jam or marmalade and an unusual blend of tea or flavored coffee.

❄ MORAVIAN SUGAR CAKE

The Moravian Protestants, also known as the Church of the Brethren, came to America from Bohemia (currently a part of the Czech Republic) to settle in Pennsylvania (1740) and Winston-Salem, NC (1753), where maintenance of the simple lifestyle exists today in the charming village of Old Salem. This gentle community is also well known for their cookies, particularly the impossibly thin Moravian gingersnaps, which require incredible patience to make … but nobody does it better.

1 med. potato, peeled and sliced
1 pkg. dry yeast
½ c. warm water
1 egg, lightly beaten
1/3 c. butter, melted
1/3 c. sugar

½ t. salt
2¼ c. all-purpose flour
1-2 T. softened butter
½ c. brown sugar
1 t. ground cinnamon
1/3 c. butter, melted

Cook potato in boiling water until tender, drain, and mash, measuring out ½ cup. Dissolve yeast in warm water. Combine ½ c. potato, lightly beaten egg, 1/3 c. melted butter, sugar, and salt, and mix well. Add yeast mixture and 1 c. of the flour, again mixing well. Stir in remaining flour to make a soft dough.

Turn dough onto floured surface and knead until smooth. Place in a well-greased bowl, turning dough to grease all surfaces. Cover and let rise in a warm place, free from drafts, until doubled in bulk (about 2 hours). Punch dough down and divide in half, pressing each half into a well-greased 8" square baking pan. Brush with softened butter, cover, and let rise again until doubled (about 1 hour). Make holes 2-3" apart in the dough using the handle of a wooden spoon. Combine brown sugar and cinnamon and sift evenly over dough. Drizzle with remaining melted butter. Bake at 400° F 20 minutes. Serve warm or wrap and give generously as gifts. Makes 2 cakes.

HORS D'OEUVRES AND SNACKS

On a cozy evening by the fire, or at your next Christmas party, satisfy holiday hungries with these easy recipes …

Sweet Champagne Mustard for Dipping, Sandwiches, Cold Meats:

2/3 c. dry mustard
1 c. sugar
3 large eggs
2/3 c. champagne vinegar

Combine mustard and sugar on top of a double boiler, stirring well until smooth. Beat in eggs and vinegar with a wire whisk. Continue beating over boiling water 5-7 minutes until slightly foamy. Immediately remove from heat and pour into a jar. Makes about 1¾ cups.

❄ VERA'S CHIPPED BEEF MOLD

1 t. dried onion flakes	2 T. mayonnaise
1 T. sherry	1 jar (4½ oz.) dried beef, chopped
8 oz. cream cheese, softened	¼ c. stuffed olives, sliced

Soak onion flakes in sherry until liquid is absorbed. Mix with remaining ingredients and shape into a mold with your hands. Cover mold with additional olives or slivered almonds for garnish.   *Vera Fick*

❄ JEZEBEL

1 #2 jar apple jelly	1 #2 jar horseradish
1 #2 jar pineapple preserves	2 oz. dry mustard

Mix all ingredients together and serve over cream cheese, with crackers.   *Zella McKnight*

❄ CHUTNEY BEEF

3½ lb. beef tenderloin	1 T. oil

Cut tenderloin into bite-sized pieces and place on a jelly roll pan lined with several layers of paper towels. Cover with plastic wrap and refrigerate overnight. To cook meat, line a broiler pan with foil and arrange meat in single layer on the pan. Pour one tablespoon of oil over the meat, stirring to coat each piece. Broil 3-4 minutes. No turning is necessary.

Chutney Sauce:

1 8 oz. jar chutney	1 t. salt
3 t. curry powder	2 T. lemon juice
1 t. ginger	6 T. butter

Mix ingredients in a saucepan and bring to a boil, cooking one minute to blend. Using a slotted spoon, put cooked meat in a chafing dish and pour sauce over. Serve when heated through with toothpicks, or over rice as an entrée.

    Libby Cox

❄ DEDE'S ASPARAGUS ROLL-UPS

1 loaf white bread (24 slices)	4 oz. bleu cheese
½ c. softened butter	25 spears fresh asparagus
8 oz. cream cheese, softened	½ c. melted butter

Steam asparagus briefly or parboil, leaving stalks fairly firm. Trim bread crusts. Flatten bread with rolling pin. Mix butter and cheeses and spread mixture on bread. Lay one asparagus spear in middle of slice and roll up bread around the spear. Slice each roll into 4 pieces and dip in melted butter. Roll in sesame seeds, if desired, and put on cookie sheet to freeze. Before serving, bake frozen roll-ups about 15 minutes at 400° F. Makes about 96 roll-ups. Great to have on hand for quick yet elegant hors d'oeuvres.   *Dede Caughman*

❄ BLEU CHEESE BITES

1 c. biscuit baking mix	2 T. margarine, melted
¼ c. cold water	1 T. chopped parsley
¼ c. bleu cheese, crumbled	paprika

Heat oven to 450° F. Mix baking mix, water, and bleu cheese with hands until well blended. Shape tablespoons of dough into balls and arrange on an ungreased cookie sheet 2" apart. Stir parsley into melted margarine and drizzle over each ball. Sprinkle with paprika. Bake until golden, 8-10 minutes. Makes about 2 dozen.

Be prepared for holiday drop-ins. Keep plenty of cocktail napkins and ice on hand. Have "ready-when-you-are's" available: instant hot drinks, spiced nuts, cookie trays and tins, wine and drink mixers …

❄ RED CAVIAR CHRIS-MOUSSE

1 envelope unflavored gelatin	1 3½ oz. jar red caviar
½ c. boiling water	2 T. mayonnaise
2 T. cold water	2 T. lemon juice
16 oz. sour cream	dash Tabasco

Dissolve gelatin in boiling water. Add cold water and then remaining ingredients, stirring to blend. Spoon into a lightly oiled mold and cover to chill in the refrigerator several hours or until set. Set mold in pan of warm water to loosen, and invert onto a serving tray. Serve with melba toast rounds or other favorite crackers. Makes about 4 cups.

Missy Scott

❄ MIDDLE EASTERN HUMMUS

3 cans garbanzo beans/chick peas	3 T. tahini (ground sesame seed)
5 cloves garlic	salt
4 T. olive oil	pepper
5 T. lemon juice	chopped parsley, parsley sprigs

Blend all ingredients except parsley in a food processor until smooth. Chill. Sprinkle with parsley and serve as a delicious dip with soft pita wedges.

❄ MEXICAN FIREBALLS

1 lb. ground chuck	2 T. Worcestershire
1 c. seasoned bread crumbs	½ t. garlic salt
1 egg, beaten	3 T. green chiles, diced
¼ c. minced onion	Tabasco, to taste
3 T. tomato paste	1 c. grated Parmesan

Combine all ingredients but the Parmesan. Form 1" balls and stuff with: sliced olives, pineapple tidbits, sliced water chestnuts, sliced mushrooms … Coat balls with Parmesan cheese and bake at 425° F for 15 minutes. Or freeze, and thaw before baking. Makes about 40.

❄ GREEK SKEWERS

Marinade:

¹/₃ c. tarragon or lemon basil vinegar	1 lb. sea scallops
½ c. olive oil	8 oz. whole mushrooms
2 cloves garlic, minced	large pitted Greek olives
chopped scallions	1 lb. medium shrimp
1½ t. salt	whole red and yellow peppers, cubed
dash pepper	dolmathes (grape leaves)
dash hot pepper sauce	

Combine marinade ingredients and pour over all remaining items except grape leaves. Cover and refrigerate overnight, stirring several times. Arrange marinated items on wooden skewers, wrapping each seafood item with grape leaf before skewering. Grill or broil 3-4" from heat, turning occasionally, until done.

❄ TERIYAKI BACON WRAPS

¹/₃ c. teriyaki sauce	1 T. honey
2 or 3 bananas	10 slices bacon, cut in half

(may also wrap pineapple chunks, chicken livers, water chestnuts, stuffed olives, shrimp, scallops …)

Combine teriyaki sauce and honey. Cut peeled bananas in 1" slices and marinate in sauce, stirring occasionally, for one hour. Wrap each banana in ½ slice of bacon and fasten with toothpick. Lay on rack in shallow baking pan and brush with reserved marinade. Broil 3-4" from heat, turning to cook on all sides, about 10 minutes. Makes 20.

❄ CHEESE TRAY

For colorful hors d'oeuvres, pour one of the following over cream cheese:

> red and/or green pepper jelly
> chutney and toasted almonds
> minced parsley and sun-dried tomatoes

Or tint softened cream cheese with food coloring or 2 t. curry powder and pipe through a pastry bag or cake decorator onto toasted party rye, buttered toast points, crackers, cucumber rounds, celery sticks … topped with a dab of caviar, pimiento, or almond sliver.

To a basic cheese ball recipe, add one or more of the following: chopped green olives, chopped nuts, crumbled bacon, crushed pineapple, chopped green pepper, chopped apples, diced pimiento, horseradish …

Instead of making a cheese "ball," shape cheese molds into holiday shapes: Christmas tree, bell, reindeer, star … and garnish to decorate.

Re"cycle" a plain wheel of softened Brie cheese:

Arrange toasted almonds on top and drizzle melted butter over all,
> broiling until soft, gooey, and delicious. Serve with crackers and/or
> crusty bread.

Spread with a lightly moistened mixture of brown sugar and chopped pecans. Broil until soft and serve with Swedish gingersnaps. Outstanding!

Wrap completely in thawed puff pastry, tucking the ends underneath, drizzle with butter and sesame seeds, bake at 350° 15 minutes, and serve with crackers.

Fill slitted snow peas, cornucopias of Lebanon bologna and salami, or mushroom caps with spiced soft cheese. Add a cheery sprinkle of chopped fresh parsley or paprika.

✳ CHEESE TIPS

- Allow ¼ pound of cheese per guest and serve at least three cheeses of varying flavor and texture.
- Arrange a cheese tray with different shapes and colors of cheese for visual and gastronomical interest.
- Serve dessert cheese at room temperature with fresh fruit.
- Cheese is a good cocktail food because of its high fat content, which tends to cut the impact of alcohol.

✳ FLAVORED POPCORN

Add one of these flavorings to ⅓ c. melted butter and pour over everybody's favorite health food, freshly popped popcorn:

¼ c. Parmesan cheese	2 T. dry ranch dressing mix
1 T. garlic salt	¼ c. grated cheddar
2 T. taco seasoning mix	2 T. bacon bits
2 t. curry powder	2 t. Italian herb seasoning
2 T. peanut butter (mix with the melted butter until smooth)	½ c. crumbled bleu cheese

It's-a-Wrap, Canned Laughter, and Other Last-Minute Snack Ideas

- Wrap soy-marinated cooked shrimp in lightly steamed snow peas and secure with a ruffled toothpick.
- Wrap fruit chunks dipped in honey in large biscuit-cutter sized fresh crepes and tie into bundles with holiday ribbon.
- Make cocktail sandwiches using these and other thrilling fillings: cream cheese and chopped stuffed olives, peanut butter and bacon, dates and walnuts in cream cheese, chicken salad and chopped pear, egg salad and spicy mustard, deviled ham and chopped apples, chopped hard-boiled egg and caviar ... or use one of these fillings to top cucumber slices, buttered toast points, or pastry shells ...
- Marinate cheese-filled tortellini, snow peas, and cherry tomatoes in Italian dressing and serve with ruffled toothpicks.
- Dip pretzels, Combos, eggrolls, hot soft pretzels ... into spiced or champagne mustard.
- Arrange canned smoked oysters, clams, and sardines on buttered and toasted pita wedges and sprinkle with a little garlic salt.

Concerning Raw Eggs

There is growing concern about the threat of salmonella contamination of raw eggs. The following recommendations should be made:

The very young, the very elderly, and the chronically ill should not consume anything containing raw egg.

Check eggs for broken shells and discard any found.

Refrigerate eggs as soon after purchase as possible.

Dishes containing raw egg should be consumed immediately.

Items containing raw egg should be kept at room temperature only as long as it takes to prepare them.

- Combine chopped black olives and smoked oysters in a small bowl, mound on a platter, and serve with crackers and a spreading knife.
- Fill "Who's Counting Fat Grams?" biscuits (from page 158 and your freezer) with a spread of store-bought liver paté and more butter.
- Dippity-Do's. Even though it's so "Eighties," everybody still loves *Hot Artichoke Dip*: one can artichoke hearts, 1 c. Parmesan, 1 c. mayo; baked 20 minutes at 350° until warmed through ...
  and *Mexican Layer Dip*: layerings of lettuce, chopped tomato, chopped green onions, grated cheese, refried beans, browned ground beef, guacamole, black olives, and sour cream ... served with a big basket of tortilla chips.
  (and Jim won't even give up, from the "Sixties" ...) *California Onion Dip*: sour cream and dry onion soup mix and a bag of Ruffles (nearly a classic ... but don't serve this at your formal cocktail party!)

COLD PUNCHES AND CHRISTMAS SPIRITS

Many ingredients make a grand Christmas feast. Set the mood with food, a blazing fire, and a cold drink to warm the spirit.

❄ SPICED SPRITZERS

5 sticks cinnamon, broken
3 whole cloves
6 c. rosé wine

2 12 oz. cans ginger ale, club soda, or lemon-lime beverage

Tie cinnamon and cloves in a cheesecloth bag. Add bag to wine in a saucepan and heat to simmer. Cool. Pour into a glass pitcher and refrigerate. To serve, pour 4 oz. of wine mixture into a wine glass and add approximately 2 oz. ginger ale (or other sparkling beverage). Fruited ice cubes add a spirited touch. 8-10 servings

❄ EGGNOG FOR TWENTY

12 eggs
1 lb. confectioner's sugar
½ t. salt
1 t. vanilla
1½ qts. milk

1 qt. heavy cream
3 c. water
3 c. bourbon
1 c. dark rum or brandy

Beat eggs. Gradually add sugar, salt, and vanilla, continuing to beat mixture. Stir in milk, cream, water, bourbon, and rum or brandy. Cover tightly. Chill at least 48 hours for flavors to blend.

❄ MIMOSA PUNCH

Mix equal parts dry ("brut") champagne and orange juice. Garnish with mint leaves or a maraschino cherry. Serve over crushed ice.

 There are three types of champagne: "brut"—unsweetened, dry white wine; "sec" and "demi-sec"—sweeter wine; "doux"—sweetest, most full-bodied of the champagnes.

❄ NON-ALCOHOLIC CHRISTMAS PUNCH

2 qts. cranberry juice	½ c. sugar
1 T. grated orange rind	5 whole cloves
2 c. orange juice	1 liter ginger ale or lemon-lime beverage

Put all ingredients except carbonated beverage into a large pot and bring to a boil. Reduce heat and simmer 10-15 minutes. Remove cloves and chill punch until ready to serve. Add ginger ale just before serving.

HOT DRINKS

To tantalize the nose and tingle the toes ...

❄ WASSAIL

"Wassail" derives from the Saxon expression, "Was Haile!" which means, "To your health!" It's the favorite drink of merry olde England.

½ gallon apple cider	3 sticks cinnamon
1 pint cranberry juice	lemon studded with cloves
¾ c. sugar	orange slices
1 t. whole allspice	1½ c. rum

Combine all ingredients in a large pot. Bring to a boil and simmer for a few hours before serving. Serve in mugs or tempered glass cups. Makes about 3 quarts

A wassail bowl is a warm greeting to visitors and frosted carolers roaming the neighborhood ...

❄ HOT BUTTERED RUM

2 c. brown sugar	8 whole cloves
½ c. butter	1 whole nutmeg
dash of salt	2 qts. hot water
5 sticks cinnamon	2-3 c. dark rum

Combine all ingredients in a large pot and simmer over low heat for a few hours, allowing the full flavor to steep sufficiently. Serve in mugs with a cinnamon stick. 8 servings

❄ GLOGG

A spicy Swedish drink ... deliciously different.

1 half gallon burgundy wine	2 doz. whole cloves
1 fifth port wine	1 c. water
1 c. light rum	1 c. raisins
1 c. brandy	2/3 c. slivered almonds
5 sticks cinnamon	¼ c. sugar

Combine spices and water in a small saucepan, bringing to a boil. Reduce heat and simmer 30 minutes. Strain out spices. In a large pot, combine spiced water with the remaining ingredients. Heat just to simmer. Serve in mugs rinsed in hot water, with a slice of lemon or orange.

He causeth the grass to grow for the cattle,
and herb for the service of man:
That he may bring forth food out of the earth;
And wine that maketh glad the heart of men . . .
—Psalm 104:15

There's nought, no doubt, so much the spirit calms, as rum and true religion.
—Lord Byron

Beverage Tips

• Mix defrosted lemonade with two cans of cold water. Freeze in ice trays and use cubes in punch drinks or apple cider.
• Freeze berries or mint sprigs into ice cubes: Freeze 1/3 of the liquid, add berry, and freeze again. Add remaining liquid and freeze until solid. Look for ice molds in Christmas shapes.
• Insert a fresh flower stem into a citrus round and float in a punch.
• Float an ice mold, flavored ice, colored ice cubes ... in punch.
• Cloved lemons and oranges add color and flavor to a hot or cold cider bowl.
• Make "Tipsy Olives" for a real splash or as a gift: Put one jar of stuffed olives and juice into a 1-quart mason jar. Add 8 oz. of wine vinegar, 3 finely chopped garlic cloves, and the juice of one lemon. Dice the lemon rind and stir into mixture. Seal tightly. Keep refrigerated until ready to use.
• Allow one pound of ice per person when serving cocktails.

❅ WINTER WEATHERER

This recipe will clear up even the stuffiest Christmas cold!

6 oz. Scotch or Irish whiskey	lemon slices
2 T. honey	¼ c. boiling water

Rinse two heavy mugs with hot water. Put one tablespoon of honey into each mug and add half the water to each, dissolving the honey. Heat whiskey in a pan (do not boil) and add to the mug. Top with a lemon slice.

Or serve:

Hot apple cider with a lemon slice and cinnamon stick
Hot cranberry juice cocktail punch with floating cloved oranges
Warmed wine heated with commercially-available mulling spices

❅ INSTANT HOT DRINK MIXES

Have on hand for surprise guests and family, or give as gifts:

Instant Russian Tea
Combine:

2 c. Tang	2 T. ground cinnamon
½ c. instant tea	3 T. ground cloves
1 envelope lemonade mix	Mix 1½ T. with boiling water.
¼ c. sugar	

Café Coca-Mocha
Combine in a blender:

¼ c. non-dairy creamer	2 T. powdered unsweetened cocoa
¼ c. sugar	Mix 1½ T. with boiling water.
1/3 c. instant coffee	

Variations:
Café à l'Orange: substitute 3 orange Lifesavers for the cocoa.
Bavarian Mint: add 1 crushed candy cane to recipe.
Café Viennese: substitute 1 T. ground cinnamon for the cocoa.

Garnish hot coffees and cocoas with flavored or regular whipped cream topped with sprinkles of nutmeg, cinnamon, or chocolate shavings ... marshmallows or cinnamon candies ... ground-up candy canes ... Or pour melted chocolate over whipped cream. Use a candy cane or cinnamon stick as a swizzle stick.

❅ FLAVORED WHIPPED CREAMS

Whip heavy cream in a chilled bowl with chilled beaters. Add 2 T. powdered sugar and ¾ t. vanilla, other flavoring extract, or liqueur. A pinch of salt will hasten whipping. Or add small amounts of:

cinnamon	grated chocolate
fruit preserves	marmalade
ginger	nutmeg

SOUPS AND STEWS

To calm the spirit, warm the heart ...

❄ CURRIED CREAM CHEESE SOUP

4 3 oz. pkgs. cream cheese   salt and pepper to taste
2 c. beef consommé   ¾ t. curry powder
1 garlic clove

Add all ingredients to blender or food processor and purée on full speed until smooth. Refrigerate and serve cold with a garnish of tiny shrimp, slivered chicken, toasted almonds, or fresh caviar. You can substitute 12 oz. plain yogurt for the cream cheese to lower fat content and calories. Serves 6.

❄ CHRISTMAS EVE OYSTER STEW

4 T. butter   1 qt. fresh oysters in liquid
dash of flour   2 t. Worcestershire
1 pint half and half   salt and freshly ground black
¼ c. milk   pepper

Melt butter and add enough flour to thicken. Stir in half and half and milk. Add oysters and liquid, Worcestershire, and salt and pepper to taste. Cook over low heat for 10-12 minutes to heat through, being careful not to let boil. Serve with parsley garnish and crackers. *Vera Fick*

❄ CAROLYN'S VEGETABLE SOUP POT

Keep this simmering all through the holidays with frequent additions of leftovers, or freeze for "fast food" on a hectic evening ...

short ribs (3-5 lbs) or stew beef   4 large potatoes, diced
2 large cans tomatoes   frozen lima beans, corn, okra
1 large can V-8 juice   whatever else sounds good
3 large carrots, sliced   seasoning to taste
2 large onions, chopped

Cover meat in water in a large soup pot. Cook until tender with tomatoes and V-8. Add carrots, onions, and limas. Add corn, okra, and potatoes about an hour before serving. Simmer and add seasonings during the last 20-30 minutes of cooking for maximum flavor. *Carolyn Gober*

VEGETABLES AND SALADS

For healthful meal-mates, try these ...

❄ MARINATED BEANS AND BLEU CHEESE

1 can blue lake green beans   sliced sweet onions
small wedge of bleu cheese,
    crumbled
favorite Italian dressing

Mix first three ingredients together and pour dressing over all. Refrigerate overnight before serving.

Soup's On

• Garnish cream soups with tiny shrimp, caviar, parsley, croutons, sliced mushrooms, sieved hard-cooked eggs ...

• For seasoning, twice the quantity of fresh herbs gives nearly equivalent flavoring as dried. Fresh is best for full flavor.

• Make a bouquet garni: In the middle of a small square of cheesecloth, mix 1/8 t. each of peppercorns, bay leaves, dried celery tops, parsley, sage, rosemary, thyme ... Tie up in a little bag to season soups.

Serving Salads and Vegetables

• Carve peeled potatoes into shapes. Boil immediately in a large pot, adding bouillon cubes to the water for flavor. Cook 30-35 minutes, until cooked through. Drizzle with butter and chopped parsley.

• To peel tomatoes: Drop tomato into boiling water for 12 seconds. Drain. Skin should peel away easily.

• To unmold a gelatin mold: Rinse the serving dish or plate with cold water. Dip mold in warm water almost to the top. Loosen upper edge of gelatin with the tip of a rubber spatula. Put serving dish on top of mold and invert. Shake firmly, holding tightly in place, and carefully lift off mold.

• Make herbed wine vinegar for salads or as a lovely gift (presented in a decorative bottle with a floating stem of fresh herbs):

1½ c. white wine
1½ c. white vinegar
2 c. chopped fresh herbs (basil, chives, rosemary, tarragon, dill ...)

Mix well. Shake before pouring.

• To get the most flavor from garlic: Flatten a peeled garlic clove with the flat side of a heavy knife by pressing down hard. Sprinkle with salt and chop thoroughly.

❄ BEST BEAN SALAD

Marinated salads last a week to ten days in the refrigerator and make good "quick meal" supplements.

1 can cut green beans
1 can white shoepeg corn
1 can tiny green peas
1 can kidney beans
1 green pepper, diced

4 celery stalks, sliced diagonally
2-3 mild onions, cut in rings
1 small jar pimientos
1 can sliced water chestnuts

Dressing:
½ c. salad oil
1 c. vinegar
1 T. salt

¼ c. sugar
1 T. water
dash of pepper (or more)

Drain all canned vegetables and mix with remaining ingredients. Pour dressing over all and let stand one day in the refrigerator before serving.
Justina Poe

❄ MIXED PASTA SALAD

Add chopped meats, seafood, olives, cheese, peppers, tomatoes, artichoke hearts, hearts of palm, early peas, pine nuts ... whatever sounds good, to cooked pasta. Marinate in an oil and vinegar dressing, spices, and herbs. Good for lunch, to finish up leftovers, or as a side dish at dinner.

❄ SWEET POTATOES AND APPLES

6 med. sweet potatoes
2 med. apples
4 T. butter, melted

½ c. brown sugar
1 T. cinnamon
1 T. honey

Bake potatoes in jackets until tender. Cool. Slice lengthwise in ½" slices. Layer half of potatoes in a greased casserole. Sprinkle with cinnamon and cover with apples, sliced thickly. Repeat layering. Dissolve sugar and honey in melted butter and pour over all. Bake at 325° F for 45 minutes.
Carolyn Gober

❄ SPINACH AND ARTICHOKE CASSEROLE

2 10 oz. pkgs. frozen chopped
   spinach
1 stick butter, melted
8 oz. cream cheese, softened

1 t. lemon juice
1 can artichoke hearts
crushed cracker crumbs

Cook spinach and drain well. Add butter, cream cheese, and lemon juice to spinach and blend well with mixer. Place artichoke hearts in bottom of greased casserole and add spinach mixture. Top with cracker crumbs and bake at 350° F for 25 minutes.
Jean Hunter

❄ CORN PUDDING

1 12 oz. can whole corn	1 t. dry mustard
2 12 oz. cans creamed corn	1 t. dried onion soup mix
4 eggs, lightly beaten	coarsely ground black pepper
½ c. sugar	½ c. butter, melted
4 T. cornstarch	½ c. milk
2 t. garlic salt	

Combine corn and eggs. Set aside. Mix sugar, cornstarch, garlic salt, dry mustard, onion soup mix, and pepper. Add butter and milk, and combine with corn mixture in greased 3 qt. casserole. Bake at 400° F one hour or until golden.

BREADS

A friend in "knead" is a friend indeed ...

❄ EASY FRENCH BREAD

All the flavor, warmth, and satisfaction of home-baked bread, with truly minimal effort! Recipe makes one loaf, but you might as well make two at a time, it goes so fast ... and makes a terrific gift!

1 pkg. quick-acting yeast	2 T. sugar
2 c. lukewarm water	1 T. salt
4 c. sifted unbleached flour	

Dissolve yeast in 1 c. warm water. While yeast softens, sift together flour, sugar, and salt into a large bowl. Stir in dissolved yeast and add a second cup of warm water, until dough becomes soft and sticky. Cover with a clean cloth and set bowl in warm place to let rise until doubled (2-4 hours). Punch risen dough down with your hand and give it a couple of good beatings. Place in a greased loaf pan and cover again with cloth. Let rise until dough just reaches the top of the pan. Brush lightly with melted butter and sesame seeds and bake at 400° F until golden brown and sounding hollow when tapped. My oven only takes 30 minutes, but it's fast. Excellent buttered and toasted, or for melted-cheese toast at breakfast.

Ginny Fick

❄ HONEY ALMOND BRAID

Extremely impressive, this recipe makes two loaves ...

2½ c. unbleached flour	1¾ c. milk
2 pkgs. yeast	¼ c. butter
½ c. honey	2 eggs
1 T. salt	4-5 c. additional flour

Combine first four ingredients in a large bowl. Blend milk and butter in a saucepan over low heat until very warm. Add eggs, then warmed liquid to flour mixture and blend until moistened. Beat 3 minutes with an electric mixer and stir in an additional 3½ c. flour to form sticky dough. Knead, adding another ½ to 1½ c. flour until dough is smooth

---

Spice Up the Holidays with ...

Spicy Christmas Scent-Sation

Combine in a pan:

 peelings of 2 oranges
 3 cinnamon sticks, crushed
 12 whole cloves, crushed
 2 cups of water

Simmer on a back burner, adding water as needed, to fill the whole house with a continuous Christmas aroma.

Or sprinkle ground cinnamon on the burners of an electric stove. When they are turned on, the incense of cinnamon fills the air. This little fragrance trick dates back to the days of Solomon, when cinnamon was a treasured spice burned to perfume the air inside the temples.

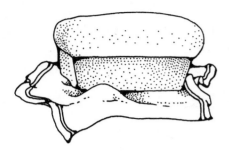

and no longer sticky. Let dough rise covered in greased bowl until doubled. Punch dough with fists and divide into two parts. To make a braid, divide each half into three ropes of equal length, braid, and seal ends with moistened fingertips. Cover and let rise again until doubled. Sprinkle with slivered almonds and brush with beaten egg mixed with a little water. Bake at 375° F until loaf sounds hollow when tapped. (If loaf turns too brown, cover with foil the last 10 minutes of baking.)

Baking Bread in Shapes

Use the sweet dough recipe for Honey Almond Braid and divide dough into several parts, using balls, ropes, and braids to create shapes (Christmas trees, teddy bears, angels, stars ...). Pieces should all be about the same thickness so they will bake evenly. Pinch seams with moistened fingertips and use a dab of fresh egg white to attach smaller pieces for features. Cover and let rise until doubled. Bake at 375° F until loaf sounds hollow when tapped.

Bread-Baking Tips

- Brush glaze on bread and rolls with slightly beaten egg white, egg yolk, or whole egg.
- Decorate sweet breads and rolls with candied fruit, colored sprinkles, crushed candy canes, dried fruit ...
- Line a bread basket with foil underneath the cloth napkin to keep bread and rolls warm while serving.
- Bake a treat in a clay pot: Clean small clay pots well in warm soapy water. Dry in warm oven two to three hours. Lacquer inside, if desired, two to three weeks before using. Fill greased pot with regular or sweet dough and a favorite filling: cheese, dried fruit, cinnamon topping, chopped apples and other fresh fruits ... Bake until golden brown at 350° F. Treat miniature clay pots the same way for making fun muffins and popovers.
- Make Herb Butter to accompany holiday feasts:

4 sticks butter, softened	1 T. freshly chopped chives
1 T. dried tarragon	1 T. crumbled dried basil
2 T. chopped fresh parsley	

Mix well and let stand 24 hours in a tightly-packed crock or jar before serving. Or mold in butter molds until firm, then roll in ground parsley, paprika, grated lemon or orange peel ...

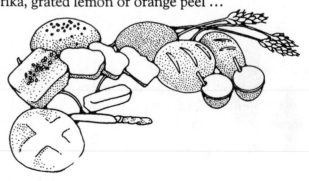

ENTRÉES

The three "E's" in my Entrées stand for "Elegant" and "Enjoyable" without incredible "Effort!"

Choose from a variety of meats for your hearty Christmas feast …

How to Roast a Duck or Goose

Preheat oven for roasting at 450° F. Lay bird on its side in a roasting pan and sprinkle inside and out with salt and pepper. For extra flavor, put freshly chopped parsley, thyme leaves, a small onion, and a garlic clove in body cavity before roasting. Reduce oven to 350° F, and place bird in center of oven. Every 20-30 minutes, depending on the size of the bird, remove fat from the pan and turn meat to the other side. When done, the bird should be a crisp golden brown. Your 4-5 pound duck or goose is usually cooked in about 1½ hours.

How to Roast a Turkey

Sprinkle washed cavity (you have taken out all the plastic wrapped giblets, etc., haven't you?) and outer skin of bird with salt and pepper. For extra flavor, insert a small onion, chopped celery tops, and parsley into the cavity. Jane's Krazy Mixed-up Salt is great for salting the skin. Place turkey in an open pan and roast in a 325° F oven, basting with juices (even if self-basting, this improves juiciness) two or three times during cooking. If turkey browns too quickly, cover with a loose tent of aluminum foil. Turkey is done when drumstick twists loosely from the body (or at about 190° F on meat thermometer).

How to Cook a Beef Roast

Always place roast fat side up in an open pan. Salt and pepper lightly and sprinkle top with a dusting of flour. A delicious accent is the addition of sliced onion rings on the top, which emerge from the oven a real treat crisply cooked.

If using a meat thermometer, insert in the thickest portion of the meat, being careful the thermometer does not touch fat.

120° F is rare　　　　　　140° F is medium
130° F is medium rare　　　150° F is well done

How to Cook a Leg of Lamb

Preheat oven to 500° F. Rub meat with a peeled garlic clove, and salt and pepper generously. Roast lamb in an open pan for 10 minutes. Reduce temperature to 325° F and cook to desired doneness. Baste meat two or three times while cooking with pan drippings. If using a meat thermometer for lamb:

Colorful Christmas Garnishes

bell pepper strips
berries/fruit peelings
black or stuffed olives
caviar
citrus slices
honeydew melon rings
mint leaves, sprigs
parsley sprigs, chopped parsley
pearl onions
pimiento
radish roses and fans
red and green cherries
thinly sliced carrots
thinly sliced cucumber
tinted onion rings (immerse in tinted water)
whole nuts

How to Make Pan Gravy and Dressing (Stuffing)

Gravy: Pour off all but one tablespoon of pan drippings. Remove from heat and add one tablespoon of flour, stirring until smooth. Stir constantly over moderate heat to brown flour (2-3 minutes). Add 1½ to 2 c. liquid (water, bouillon, broth, or milk) and season to taste. Cook over high heat until desired consistency. Add boiled giblets, onion soup mix, or yogurt for added flavor.

Oyster Dressing: Boil 1 pkg. frozen chopped spinach and drain. Cook 4 T. butter with 3 diced celery stalks and 1 diced onion until tender. Add 1 large package of seasoned dressing mix, cooked spinach, and chicken broth to moisten. Chop 1 pint shucked oysters, reserving ¼ c. liquid, and add both to dressing mixture, stirring well with 2 T. sherry, 1 t. salt, 1 t. pepper. Bake in 13" x 9" casserole, covered, at 325° F about 45 minutes.

Wild Rice/Chestnut Dressing: Rinse 2 c. wild rice. Bring 4 c. water and 2 chicken bouillon cubes to a boil and add rice. Bring to a second boil and cover, reducing to simmer, 40-45 minutes. Drain. Heat 2 lbs. chestnuts (in shell) covered with water to boiling. Cook on medium heat 10 minutes. Shell and chop chestnut meat. Melt 6 T. butter with 3 diced celery stalks and 2 small diced onions until tender. Add chestnuts, wild rice and the following seasonings: 1 t. salt, 1 t. cracked pepper, ½ t. sage, ½ t. thyme Bake in 13" x 9" casserole 45 minutes at 325° F.

(Either dressing can be used to stuff a 10-15 lb. turkey.)

145° F is rare   175° F is extremely well done
160° F is medium to well done

Serve lamb always with a delicious mint jelly.

How to Cook a Ham

Select a shank or butt portion cured ham without too much fat. Ask the butcher to cut the shank end off your shank portion ham for flavoring beans, soups, or stews. Bake in a pan at 325° F twenty minutes per pound. During the last 30 minutes of cooking, pour a sweet sauce over meat. Coca-cola, honey, orange juice, and marmalade all work well. That sugar burns on the pan bottom to give the ham a sweet smoky flavor.

How to Make the Best Grilled Pork Tenderloin in Town

Marinate tenderloin in Dale's Seasoning Sauce or teriyaki sauce overnight. Pepper heavily and grill until meat is white but still juicy. Slice thinly, for an hors d'oeuvre served with rolls or party rye bread, or more thickly as a main course. Serve with currant chutney.   *Kaki McCloud*

How to Marinate and Cook Venison

Soak venison 24 hours or overnight in a mixture of red wine, sliced onions, and fresh garlic cloves. Turn occasionally to cover meat thoroughly. Salt and pepper to taste. Cook on a rack in a covered pot at 325° F until well done, spooning marinade over roast two or three times during cooking. Cook 20 minutes per pound for rare meat, 22 minutes for medium. Turn up heat to 450° F during last 15 minutes of cooking for a nicely browned crust.   *Frances Gober*

Saucy Accompaniments

❄ ORANGE SAUCE

For goose or duck, ham, chicken, or turkey

2/3 c. orange juice	2 t. flour
3 T. sherry	¾ t. grated orange rind
1 T. chopped parsley	

Bring all ingredients to a boil, stirring constantly. Pour over meat and bake as directed, basting occasionally during cooking.

❄ MUSTARD SAUCE

For beef or ham

Spread your favorite prepared mustard generously over a beef roast or cured ham before cooking. Makes a delicious crust and adds a piquant flavor.

❄ GRILLED BEEF MARINADE

Great for a London broil or flank steak

3 oz. soy sauce   2 cloves garlic
½ T. lemon juice   2 t. bourbon whiskey
2 T. brown sugar   ¼ t. ground ginger

Mix all ingredients and marinate beef overnight in a zipped plastic bag, tossing occasionally to distribute flavoring evenly. Grill to desired doneness. Slice thinly on the diagonal to cut through tough fibers.

❄ CHRISTMAS CURRANT CHUTNEY

Zesty with chicken, lamb, or ham; makes 12 ½-pint jars for gifts and for keeps

1½ lbs. crystallized ginger   4 lemons, sliced and seeded
½ lb. red pepper   1 c. currants
½ lb. green pepper   3 c. apple cider vinegar
1 lb. onions   ½ t. salt
½ lb. cucumbers   1 t. cayenne pepper
2 c. raisins   7 c. sugar

Cut 1 lb. ginger and ¼ lb. red pepper into narrow strips. Dice remaining peppers, onions, and cucumbers. Put raisins, seeded lemons, and remaining ginger into a food processor to grind. Combine all ingredients in a large heavy pot and bring to a boil. Reduce heat and simmer one hour, stirring occasionally. Pour into sterilized jars and seal with melted paraffin.

Chestnuts Roasting on an Open Fire ...

With a sharp knife, make a cross on the soft end of whole chestnuts to facilitate peeling. Place in a heavy skillet or fireplace roaster and lay on a grate or bed of hot coals. Nuts will crack and pop and, when peeled, make a delicious Christmas treat. Honest.

A bellyful is a bellyful ...
—Francois Rabelais

More Meat Cooking Tips

• Turn cooking meat with tongs instead of a fork, which pierces the meat, allowing juices to escape.
• Let roasts stand at least 15 minutes before carving, after removing from the oven.
• Decorate fowl with leg frills for a festive appearance at the table.
• Surround meat on a platter with fresh parsley, greenery sprigs, cherry tomatoes, radish roses, carved potatoes, or other decorative garnish.

And now, for something completely different, break tradition for Christmas dinner with:

❄ STUFFED RED SNAPPER

Leave head and tail on fish. Clean inside and outside well, and salt lightly after rubbing entire fish with olive oil. Set aside and make dressing:

Frosty Grapes and Other Fruit Flavors ...

• Drain washed grapes. Dip clusters into frothy beaten egg whites. Shake off excess and dip into powdered or granulated sugar until completely covered. Dry on baking rack. Also frost mint leaves, raspberries, blueberries, strawberries ... as festive garnish for desserts.
• Tint baked pears or apples with food coloring added to the syrup, or with red cinnamon candies added while baking.
• Cut cranberry jelly into shapes for Christmas dinner.
• Cut citrus in half, flute the rim, remove pulp, and use as a basket to serve berries, mixed fruit, pasta salad, seafood salad, birdseed ...

1 large pkg. seasoned stuffing mix	¼ c. chopped green olives
1 green pepper, chopped	4 T. butter, melted
3 stalks celery, chopped	enough chicken broth to moisten dressing
1 small bunch green onions, chopped	

Combine all dressing ingredients in a saucepan over low heat until soft but not brown. Stuff fish and decorate outside with lemon slices, tomato slices, and olives. Sprinkle over all with dillweed and put in oven at 350° F. Cook uncovered 25-30 minutes per pound of fish. When thick part of fish flakes with a fork, it's done. If garnishes begin to brown, cover with foil about halfway through cooking time.   *Vera Fick*

❄ PASTA WITH CAVIAR

... appetizing with your Christmas Eve oyster stew

1½ c. heavy cream	1 small jar caviar
juice of ½ lemon	cooked angel hair pasta

Warm heavy cream over low heat. Stir lemon juice and caviar into cream and heat through. Drain cooked pasta and pour sauce over. Toss and serve with additional caviar or shrimp garnish.

FRUIT

... as a side dish or dessert ...

❄ HOT CURRIED FRUIT

1 can each: pears, apricots, pineapple chunks, dark cherries	2 T. cornstarch
¾ c. raisins	1 T. curry powder
⅓ stick butter	1 c. brown sugar

Drain fruit and reserve ¾ c. of mixed juices. Stir fruit in a casserole dish. Combine reserved juice with remaining ingredients and cook over low heat until sauce thickens. Pour over fruit. Bake at 350° F for 30-40 minutes.   *Helen Covington*

❄ FROZEN FRUIT SALAD

Great to have on hand. Freeze in individual paper baking cups in a muffin tin, and store in a plastic bag for impromptu dessert or sweet meal-mates (cool, creamy complement to hot soup) ...

8 oz. cream cheese, softened	1 c. pineapple chunks, drained
¼ c. lemon juice	8 oz. container frozen whipped topping
14 oz. can condensed milk	
1 c. chopped pecans	
	1 can cherry pie filling

Combine cream cheese and lemon juice, beating until smooth. Stir in milk, pecans, and pineapple. Fold in whipped topping and pie filling. Freeze in 24-30 paper baking cups, muffin tins, or 13" x 9" casserole at least 6 hours before serving.   *Ginny Fick*

❊ HOMEMADE CRANBERRY SAUCE

1 c. sugar
1 c. water
2 c. clean cranberries

Boil sugar and water together for five minutes to make syrup. Add cranberries and cook until skins split (about five more minutes). Cool. Refrigerate until thick.

❊ CANDIED FRUIT PEEL

Great in baking or as a garnish … can be dipped in chocolate …

Peel well washed citrus fruit in strips. Cover peel with cold water and bring to a boil, cooking 3 minutes. Drain. Repeat process with additional cold water. Drain. Repeat a third time, covering once again with cold water. Measure amount of peel remaining and add an equal amount of granulated sugar to the pot. Stir, cooking until peel is well coated with glaze. Sprinkle with sugar while still hot and tint if desired. Use in baking, or as a garnish.

Lila Maddox

Toast coconut, almonds, and other nuts in the microwave on high, stirring once or twice for one to two minutes. Or mix with one tablespoon of butter and toast in the oven, stirring occasionally until golden.

HOLIDAY SWEETS

Lovely to look at, delightful to … gulp!

Dessert elegance is in the serving: silver bowls filled with well-formed scoops of ice cream or sherbet lavished with rich toppings and garnishes … sparkling parfait glasses layered as rainbows … crystal plates offering up scrumptious slices of pound cake decorated with orange slices and piped flavored cream … cakes mounded with lime sherbet or pistachio ice cream and a waterfall of fudge … flaming fruit … frozen mousse topped with caramel sauce and toasted coconut …

Mold, decorate, garnish, design … something unusual, artistic, tantalizing for the grand finale to a delicious meal …

❊ POUND CAKE WITH ORANGE GLAZE

… serves many, wonderful to have on hand …

2 sticks butter
1 stick margarine
1 box confectioner's sugar
6 eggs
3 c. sifted unbleached flour
1 t. vanilla
1 T. lemon juice
1 t. almond extract

Cream butter and sugar. Add unbeaten eggs, one at a time. Stir in flour and then flavorings. Pour in greased tube or Bundt pan and bake at 325° F for one hour or slightly longer, until toothpick inserted in center comes out clean.

To glaze: Mix 2 t. grated orange rind with 1 c. granulated sugar. Add ½ c. orange juice and stir until sugar is dissolved. Pierce cake top with fork tines and pour glaze over warm cake. May substitute lemon rind and fresh lemon juice for the orange.

Ginny Fick

❄ SCOTT'S FAVORITE CUSTARD PIE

5 eggs	3 c. milk
1 c. sugar	1½ t. vanilla
1½ t. salt	unbaked 9" pie crust
¼ t. nutmeg	

Mix all ingredients together and pour into unbaked pie crust. Bake 20 minutes at 400° F, then 30 minutes at 325°.   *Frances Gober*

❄ CARAMEL PECAN PIE

36 caramels, unwrapped	¼ t. salt
¼ c. water	½ t. vanilla
¼ c. butter	1½ c. chopped pecans
¾ c. sugar	unbaked 9" deep dish pie crust
3 eggs, lightly beaten	

Melt together caramels, water, and butter. Add remaining ingredients and mix well. Pour into unbaked pie crust and bake at 350° F 30-45 minutes, or until golden.   *Frances Gober*

❄ SIMPLY DIVINE CHEESECAKE WITH CHOCOLATE DRIZZLE

1½ c. graham cracker crumbs	4 8 oz. pkgs. cream cheese,
1½ c. sugar, divided	softened
1 t. cinnamon	1 T. lemon juice
1/3 c. butter, melted	½ t. vanilla
4 eggs	dash of salt
	2 c. sour cream

Mix crumbs, ¼ c. sugar, cinnamon, and butter to make a crust in the bottom of a buttered 9" or 10" springform pan. Beat eggs and 1 c. sugar until thick. Add cheese, lemon juice, vanilla, and salt, beating until mixture is smooth. Pour over crust and bake at 375° F for 30 minutes. Remove from oven. Fold remaining ¼ c. sugar with sour cream, spread over warm cake, and return to oven reset at 475° F for ten minutes. Cool and refrigerate before serving, at least 3 hours. Just before serving, drizzle melted semisweet chocolate or easier yet, Magic Shell, over cake. Decorate with fresh raspberries, if available.

❄ MICRO-FAST PEAR CRISP

1 can Bartlett pears	½ c. shredded coconut
1 T. grated lemon peel	1/3 c. chopped pecans
2 T. cornstarch	2 T. each: sugar, flour, butter

Drain and slice pears, reserving ½ c. juice. Combine pear juice, lemon peel, and cornstarch in microwave-safe glass casserole and cook on high for 2 minutes, until thickened, stirring after 1 minute. Add pears and cook on high for 2½ minutes, or until heated through. Combine coconut, pecans, sugar, and flour, and cut in butter until crumbly. Sprinkle over pears and broil in conventional oven until coconut is toasted, 2-3 minutes. Serve with vanilla ice cream. 4-6 servings

❈ HOMEMADE FRENCH CREPES

1 c. sifted flour	1 c. milk
1 t. baking powder	2 eggs
1 T. sugar	1 t. oil
½ t. salt	

Sift first four ingredients together neatly onto waxed paper. Put remaining ingredients in blender and process until well mixed. Add half of the dry ingredients and mix well. Add remaining flour mixture and stir until batter is smooth. Grease a 6" fry or crepe pan with butter and heat on high. Pour approximately 3 T. batter into pan, rotating quickly to spread batter evenly over the entire bottom of the pan. Cook until thin cake is lightly browned; turn and brown opposite side. Stack cakes until all are cooked.

Fill crepes with preserves and a sprinkling of confectioner's sugar, chocolate mousse or pudding, vegetable or meat filling, cream cheese and sour cream, smoked salmon and cream cheese with capers, scrambled eggs and salsa, chunks of honey-dipped fruit tied into a bundle with holiday ribbon ...   *Dave Fick*

❈ SWEET GINGERBREAD WITH HARD SAUCE

½ c. butter, softened	½ t. cloves
½ c. sugar	1 t. baking soda
2 eggs	½ t. salt
1½ c. flour	½ c. molasses
1½ t. ground ginger	½ c. applesauce
1½ t. cinnamon	

Cream butter and sugar in large mixing bowl, and beat in eggs. Mix together flour, spices, soda, and salt. Stir flour mixture into butter, and stir in molasses and applesauce until just blended. Bake in greased 8" square baking pan at 350° F for 30 minutes or until tested done.

Serve warm with hard sauce or lemon sauce ... or cooled, with powdered sugar sifted and stenciled through a lace paper doily.

Hard Sauce:

Cream 1/3 c. softened butter and gradually add 1 c. sifted confectioner's sugar. Add ½ t. vanilla, beating until sauce is light and fluffy. Chill or serve at room temperature. May add other flavorings to taste ... . lemon, brandy, orange, coffee, rum ...   *Margaret Johnson*

❈ PEAR OR APPLE OVEN PANCAKE

2 T. butter	1 c. milk
3 pears/apples, peeled and cut in wedges	1 c. flour
2 T. brown sugar	1 t. sugar
1 t. cinnamon	pinch salt
4 eggs	

Melt butter and add fruit, brown sugar, and cinnamon, cooking until soft. Remove from heat. Combine eggs and milk in a blender and mix at high speed, adding flour, sugar, and salt until smooth. Coat bottom

and sides of heavy ovenproof skillet with butter. Pour in batter and spoon fruit evenly on top. Bake at 425° F in the center of the oven about 20-30 minutes (until puffy and golden). Sprinkle with confectioner's sugar and serve warm. 6-8 servings

CHILLY HOLIDAY THRILLERS

Baskin-Robbins has made a mint (and praline, and chocolate chip ...) out of creative ice creams. Just think of your own favorite flavors and mix them with a few scoops of chocolate or vanilla (or whatever) and you're in business, too. Ice cream is delicious any way you look at it (especially when it's riding on a spoon toward your mouth!). Put it in a bowl, on a pie or cake, or between cookies ... Mold it, drench it, fruit it, liqueur it ... Top or lace it with nuts, candies, cookies, cookie dough(!), fruits, marshmallows, licorice ...

Flaming Desserts

Not many people are left unimpressed by a flaming dessert, no matter how many times they have seen one. Imagine how exciting the grand finale would be at Christmastime ... turn off all the lights except those on the tree (and the candlelight at the table), and set aflame some saucy cherries or bananas ...

Sauces and fruits to be set aglow need to be warm (heat in saucepan prior to flaming) and the brandy, rum, or flavored liqueur used to flambé should also be delicately heated. Put the fruit in a heated chafing dish, sprinkle with granulated sugar, pour the warmed liqueur over all, and ignite, touching the edge of the dish with a long match or taper.

When flambéing, always use good common sense. Advise guests to stand back and be amazed as you light this marvelous dessert.

❈ CHERRIES JUBILEE

2 cups pitted cherries ½ c. slightly warmed brandy

2 T. kirsch

Follow above procedure with these ingredients and ignite. Serve cherries over ice cream.

❈ PEPPERED STRAWBERRIES

¼ c. butter
4 T. sugar
Grand Marnier

2-3 c. fresh strawberries, or 2
    boxes frozen berries
freshly ground pepper
vanilla ice cream

Preheat a chafing dish, stirring in butter and sugar until melted and syrupy. Add 3 T. or slightly more of Grand Marnier. Stir in strawberries to coat and grind plenty of fresh pepper over all (more than you would over a salad, but not so much as to make everybody sneeze!). Pour over 2 T. additional Grand Marnier, stirring constantly. Ignite with a long match and flambé 30 seconds. Pour over ice cream and enjoy! *Hilli Evans*

More Ice Creamy Delights

- Froth softened ice cream in a blender with a favorite liqueur. Serve in a tall parfait or champagne glass topped with toasted almonds.
- Mix softened vanilla ice cream with sherry-soaked macaroons and toasted almonds. Return to the freezer to harden, and serve in champagne glasses with a whole macaroon on the side. (Gailyn Thornton)
- Make an ice cream cake or pie, layering two or three of your favorite flavors, filling the center with fruit or crushed candy or nuts, and topping with whipped cream or drizzled chocolate.
- Frost an angel food cake with sherbet for a deliciously light after-dinner treat.
- Soften ice cream slightly and spread in a jelly roll pan lined with buttered wax paper. Freeze to harden. Using cookie cutters, cut ice cream into shapes and sprinkle with tinted or toasted coconut mixed with chopped nuts, colored sugar, sprinkles, grated chocolate … Top with tiny cinnamon candy decorations or a whole maraschino cherry.
- Make a Vermont Maple Walnut sauce: Bring 1½ c. real maple syrup to a boil and cook until it begins to thicken. Remove from heat and add ½ c. coarsely chopped walnuts. Cool and serve on ice cream. Store in the refrigerator.

> Use melted chocolate to coat: pretzels, raisins, caramels, animal crackers, Oreos, nuts, Chinese noodles, marshmallows, mandarin oranges … Dip item in chocolate using a slotted spoon, tongs, or a small strainer. Cool on wax paper in the refrigerator and store in an airtight container.

A CHOCOLATE-LOVER'S CHRISTMAS

Chocolate has to be the single most favorite food of anyone with good taste. Nowadays, individuals will go to great lengths to create new and interesting forms of the treat. A substance that lends itself well to creativity, chocolate is easily molded, colored, shaped, and flavored in as many ways as there are M&M's in a 25-lb. bag! You can buy the stuff powdered, liquefied, solid, chipped, or chunked. Use it to enliven cookies, cakes, pies, drinks, and ants … popcorn, potato chips, and pretzels.

For totally captivating your culinary audience, create some tempting chocolate treats this Christmas.

❋ CHOCOLATE-COVERED CHERRY COOKIES

1½ c. flour	1 egg
½ c. unsweetened cocoa	1½ t. vanilla
¼ t. salt	maraschino cherries
¼ t. baking powder	6 oz. chocolate chips
¼ t. baking soda	½ c. condensed milk
½ c. butter	4 t. cherry juice
1 c. sugar	

Stir together dry ingredients. In a separate bowl, cream butter and sugar, gradually adding egg and vanilla. Beat well. Add dry ingredients and blend all together. Shape dough into 1" balls and place on an ungreased cookie sheet. Press each center with your thumb and put a cherry in the indentation. Combine chocolate chips and condensed milk

Make it Easy on Yourself

If you can't or don't want to make chocolate goodies yourself, decorate with glass bowls full of red and green Hershey kisses, foil-wrapped chocolate balls, holiday M&M's, dome-covered plates of elegant molded chocolates or truffles ... intoxicating! Keep extras on hand, as this "decoration" does a fast disappearing act!

in a saucepan and heat to melt and blend. Add cherry juice. Spoon frosting over cookie to cover cherry. Bake at 350° F for about 10 minutes. Cool. Makes 4 dozen.

❈ EASY CHOCOLATE FUDGE COOKIES

1 12 oz. pkg. chocolate chips	1 t. vanilla
¼ c. butter	1 c. flour
1 can sweetened condensed milk	1 c. chopped pecans

Melt chocolate chips and butter in microwave or double boiler. Add condensed milk and vanilla. Remove from heat and stir in flour and pecans. Drop by tablespoonsful on ungreased cookie sheet and bake at 350° F 8-10 minutes. Take out when slightly undercooked for chewy brownie consistency. These freeze deliciously.   *Dixie Purvis*

❈ CHOCOLATE FONDUE/SAUCE

3 3 oz. Toblerone chocolate bars	2 T. kirsch, orange or cherry
½ c. evaporated milk	liqueur, or brandy

Break up chocolate and melt pieces with milk in the microwave (2-3 minutes on full power) or in a saucepan over moderate heat. Stir until fully blended. Add flavoring. Serve as fondue dip with pound cake squares, fruit, marshmallows ... or as a fantastic chocolate sauce over ice cream.   *Dale Aiken*

❈ CHOCOLATE STRAWBERRIES

2 dozen large fresh strawberries	1 t. butter
1 lb. Baker's semisweet chocolate	

Wash and dry strawberries. Chop chocolate in small pieces and melt slowly with the butter in a double boiler or in the microwave, stirring occasionally. Dip berries in chocolate and cool on a wax paper-lined cookie sheet in the refrigerator. Great as a garnish or after-dinner pièce de résistance.

❈ SINFULLY CHOCOLATE FROZEN MOUSSE CAKE

1 c. shredded coconut	4 egg yolks
3 c. semisweet chocolate chips	8 egg whites
2 c. whipping cream, divided	

Toast 2-3 T. coconut. Melt chips in heavy saucepan (or microwave) slowly, so chocolate doesn't dry out. Remove from heat and stir in 1 c. cream and remaining fresh coconut. Cool to room temperature. Whisk egg yolks until blended and stir into chocolate mixture. Beat second cup of cream until soft peaks form and fold into chocolate. Beat egg whites until soft peaks form and fold into chocolate mixture. Sprinkle toasted coconut onto bottom of 10" springform pan and pour mixture over. Cover and freeze overnight. Run knife around edge before removing mousse from pan. Serve frozen in slender wedges with warm caramel sauce and a sprinkling of toasted coconut. Serves 10-12 ... to 20 ... extremely rich!

Caramel Sauce:

1¼ c. sugar   ½ c. butter
⅓ c. water   1 t. vanilla
1 c. whipping cream

   Mix sugar and water over low heat until sugar is dissolved. Turn up to boil until sugar is light brown caramel color. Watch constantly. Add cream (don't let it bubble over!) and stir until smooth and creamy. Remove from heat and add butter and vanilla. Stir to melt butter and serve. Store remaining sauce in refrigerator covered.

Dixie Purvis

❈ LACY CHOCOLATE BASKET

2½ 4 oz. bars German sweet baking chocolate

   Cover a custard cup, small ramekin, or banana split bowl with heavy-duty foil and chill in the freezer. Melt German chocolate slowly in a double boiler or microwave, stirring until smooth. Using a small spoon, drizzle half the chocolate randomly over bottom and sides of foil-covered container, overlapping in a lacy pattern. Return to freezer to harden (about 5 minutes). Slowly reheat chocolate if it becomes too thick. Drizzle rest of chocolate to cover and return to freezer to chill. Carefully lift chocolate-coated foil from dish and slowly peel foil away. Transfer basket to a chilled platter and keep in freezer until ready to use. Inside your chocolate basket, serve cookies, cakes, chocolate-dipped fruits, petit fours or truffles, fresh berries, puddings and ice creams ...

Molding Your Own Chocolates

   Chocolate tennis rackets, golf balls, reindeer, and Santa ... what marvelous gifts! There are plastic and rubber molds available in many shapes and designs just for the purpose of molding chocolates — and wafers of real and colored "chocolate" for melting and decorating. Use the Yellow Pages to find a candy-making specialty store or kitchen shop where you can find these items and information on how to use them.

More Chocolate Lover's Holiday Treats

• Make chocolate leaves: brush melted chocolate over a silk leaf and chill in the refrigerator. When hardened, peel leaf away. Use chocolate leaves to decorate chocolate strawberries, or as a garnish.
• Curl chocolate: With a slightly warmed potato peeler, pull the blade over a smooth surface of room temperature chocolate to make long curls.
• Grate chocolate: Refrigerate chocolate and hand grater until cold. Grate blocks of chocolate and refrigerate immediately, to prevent lumping, until ready to use.
• Make your own truffles for gifts and dessert-toppers:

2/3 c. whipping cream
3 T. unsalted butter
1 T. sugar
6 oz. semisweet chocolate

2 T. flavoring (brandy, rum, amaretto, kahlua, crème de menthe)
cornstarch

Cook cream, butter, and sugar in saucepan until melted and hot. Remove from heat and stir in the semisweet chocolate until well blended. Add flavoring. Pour into chilled bowl, cover, and refrigerate at least 1 hour, stirring frequently. Roll into balls on baking sheet lined with waxed paper and chill 30 minutes until firm. Roll balls in cornstarch and brush off excess. Melt dipping chocolate (see Chocolate Strawberries). Drop candies into chocolate one at a time and remove with long-tined fork, shaking off excess chocolate. Twist fork to swirl top. Store in cool, dry place.

- Create "white chocolate" snowflakes as dessert garnish: Press melted "white chocolate" through a pastry bag onto a cookie sheet, drizzling in spun sugar shapes or symmetrical snowflake shapes. Before substance hardens, add sprinkles or silver dragees for ornamentation. Put into freezer to harden and scrape off sheet with a spatula. Great on cheesecakes, frosted cakes, dessert trays ...

CHRISTMAS COOKIES

❋ JIM'S FAVORITE SCOTCH SHORTBREAD

1½ c. butter, softened
1 c. sugar

1 c. rice flour
2¼ c. unbleached flour

Cream softened butter with sugar. Sift rice flour into mixture and stir well. Gradually add remaining flour, stirring until dough no longer sticks. Knead with hands and spread on greased cookie sheet, flattening dough until it is about ½" thick. Prick with fork tines for decoration and bake at 325° F until golden (about 20-30 minutes). Cool on pan for five minutes and cut into small squares.

❋ MORAVIAN CHRISTMAS COOKIES

1 c. molasses
¾ c. brown sugar
¼ c. butter, melted
¼ c. shortening, melted
1½ t. cinnamon

1 t. cloves
1 t. ginger
¾ t. baking soda
3 c. unbleached flour

Add sugar to molasses and mix well. Stir in melted and cooled butter and shortening. Sift spices and soda with 1½ c. flour and add to molasses mixture, stirring well. Stir in remaining flour until dough is stiff. Let dough stand overnight. Roll *very, very* thin on pastry cloth sprinkled with flour, and cut into shapes. Bake on greased cookie sheets at 325° F until crisp. Makes about 1½ lbs. (which is LOTS!).

❄ CINNAMON YULE LOGS

1 c. butter
1 t. almond extract
3 T. sugar

2 c. flour
1 T. cinnamon

Mix butter with almond extract and gradually stir in remaining ingredients. Roll into logs about 2" long. Bake on ungreased cookie sheet at 300° F for 20-25 minutes. Cool slightly. Roll in a mixture of sugar and cinnamon while still warm.

❄ PEANUT BUTTER KISS COOKIES

2 ⅔ c. sifted flour
2 t. baking soda
1 t. salt
1 c. butter, softened
⅓ c. crunchy peanut butter

1 c. sugar
1 c. brown sugar, firmly packed
2 eggs
2 t. vanilla
5 doz. Hershey kisses

Preheat oven to 375° F. Sift first three ingredients and set aside. In a large bowl, beat butter and peanut butter until well blended. Add both sugars and beat until fluffy. Beat in eggs and vanilla until smooth. Stir in flour mixture until soft dough forms. Using level tablespoon, shape into 5 dozen balls, roll in granulated sugar, and place 2" apart on ungreased cookie sheet. Bake 8 minutes and remove from oven. Press chocolate kiss into each center and bake one additional minute. Cool.

Carol Cleveland

❄ FRUIT-FILLED SWEETIE PIES

2 frozen pie crusts
1 c. dried apricots
½ c. almonds

½ c. sugar
2 T. water

Thaw pie crusts. Place apricots and nuts in food processor until finely chopped. Combine with sugar and water, cooking over low heat until warm. Cool. Roll out crusts, smoothing seams, and cut with 2½" scalloped biscuit cutter into rounds. Place rounds on cookie sheet and spoon filling on half, fold, and press edges together to seal, moistening with egg white. Crimp for decoration. Bake at 375° F for 5-7 minutes. Brush with a little beaten egg white and sprinkle with granulated sugar. Return to oven 2 more minutes until golden. Dip ends in melted chocolate, if desired.

Variations on a filling: raspberry or strawberry preserves with macadamia nuts, pineapple preserves with flake coconut, orange marmalade with chopped pecans, chopped dates and walnuts cooked with sugar and water until tender (as above).

❄ LACY COOKIE CRISPS

¾ c. butter
¾ c. granulated sugar
½ c. light molasses

2 t. ground ginger
1½ t. vanilla or bourbon
1½ c. sifted unbleached flour

Heat butter, sugar, molasses, and ginger in a heavy saucepan until butter melts, stirring to blend. Remove from heat and stir in flavoring and flour. Drop one tablespoon of dough on greased cookie sheet, allowing room for spreading to 3" cookie. Bake about 4 cookies at a time at 300° F for 8-10 minutes. Cookies will bubble and become lacy in texture. Remove from oven and cool for 2 minutes. Lift off cookie sheet with spatula, quickly rolling around the handle of a wooden spoon, before cookies become crisp. Cool on rack and store in airtight container.

❋ JEAN'S MINTY SURPRISE PACKAGES

2 egg whites
½ t. cream of tartar
¾ c. sugar

2 drops green food coloring
few drops peppermint extract
6 oz. semisweet chocolate chips

Preheat oven to 350° F. Beat egg whites with cream of tartar to make soft peaks. Reduce mixer speed to low and gradually stir in sugar. Increase speed to high and beat to stiff peaks. Add food coloring and extract. Fold in chocolate chips. Line baking sheet with waxed paper or parchment. Drop meringue to form kiss shapes. Place in oven, shut door and immediately turn off oven. Leave six hours or overnight. Store in airtight container.

Jean Hunter

❋ BASIC SUGAR COOKIE DOUGH

½ c. butter, softened
1 c. sugar
1 egg
1 t. vanilla

2 c. unbleached flour
¼ t. salt
½ t. baking powder

Cream butter and sugar, add egg and vanilla, and sift in remaining ingredients, stirring with mixer until well blended. Knead until dough sticks together, wrap tightly in plastic, and refrigerate until needed. Roll out 1/8" thick on floured surface and cut into shapes, or form into a roll and freeze for slice-and-bake quick and hot cookies. Bake at 325° F 7-9 minutes.

❋ BASIC GINGERBREAD COOKIE DOUGH

2⅓ c. flour
1 t. cinnamon
1½ t. ginger
½ t. salt
2 t. baking soda

1 c. sugar
¼ c. light molasses
1 egg
2/3 c. shortening

Sift together dry ingredients. Cream sugar, molasses, egg, and shortening and add flour mixture, stirring or mixing with your hands until well blended. Cover and chill at least one hour before cutting and baking. Roll dough out about 1/8" thick on floured surface and cut into shapes. Place on cookie sheet about 1" apart and bake 7-8 minutes at 375° F. Remove from sheet while still warm.

More Christmas Cookie Tips

- Flour cookie molds and decorative stamps before using. Dip cookie cutters in cold water to prevent sticking.
- When freezing dough or pastry, wrap tightly in a ball or roll. Thaw

at room temperature.

- Sprinkle sugar on cookies and cakes while still warm for best adhesion.
- Use a nutmeg grater to grate flakes off whole nutmeg for fresh flavor.
- Keep ground spices tightly stored. Exposure to air and heat will alter flavor and fragrance. Most herbs and spices dull in taste and appearance after one year's storage.
- When cookie decorating strikes your fancy ...

❄ COLORFUL FROSTINGS FOR COOKIE AND CAKE DECORATING

1: Beat 2 egg whites just until stiff, add 3½ c. confectioner's sugar, 2 t. vanilla (or other flavoring), 1-2 drops glycerin (for shine), and food coloring ... this is the thicker variety.

2: Beat 1 lb. of confectioner's sugar with 5-6 T. milk and food coloring.

3: Beat 2 c. confectioner's sugar with 2 T. water, 1 t. vanilla, and food coloring.

- Make cookie "paint": Mix evaporated milk with food coloring. Add water to desired consistency and paint cookie before baking. Mixing egg yolks or corn syrup with food coloring produces a textured effect.
- Grind hard candies for sprinkle decoration. Put inside a zipped bag and pound to desired fineness.
- Dip cookies and candied fruit peel into, or drizzle with, melted chocolate.
- Make a cookie bowl for holiday cookies: Cover the outside of a round glass casserole dish with foil and rub foil with shortening. Roll out gingerbread or sugar cookie dough and cut a large (about 9" diameter) circle, using a wax paper pattern. Trim edges to make a scalloped pattern. Invert dough over foil and bake at 350° F about 15 minutes, or until light brown around the edges. Cool on wire rack and remove bowl from casserole. Carefully peel away foil and fill with fun.
- Collect recipes of favorite international Christmas cookies and try a new one each year.

Other Holiday Dessert Ideas

- Make a shape cake: bake a sheet cake using a simple butter cake mix. Freeze cooled cake 30 minutes. Using cookie cutters or a sharp knife, cut cake into shapes or pieces to arrange into one big figure (Christmas tree, Rudolph, Santa face, angel, nutcracker ...). Frost and decorate.
- Use extra pastry dough to make shapes and designs as an upper-crust decoration on pies.
- Coat raisins and other dried fruits lightly with flour before adding to cake batter to prevent their settling to the bottom.
- When whipping up meringues, remember that superfine sugar dissolves better than does granulated sugar. Beat 2 egg whites with a

Make it Easy on Yourself

If you don't enjoy this or can't fit baking into your holidays, don't feel the least bit guilty about picking up something sinful and delicious from the neighborhood bakery or catering service. Excessive baking can put an unbearable weight on the season anyway ...

or ...

Have a neighborhood cookie swap. Organize a party of several Betty Crockers, inviting each to bring 5 dozen of one kind of cookie. Set each tray on a table, provide boxes (buy them from a bakery), and allow each guest to select 5 dozen of an assortment to take home. Each of you gets variety without having to make several different things all by your lonesome.

Della Robbia ...

was a 15th century Italian sculptor. A Della Robbia wreath consists predominantly of fruits and nuts.

dash of salt to soft peaks. Gradually add ½ c. sugar, beating until stiff. Make baskets by swirling meringue into a full circle shape (make a wax paper pattern, if necessary) and depressing the center with a spoon. Bake at 275° F 45 minutes or until crisp. These may be frozen until ready to use. Fill meringue baskets with ice cream topped with fresh or hot fruit, fudge or caramel sauce ... for a snowy mound of sweetness.

- Egg whites are best whipped at room temperature. They must be totally free of yolk. A pinch of salt hastens stiffness.
- When a recipe calls for cream and you don't have any, use these equivalents:
  1 c. light cream = ⅞ c. milk + 3 T. butter
  1 c. heavy cream = ¾ c. milk + ⅓ c. butter
- Whip chilled cream in a chilled bowl with chilled beaters. Add ginger, vanilla, cinnamon, nutmeg, rum ... for flavoring, and 2 T. powdered sugar for sweets.
- Freeze dollops of whipped cream on a cookie sheet. Thaw at room temperature 10-15 minutes for instant toppings.
- Soak squares of sponge or angel cake in your favorite liqueur and serve with flavored whipped cream.
- Flavor sour cream with your favorite extract or liqueur, brown sugar, or Tang orange drink mix, and serve over fresh fruit, cheesecake, or pound cake.
- Use colorful marzipan fruits, mint flowers, or other Christmas shapes to garnish a cream pie or cheesecake, Della Robbia-style.

❋ MARZIPAN

4 oz. almond paste	food coloring
½ c. powdered sugar	cocoa
1 T. light corn syrup	

Break up paste in a small bowl and knead with sugar and corn syrup using your bare hands. Add food coloring or cocoa to color. Form into shapes, using small knife, ice pick, and other kitchen tools to sculpt fruits, flowers, leaves, or holiday figures ...

Or paint completed sculpture with food coloring and a small paintbrush, let dry, and glaze with egg white slightly diluted with water.

❋ BUTTER MINTS

⅓ c. light corn syrup	½ t. salt
¼ c. butter	1 box confectioner's sugar
1 t. peppermint extract	food coloring

Combine first four ingredients in a small mixing bowl. Sift in confectioner's sugar, stirring frequently to mix well. Using your hands, form dough into a smooth ball and divide into separate balls as desired for different colorings. Knead food coloring into dough with fingers, shape as desired, and air dry overnight. Store in airtight container.

A GRAND FINALE

Add sparkle to after-dinner fireworks with a colorful liqueur, brandy, flavored coffee, or distinctive "pousse-café" to follow or accompany your elegant dessert ...

❄ POUSSE-CAFÉ

(French for "coffee-pusher.") Select two or three different colored liqueurs. Pour one at a time slowly down the side of a cordial glass. Refrigerate. The heavier liqueurs will sink to the bottom, the lighter ones remain on top, for an eye-popping layered effect.

KIDSKITCHEN

Cook up a little fun ...

While it is true that too many cooks spoil the stew, a well-organized committee of parent(s) and children can comfortably create lots of delectables in the Christmas kitchen. The adult should certainly be in the mood for such an undertaking and carefully supervise the little ones by advising of any and all conditions to their invasion of "grownup" territory. Any breach of contract — whining, impatience, disobedience, playing with knives—must promise instant removal from the scene ... "to your room!"

The "K-Team" should be well rested, well fed, and well prepared at the outset. Play soothing Christmas music in the background, give each participant an apron, and clear off plenty of workspace so everybody can help and/or watch.

Allowing children some time in the kitchen is the perfect opportunity to give them exposure to food preparation, nutritional information, practical math skills (!), and cooperative contact with Mom and Dad. Keep it light and fun, and clean up the mess cheerfully when it's all over!

Holiday Lunches

❄ CRAZY CHRISTMAS SALAD

Employ fruits, vegetables, cheeses, nuts, cooked pasta shapes, and garnishes to create your own Christmas lunch. Your plate will be the canvas, the foods your palette — and you will treat your PALATE to something "nutritious-delicious!" With these foods, make faces, Christmas trees, gift-wrapped packages, snowmen, Santas, angels ... See who can make the scariest monster—then gobble 'em up before they getcha!

Kids' Own Cookbook

Over the years, collect favorite family recipes suitable for your KidsKitchen. Create your own "cookbook" typed or printed on colored index cards. Punch a hole in the left-hand upper corner and bind the book together with ribbon, yarn, or metal rings (available at office supply stores) ... Kids will love having their very own cookbook! Add a few empty cards for their own additions. Who knows? You might just inspire a junior Julia Child or Paul Prudhomme!

 Put ice cubes made with cranberry juice in club soda for a refreshing holiday sparkler that should appeal to just about anybody.

❄ HOMEMADE PEANUT (OR CASHEW) BUTTER

In a food processor or blender, mix:

1 c. peanuts (or cashews)   ½ t. salt (if using unsalted nuts)
2 T. vegetable oil

If peanut butter is too runny, add a few more peanuts. If too stiff, add a drop or two more oil. Serve fresh peanut butter with applesauce, bacon, chopped dates and bananas, maple syrup, honey, cream cheese and chopped dried fruit, diced ham, shredded carrots ... jelly?

❄ SANTA CLAUS APPLE

With a juicy red apple for his body, a marshmallow for his head (attached with toothpicks), candy for his eyes, and a split cherry for his mouth ... Santa comes to lunch at Christmas.

String a short string with popcorn for his collar and make a red paper cap for his head. Pieces of broken toothpick will attach many of the garnishes to whole fruit for making fun food figures.

❄ PICASSO'S "PAINTED" CRACKERS

Tint softened cream cheese with red and green food coloring and spread or pipe onto crackers and toast points. Decorate with anchovy paste, contrasting colors of cream cheese, boiled egg yolk mixed with mayonnaise, carrot curls (use a vegetable peeler to curl long strips), caviar, pimientos, nuts, olives, tinted coconut, dried fruits ...

❄ CARVED FRUIT AND VEGETABLE STAMPS

Apples, potatoes, melon, or carrots can be carved to make decorative stamps for dipping into food coloring and printing onto cheese, bread, or a hard-boiled egg. After so colorful a lunch, eat the stamp for dessert!

❄ MAKE-YOUR-OWN PIZZA

Make or buy pizza dough or crust, or use sliced bagels or English muffins as the basis for a wonderful relationship between: tomato sauce, grated cheese, sliced pepperoni, olives, anchovies, sliced peppers and mushrooms, grilled onions, browned ground beef, leftover chicken and shrimp ... and all kinds of other good things. Top all with Italian seasoning and a sprinkling of Parmesan cheese, and bake until toasty, bubbly, and GOOD.

❄ RED AND GREEN INCREDIBLE EDIBLES

tomato soup topped with chopped parsley
oatmeal topped with green tinted coconut and red cinnamon candies
lime sherbet in cranberry punch
red and green Kool-Aid, Jello, jellybeans, or maraschino cherries
vanilla ice cream ball rolled in green tinted coconut and topped with a
    cherry
green eggs and ham

Snacks

❄ GELATIN CUTOUTS

2 pkgs. unflavored gelatin   1½ c. cold water
1 6 oz. pkg. flavored gelatin   1 c. boiling water

Dissolve unflavored gelatin in 1 c. cold water. Dissolve flavored gelatin in 1 c. boiling water. Stir ½ c. cold water into flavored mix and then plain dissolved gelatin. Add $\frac{1}{8}$ c. sugar or artificial sweetener if desired. Chill in a greased jellyroll pan until firm. Cut out shapes with cookie cutters.

❄ SNOW CREAM

May all your Christmases be white enough for snow cream!

1 c. milk   1 t. vanilla (or other flavoring)
¼ c. sugar   Mix well and pour over a bowl of
                         fresh clean snow.

❄ ELF MIX

This is the original dump recipe—any combination of the following tastes terrific all dumped together and will quickly, if not magically, disappear. Add more as you munch.

raisins	mixed nuts
coconut slices	Bugle corn chips
sunflower seeds	popcorn
Chex cereals	Goldfish crackers
pretzel sticks	corn nuts
carob or chocolate chips	Cheerios
dried fruit	M&M's
toasted pumpkin seeds	Reese's Pieces
banana chips	yogurt-covered nuts/raisins

Store in an airtight container. Serve in cloth-lined baskets for emergency snacks in the wink of an eye. Or fill a Lucite box or photo cube for a wonderful gift.

❄ POPCORN-MARSHMALLOW TREATS

Deck the halls with popcorn balls …
Mix up the following ingredients to make shapes and figures for decorating and snacking as well. These also make great party favors wrapped in clear cellophane and tied with a bow …

About Jello

While somewhat lacking in nutritional content, Jello is a funtastic invention for little kids. Between the wobbles and the wiggles, the glimmers and the shimmers, and the rainbow of colors (they even have BLUE now!), it's the eighth natural wonder of the kitchen. There are endless possibilities for its use: cut it into shapes, pile it up in cubes, mold it, suspend fruits and other suspicious characters in it, mix it with whipping cream or juices, build a sundae or parfait with it … use your imagination. And when holiday upset stomachs occur, don't forget to serve Jello to patients who can't take solids but are still a little hungry.

People who *know* say the elves eat this all day long as they work in the toy factory, energetically preparing for Santa's sleigh ride around the world.

Lollipop Cookies

Insert a popsicle or lollipop stick into a sugar or gingerbread cookie before baking to achieve the lollipop look. When cookie is cooled, decorate with colorful frostings. Wrap in clear cellophane tied with a bright ribbon for party favors or gifts, or "plant" several in a decorative clay pot filled with wrapped chocolate kisses as the "growing medium!"

1 lb. bag marshmallows	6 qts. popped popcorn
¼ c. butter or margarine	

Melt marshmallows and butter in microwave or over low heat until smooth, stirring occasionally. Add food coloring or 2 T. dry flavored gelatin for color and flavor if desired. Stir until well blended and pour over popcorn, mixing with clean hands until well coated. You might stir in nuts or candies too, to give the popcorn added dimension and texture. Form into shapes (snowballs, snowmen, Christmas trees ...) and press in candy decorations (M&M's, cinnamon candies, chocolate chips, silver dragees ...) while still warm.

NOT FOR KIDS ONLY

❄ STAINED GLASS COOKIES

Using Basic Sugar Cookie dough (see page 184), form narrow strips of chilled dough into the shape of window panes, trees, wreaths ... on a foil-covered cookie sheet. Bake 5 minutes at 375° F. Put colored hard candies into a zipped plastic bag and hammer to crush moderately. Use crushed candy to fill in spaces between the "window panes" and return to the oven for an additional 4-5 minutes, watching carefully, and remove when all candy has just melted. Cool at room temperature and peel foil from backs of cookies.

If you intend to hang these as decorations or ornaments, make a hole in the dough before baking and run a string, cord, or ribbon through hole when cookie is cooled.

❄ CORNFLAKE WREATHS

½ c. butter	green food coloring
8-10 oz. marshmallows	3½ c. cornflakes
½ t. vanilla	red cinnamon candies

Melt butter and marshmallows, adding vanilla and enough green food coloring to make a bright Christmas green, stirring well. Add cornflakes and coat thoroughly with marshmallow mixture. Line cookie pans with waxed paper and butter your fingers. Shape mixture into Christmas wreaths the size of a small cookie. Decorate while still warm with cinnamon candies. These are fantastically festive.

❄ BUTTERY "SPRITZ" SPURTED COOKIES

1 c. butter	½ t. vanilla
½ c. brown sugar	2½ c. unbleached flour
1 egg	1 t. baking powder

Cream butter and brown sugar. Add egg and vanilla and blend thoroughly. Sift flour and baking powder, beating into butter mixture. Never chill spritz dough. Push dough in different shapes through a cookie press onto an ungreased cookie sheet and decorate with colored sugars. Bake at 375° F about 7-8 minutes, or until edges are crisp but not brown. Makes about 6 dozen melt-in-your-mouth cookies.

❄ GINGERBREAD HOUSE

Every Christmas should have one—elaborate or simple. Involve the whole family in the baking or at least the decorating. Create a simple cottage, a small village, or even a replica of your own home!

Use the recipe for Basic Gingerbread Cookie Dough (see page 184). Make patterns with wax paper and press each piece against dough rolled out 1/8" thick on a floured surface. Cut around patterns with a sharp knife edge and bake pieces on greased cookie sheets at 375° F about 10-15 minutes, depending on size. If you want to get fancy, add texture ("architectural detail") to unbaked cut dough with kitchen tools, fork tines, knives … Trim edges of baked cookie pieces with a sharp knife and cool.

Dip edges of house parts into Sticky Sugar Glue and hold together until stuck fast. Place glued house on a foil-covered piece of heavy cardboard or a flat plate for decorating.

Sticky Sugar Glue:

Melt 1 c. granulated sugar and 1 t. white vinegar in a saucepan over low heat. When color is light brown and sugar is totally dissolved, dip pieces and glue. Work quickly, as this "glue" hardens fast.

Decorative Frosting ("Mortar"):

Beat 1 egg white with a pinch of salt until stiff. Beat in 2 c. powdered sugar and squeeze designs out of a pastry tube to decorate house. You may wish to color part of the icing with a drop or two of food coloring, or use easy ready-made frosting available in tubes or cans.

Decorate and accessorize cookies, cakes, and gingerbread houses with:

candied fruits	licorice whips
candy canes	Lifesavers
candy kisses	M&M's or Reese's Pieces
chocolate chips	marshmallows
chocolate stars	nonpareils
cinnamon candies	nuts
colored sprinkles	peppermint patties
colorful hard candies	peppermints
frosting	raisins
Fruit Loops	silver dragees
gumdrops	sugar cubes
gummy bears	tinted coconut

- Small sticks of gum make excellent roof tiles!
- Inverted and frosted sugar cones can be trimmed as Christmas trees.
- Candy sticks can be columns, with green tinted popcorn garlands.
- Use tubed gel icing to "polish" windows.
- Knead food coloring into unbaked sugar cookie dough and bake little shutters, flower pots, doors, awnings … attaching to your gingerbread house with Sticky Sugar Glue.
- Let your imagination run wild with creative "home-making" techniques!

❄ Make it Easy on Yourself

If baking and designing an elaborate gingerbread house is way beyond your reach, try using whole graham crackers for your house pieces, held together with Sticky Sugar Glue or the decorative frosting "mortar." Ready-made frosting adds doors, windows, shutters … and candy accessories assist the do-it-yourself remodeling job, turning plain graham crackers into a sugary holiday fantasy. This is quick, and just as much fun.

Make it Easy on Yourself (from the "I Hate to Cook" kitchen)

If you haven't the time or inclination to cook Christmas gifts, give:

assortment of unusual spices, teas, coffee beans, cocktail nuts ...

bag of pecans, walnuts, and almonds (give early to a Christmas baker)

bag or basket of fresh fruit

bottle of wine, box of crackers, wedge of Brie in a basket

fresh-from-the-bakery croissants, bagels, breakfast bread, dinner rolls, beignets, coffeecake

genuine Vermont maple syrup in a jug

jar each of red and green pepper jelly

specialty box of chocolates

spicy mustard and pretzels for dipping

TASTEFUL PRESENTATIONS FOR FOOD GIFTS

The barely hidden fact that I am somewhat of a food freak, *and* my celebration of the delights of holiday feasting in these pages, give weight to my hearty recommendation of food and creative kitchen items as just about the most perfect Christmas gift of all.

Many items from "A Festival of Feasting" can be presented to neighbors and friends, relatives, teachers, special service people, and children, leaving the giver reasonably assured that his or her gift will be relished and remembered, long after the last lovingly-prepared morsel is gone.

Make your presentation even more memorable and impressive with the clever gift-wrapping of your culinary artistry. Unusual containers of all sorts, sizes, and degrees of sophistication will convey extra-special thought, making the recipient feel extra-deep-down good inside.

Wrap food gifts in containers that are:

Cheaply Chic

Decorated:

canister with plastic top	milk carton
coffee can	oatmeal box
egg carton	shoe box
empty candy box	whipped topping or margarine container ...

Painted or sticker-decorated:

clay flower pots	paper sacks
leftover jelly jars	wine bottles ...
mason jars	

Ribbon-trimmed:

mushroom baskets	plastic berry baskets ...
peach baskets	

Unusually Useful

apothecary jar	kitchen canisters
brandy snifter	large kitchen scoops
bread pan	lidded mixing bowl
Christmas stocking	Lucite container
coffee mugs	new cookie/cake pan
cookie jar	stoneware crock
cooking utensil	straw planter basket
decorated wood crate	travel thermos
decorative tins	wire fruit basket

Extravagantly Elegant

antique container
ceramic cache-pot
ceramic ginger jar
ceramic/copper mold
ceramic/copper teapot
Christmas china
clay wine cooler
cocktail tray
crystal vase or pitcher
decorative pottery
French wire planter

hand-painted basket
holiday mugs/glasses
jewelry chest
marble cheese board
painted box
pewter bowl
picnic basket
silver ice bucket
truffle bowl
wooden salad bowl

Gift Containers for Kids

Kids thrill to their own private stash of holiday goodies. Pack in one of these and your present will be the hit of the season:

decorative tin for future "treasure" storage
Lucite photo cube
lunch box with thermos
McDonald's/Burger King/sports team ... giveaway glasses or cups
piggy bank
plastic miniature wheelbarrow or wagon
plastic sand bucket with shovel
small toy tote/crayon box (personalized)

Helpful Hints and Loving Touches

- Decorate containers with self-sticking labels, stickers, Contact paper cutouts, decoupaged greeting cards or gift wrap, glued-on paper silhouettes, doilies, colored cellophane or tissue paper, fabric, ribbons, paint pens, gilded pasta shapes ...
- Soak off old jar labels in warm water, using lighter fluid to remove stubborn adhesive.
- Line containers with foil, tissue paper, cloth napkins, a new dish towel, excelsior, shredded paper ...
- Have labels printed "Just for you from the kitchen of ... " or other appropriate logo, if you frequently give food gifts.
- Put a recipe and its ingredients in a new cake or muffin tin.
- Use paper baking cups to separate an assortment of cookies in a tin.

 Wrap all food gifts in plastic wrap or bags, aluminum foil, clear cellophane, or wax paper, to maintain freshness and preserve, as indicated. Label each package with care instructions: "Refrigerate after opening," "Store in warm dry place," "Stays fresh 10 days ... " "Warm before serving ... "

Jazzy Jelly Jars

• Give jellies and preserves in mugs, ice cream parfait glasses, champagne or odd wineglasses, brandy snifters ... To prevent glass from cracking, run under hot tap water, dry, and put a metal spoon into the glass before pouring in the hot jelly. Remove the spoon and seal with paraffin.

• To whip paraffin for elaborate jelly tops: Let melted paraffin cool 5-10 minutes until it begins to solidify. Whip with an egg beater or wire whisk until foamy. Spoon immediately on top of thin base layer of paraffin already hardened over the jelly or preserves.

• Attach recipes to a wooden spoon, paint or decoupage printed instructions on the gift container or lid, spear a recipe onto a small skewer attached to the gift or container, glue a card to a popsicle stick or skewer, punch a hole in a recipe card and tie on with cord or curling ribbon ...

• Hang individually-wrapped candies or cookies with ribbon on a houseplant or small tree.

• When molding cheeseball shapes to give as gifts, line the mold with plastic wrap, leaving enough extra to wrap up the cheese and tie with a ribbon after chilling.

• Give fresh pasta with a jar of your favorite sauce, or tortilla chips with some homemade salsa.

• Pack a bowl or basket with goodies and decorate with unique or useful kitchen tools: cookie cutters, butter molds, pizza slicer, rosette iron, wooden spoons, spaghetti measure, melon ball scoop, lemon zester, nutmeg grater ... or attach an assortment of these to a kitchen wreath for a decorative as well as useful gift.

• Homemade dressings, vinegars, wines, and liqueurs are potently presentable in old-fashioned vinegar bottles, decorative wine bottles, decanters ... To seal a bottle containing a cork, dip the cork in melted paraffin before inserting into bottle.

• Recycle old unused items you already have for interesting and unique gift containers. There is just no telling what you may find around the house ...

TEN

The Traditions of Christmas
Here, There, and Everywhere

Hath not old custom made this life more sweet?
—William Shakespeare

Tradition ... it's the tea in which Christmas is steeped. Tradition gives Christmas its deep, rich color ... its warming memories ... its satisfying aftertaste.

The traditions of Christmas are what heighten our anticipation and bring our friends and family together. These ways of celebrating may have been centuries in existence, or they may be new, just beginning. Every Christmas has some — with the tree, stockings, freshly-baked cookies, the giving of gifts, feasting, and festivities ... And every Christmas can use some more.

MEMORABLE TRADITIONS FOR YOUR FAMILY CHRISTMAS

- Make a yearly family ornament (or ornaments) dated each year of your holidays together.
- Hold a stocking-hanging ceremony every Christmas Eve, with music, a fire, and perhaps the ritual reading of a favorite Christmas story or poem.
- Celebrate the season of Advent with calendars and candles, singing, or services used by your church.
- Leave milk and cookies (or pizza) out for Santa on Christmas Eve, and an apple or some "reindeer biscuits" for Rudolph and the gang.
- Coordinate a traditional family feast and serve it yearly for Christmas Eve or Christmas Dinner. We have Oyster Stew, fruit, cheese, black olives (family favorite!), and samplings from a trayful of Nana's home-made cookies ... every Christmas Eve.
- Celebrate each Christmas with a holiday meal from a different country. Study international menus and create an authentic feast, with all the trimmings, music, customs, and lore.
- Research international customs and select a favorite international

Special Projects — Special Treasures

Take one year or several to make or collect something extraordinarily wonderful for you and your family to keep and treasure for generations:

Christmas quilt or afghan
Christmas scrapbook or photo album
Christmas village
crèche for the mantel, hall, or foyer table ...
electric train village
hand-crafted miniatures
hand-worked stocking collection, tree skirt ...
holiday hope chest
life-sized Mr. and Ms. Santa
Victorian dollhouse
yearly issue of: ornament, needlework, pillow, miniature, porcelain plate, hand-crafted nativity figure

Always sign and date your work.

The Yule Log

One of the most enduring traditions of Christmas in Europe is the lighting of the Yule Log.

Family custom required cutting a large tree to acquire a log big enough to burn all through the twelve days of Christmas. The new log must be lit with a piece from the previous year's log and only by one with scrupulously clean hands (or the fire absolutely will not burn!).

Ashes from the Yule Log were said to cure diseases, and scrap pieces were kept for the next year's kindling, to ward off evil spirits ... again reserving a special piece for the next Yuletide fire.

Today the tradition of the Yule Log lives on, in practice, legend, and song ... and in the perhaps more popular *buche de Noël*, a scrumptious cake filled with cream, rolled and frosted with chocolate to resemble a Yule Log. While eating a piece of *buche de Noël* does not guarantee to free you from evil spirits, it's my firm belief that we must give it a hearty try all the same!

tradition to be repeated year after year.

- Invite family and friends to a "birthday party" for baby Jesus, complete with cake and presents (which might eventually go to a shelter or an empty stocking drive).
- Record each season with photographs, slides, video or audio tapes. Capture family and friends in party clothes, the wrapping and unwrapping of gifts, the tree, best snowman, Christmas dinner table, visiting friends and family, favorite new toys and treasures, new grandchildren ... A "review" of Christmas Past could be a Christmas Eve tradition.
- Take a photograph of the family in the same place, same position, every year ... for an annual record of growth and change.
- Begin Christmas morning by letting Mom and Dad enter the Tree Room ahead of everyone else to turn on the lights, start the music, light the fire ... and let the ringing of a small Christmas bell hanging on the tree invite everyone else to slide down the banister and into the festivities.
- We always had an "Uncle Louie"—an anonymous gift-giver invented by our Santa to give fun and funny gifts to various family members. It took some of us a long time to figure out there was no such person (sound familiar?). Invent your own legendary secret gift-giver(s).
- Select some lucky individual to be the recipient of "Twelve Days of Christmas" gifts.
- Begin a family add-on gift: Christmas music, collectibles, ornaments, books, electric train accessories ... and give one to the family each year, or pick out something all together.
- Keep a "Growth Stick" of each child's height as he grows from one Christmas morning to the next.
- Gild the Thanksgiving turkey's wishbone and hang it on the tree as an ornament. On Christmas morning, pull it apart and make a wish. Whoever holds the largest piece will have her wish come true.
- Reenact the nativity as a family, and/or with friends. Improvise the story of Jesus' birth with as many characters as you have people. Let the kids carry out their own interpretations and chuckle—in private —at their renderings.
- Put traditional breakfast in each stocking: a plastic-wrapped sweet roll or croissant, box of juice, raisins or tangerine, snack box of dry cereal ...
- Adopt a family, a retirement home, or an individual. Secretly prepare a meal and/or gifts, baked goods, and Christmas cheer for the lonely and less fortunate. Social service agencies can serve as liaisons between your good-hearted charity and a worthy recipient.

 "Yule" is derived from the Scandinavian "Juul"—a celebration during which Norsemen burned the log in honor of Thor, god of the sun. The shortest day of the year was over, and "rebirth" had begun ... a cause for joyous merry-making.

- Make plum pudding the Saturday after Thanksgiving. It takes about a month to develop that memorable flavor.
- If you have no extended family to spend Christmas with, organize a group of friends or families to share the day and co-op a Christmas brunch or feast.
- Take an annual hayride with several friends and family, riding through the wintry streets, admiring decorations and lights, singing Christmas carols, and finishing up with a toasty fire and cocoa.
- Harriet Kirkpatrick's family has a "Secret Santa Claus." Draw names among family members and play "Secret Santa" all through the month of December, doing thoughtful and imaginative little things to make your selected individual feel especially happy and loved. Reveal names on Christmas Eve.
- To make taking down the tree a little less painful, wrap a set of extra gifts in gold paper and put them deep under the tree, to be opened only after all the dismantling is complete. These "gifts of gold" are from the three wise men and were presented in their day on January 6, Epiphany. Don't leave the tree up past then!
- As an individual or as a family, share in the true meaning of Christmas—give of yourself, your time, and your resources that others may find happiness in your spirit.

HOW TO BUILD THE PERFECT FIRE (AND KEEP IT GOING ...)

Perhaps one of the oldest traditions of Christmas is the good-natured (sometimes) argument (most often) about how to get and keep a roaring fire going. Husbands and wives, fathers-in-law and their sons by marriage, rarely agree on the best way to build a fire. Research indicates this phenomenon predates even the reason for the holiday itself, originating with the earliest inventive man.

While not much has changed in the ensuing millions of years, the following is an effort to avoid one cherished relative being branded by a burning poker in the hands of another. Try this simple scientific procedure for building the perfect fire:

Recognize the principle of air space. Leaving room under, around, and between logs allows heat to rise and keep the home fires burning all through the happy season.

1. Keep a low bed of ashes in the fireplace under your andirons or wire grate.
2. Crumple up some newspaper and place over the ashes, or use a commercial firestarter from the hardware store.
3. Lay small pieces of wood (kindling) at spaced intervals crosswise over the newspaper. Add another layer of kindling checkerboard-style across the first (see illustration).
4. Build a pyramid of three smaller logs over the stacked kindling.
5. Light the newspaper with a match.

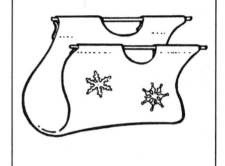

Make a Yule Log Carrier

Select heavy canvas as colorful as you can find. Cut in a rectangle large enough to support the weight of a few good logs. Cut out "handle holes" at each end (as illustrated), hem and insert large dowels or curtain rods for handles. Hem edges and decorate with trim or acrylic paint for maximum spirit.

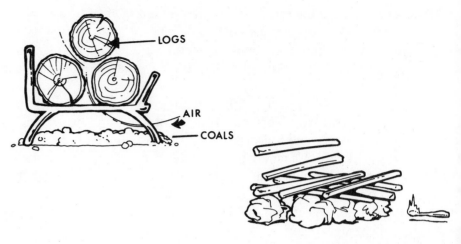

If your wood is nice and dry, and there is plenty of space for the hot air to flow between logs, you should be warm and content (until your son-in-law starts fooling around with the logs again!). Green split hardwoods (oak, hickory, apple) burn best and longest. Dried out wood is best for starting the fire, as it burns faster.

Keep a screen up before the fireplace opening to prevent sparks from peppering the hearth rug, carpet, or hardwood floors, and don't forget to open the flue!

CELEBRATIONS ... HERE, THERE, AND EVERYWHERE

One of the biggest mysteries of Christmas, the thing that kept me constantly puzzled as a child was, "How does Santa get to every house of every little boy and girl all over the world in the course of one evening on a *sleigh* driven by *reindeer*—and *how* does he carry ALL THOSE PRESENTS???"

The answer eludes me still, and I found myself resorting to the easy way out "Magic!" response when the same question occurred to my own little ones.

Past trying to figure it all out now, my grownup curiosity has traveled more toward the fascinating study of Christmas around the world.

Some holiday customs seem to be universal. Most are not. While countries that celebrate Christmas recognize the religious ceremony with church services and the crèche, carols, and the story of Christ's birth ... the traditions of gift-giving, trimming a tree, decorating, feasting, and celebrating vary from country to country, province to province, house to house.

You and your family might enjoy digging back into your roots for "old country" customs over the holidays.

And while it is true that customs often vary from family to family, there are many interesting traditions and beliefs held by individual countries each colorful Christmas season.

And I heard him exclaim as he drove out of sight—
"Good Grief! It's 3 a.m. and I haven't even done Asia!"

CHRISTMAS CUSTOMS AROUND THE WORLD

- Italians fast the entire day from sunset December 23 to sunset December 24 before the large Christmas Eve feast around the *presepe* —the manger. A candlelit *ceppo*, another part of the celebration, is a light wood frame shaped like a pyramid, which holds candles, a tiny crèche scene, and small gifts and sweets for the children.
- The Mexican *Posada*, from December 16-24, is a colorful birthday celebration with numerous nativity plays, joyous processionals, and the breaking of a piñata on the final day before Christmas.
- In Poland, the Christmas Eve feast may begin only when the light of the first evening star is seen shining in the sky.
- Norwegians place a three-pronged candleholder on the Christmas treetop signifying the Three Wise Men. Its light welcomes weary travelers and wards off evil spirits.
- Chinese Christians usher in the holiday with a spectacular fireworks display.
- An empty chair is left at the table of Czech feasts for the spiritual presence of the Christ Child.
- In Germany, an Advent wreath is hung from the ceiling with bright red ribbons.
- Scandinavians use straw and wheat in their decorating as hopeful harbingers of a good harvest in the coming spring. Sheaves of the previous fall's best grain are put on housetops and on top of poles for the birds' Christmas feast.
- The Dutch have a custom of hiding a large gift and handing out elaborately wrapped clues until the present is found. Occasionally, a tiny gift is hidden in a huge box, some pudding, or a piece of fruit.

GIFT-GIVERS AROUND THE WORLD

- In Spain and Mexico, children put shoes filled with hay on the balcony. The Wise Men's camels eat the hay and the Wise Men leave gifts behind, according to custom.
- In Italy, *La Befana* is an old woman supposedly too busy sweeping when asked to accompany the Wise Men on their journey to Bethlehem. Later, regretting her decision, she went out (riding on her broomstick, according to legend) looking for the Christ Child, leaving gifts for all children in case one might be the special one she sought. *La Befana* comes on Twelfth Night, the eve of Epiphany, when the Wise Men were said to have arrived in Bethlehem.
- St. Lucia is the gift-giver in Sweden. She was a generous and kind girl who gave her wealth to the poor and is pictured wearing a crown of burning candles to symbolize light and the happy season to come. St. Lucia's Day is celebrated on December 11, ushering in the Christmas season with traditional festivals and feasts.
- In Holland, Belgium, and parts of France and Germany, December 6 is St. Nicholas Day. Children leave out their wooden shoes to be filled with candies and gifts. The old saint is said to carry a birch

Many Names—for Yuletide Gift-Givers

England: Father Christmas, Kris Kringle, St. Nicholas
France: Père Noël, le Petit Jésus, le Petit Noël
Germany, Switzerland, Austria: Christkind ("Christ Child")
Italy: La Befana
Austria, Belgium, Holland: St. Nicholas
Finland: Joulupukki (Old Man Christmas)
Sweden: Jultomten, St. Lucia
Spain and Mexico: Three Wise Men or Three Kings
Brazil: Papa Noël
Syria: the smallest camel of the Wise Men's caravan
Poland: Star Man
Russia: Babouschka (baby)
U.S.A.: SANTA CLAUS!

Traditional Christmas Plum Pudding

Where are the ... plums?

(Make Thanksgiving weekend so your pudding will be "ripe" by Christmas)

1 c. all-purpose flour
1 t. baking soda
1 t. salt
1 t. ground cinnamon
1 t. ground nutmeg
½ t. ground allspice
1½ c. chopped raisins
1 c. diced citron
¾ c. mixed diced candied
    lemon and orange peel
½ c. chopped almonds
1½ c. soft breadcrumbs
1 c. firmly packed brown sugar
3 eggs, beaten
1/3 c. currant jelly
¼ c. sherry or brandy
2 c. ground suet

Combine flour, soda, salt, and spices. Add fruit, almonds, and breadcrumbs; mix well. Stir together brown sugar, eggs, jelly, and sherry (or brandy). Add to fruit mixture along with suet, mixing well. Pack into a well-buttered and sugared 1½ quart mold, covering tightly with aluminum foil. Place mold on shallow rack in a large, deep kettle with enough boiling water to come halfway up the mold. Cover kettle. Steam pudding about 5½ hours in continuously boiling water (replace water as needed). Wrap tightly in foil and store in refrigerator several weeks to ripen. Unmold and serve with Hard Sauce: ½ c. butter, softened; 1 c. powdered sugar; ¼ c. brandy ... Cream butter and sugar until smooth and beat in brandy until fluffy.

Zella McKnight

rod, so bad girls and boys can expect whippings instead of toys!

- *Julenisse*, in Norway and Denmark, are little gnome-like creatures who play mischievous tricks if all work is not done before Christmas celebrating begins.

WORLDWIDE HOLIDAY FARE

Many countries hold the superstition that the bigger the Christmas feast, the better the family fortune in the coming year.

- Cooked goose, roast beef, Yorkshire pudding, plum pudding (containing not a single plum!), boar's head, and mince pie make up the traditional English holiday menu.
- Germany is native land to most of the famous Christmas cookies, and their dessert tray is likely to include:
  Pfeffernuss—"pepper nuts"
  Lebkuchen—"life cake" (a heart-shaped cake with spices and nuts)
  Springerle — stamped cookies made with a carved mold or carved rolling pin
  Stollen—sweet cake filled with currants and frosted with white icing
  Spritz—"spurted from a press" sugared butter cookies
- Sweden offers *Pepparkakor* or gingersnaps, and "Lucia buns" made of sweet dough and saffron, served in a "Smorgasbord" of pickled vegetables, Swedish pancakes, lots of fish, and Swedish meatballs.
- The Swiss make tree ornaments of bright tissue figures, hiding delicious Swiss chocolates inside (which children are allowed to eat while dismantling the tree).
- In France, the *Buche de Noel* ("Yule Log" — a chocolate-frosted cream-filled cake roll) and marzipan are traditional.
- *Baklava*, a diamond-shaped, honey-soaked, flaky nut pastry, is the favorite treat in Greece.
- In Norway and Denmark, rice pudding sprinkled with cinnamon and hiding a magic almond inside is a favorite. Whoever finds the hidden prize receives a special treat (or is the next to be married!). Whoever finds the hidden raisin must do the dishes! ▮ Scandinavians also serve roast goose stuffed with apples and prunes.
- A Christmas bread filled with fruits, *panettone* is a favorite with Italians.
- Moravians from Bohemia, now settled in Old Salem, NC, and Pennsylvania, enjoy the most delicious sugar cakes and impossibly thin rolled out Moravian cookies.

 I would have to question the intelligence of one who receives the dreaded raisin and actually confesses the discovery! A stealthy swallow-it-down makes much better sense.

DECK THE HALLS WITH INTERNATIONAL ORNAMENTS

Many countries have favorite ornaments and hand-crafted decorations born of their unique culture. Often, these reflect a specific national art or craft. Collecting ornaments wherever you travel recalls, each holiday, the happy wanderings of days past.

- Germany: delicate blown-glass balls and figures (created in Lauscha, formerly East Germany)
- Czech Republic: painted eggshells
- Sweden: straw figures of animals, small carved wooden ornaments
- Denmark: bells, paper hearts
- Japan: pastel paper fans and butterflies, bright-colored origami
- Poland: ribbons and colored papers, carved animals
- Norway: edible trimmings, gilded nuts for good luck
- Mexico and Spain: colorful embroidered and stuffed animals and figures, papier-mâché objects
- Switzerland: tissue paper figures hiding delicious chocolates inside

Say "Merry Christmas!" in Many Languages

Joyeux Noël—France
Feliz Navidad—
 Spain and Mexico
Glaedelig Jul—Denmark
God Jul—Sweden
Frohliche Weihnachten—
 Germany
Wesotych Swiat—Poland
Buon Natale—Italy

ELEVEN

Yes, Virginia
There IS Life After Christmas

… ten thousand years from now, he will continue to make glad the heart …
—F.P. Church

I t's over—it was great! wonderful! can't wait to do it all again next year …

But wait. What do I do with all this momentum? How do I come down smoothly into dreary old January without crashing into a snowdrift of post-Christmas blues?

That's terrific—you really enjoyed Christmas this year. So much so that you're not even overcome with relief that it's over.

January does loom drearily in the wake of colored lights, warmth, and wonder. Maybe that's why Christmas is followed so closely with a New Year—in order to give us a fresh start, a chance to take our positive resolutions to heart, give renewed purpose to our very being.

MAKE THE MOST OF THE NEW YEAR

- Fix up a tray of leftover cookies, cake, and other holiday temptations to take to a shut-in, nursing home … you spread good cheer without further spreading your derriére!
- Shop after-Christmas sales for great buys on next year's gift wrap, cards, ornaments, and other holiday supplies.
- Flip back through "How to Entertain … " to find an inexpensive but festive party idea and keep the spirit flowing.
- Pamper yourself and those you love—simply enjoy being together without submitting to cabin fever: begin a Monopoly marathon, enjoy reading new books, listen to new music, spend all afternoon at the movies—do some of the lazy, relaxing things you couldn't do during the busy holiday season.
- Start a new diet or exercise program (sounds dreadful, but after a week or so of the regimen, you will begin to enjoy the new you!).
- Begin keeping a journal—of thoughts, activities, ideas, and those adorable (and not so adorable) quotes from the kids …

A wonderful gift to a newly married couple or new family would be a handmade scrapbook created especially for keeping Christmas mementos and memories ...

- Organize that big stack of the past five years' worth of photographs into an album or a scrapbook.
- Write leisurely thank-you notes and enjoy a literary visit with long-distance friends and family.
- Begin making a special treasure for next year's Christmas—quilt, crâche, ornaments, those new stockings you meant to make this year.
- Go ahead and send out the Christmas cards you never got around to addressing in December. This will be a welcome piece of mail beside the tax forms and credit card bills.

MAKE A CHRISTMAS SCRAPBOOK

December 25 brings with it so many treasures, both tangible and sentimental. What better way to keep your seasonal souvenirs and memories than in a Christmas scrapbook?

As a family, you could make a Christmas book as simple or as elaborate as you like and fill it with holiday photographs, *Nutcracker* ticket stubs, *A Christmas Carol* playbill, each year's Christmas card from your family and favorites you received, children's artwork, letters to Santa, school play programs, party favors and invitations, written records of events and emotions, personal poetry and prose ...

Books to collect all this together can be found in stores, so you could buy one, or just browse through some, getting ideas for format in designing your own, like: "Eli's first Christmas ... " "Christmas Travels ... " "Christmas Dinner Menus ... " "Michael's favorite gift this year was ... " "Next Christmas, we'd like to ... " "Best Christmas Memory ... " "I gained _____ pounds this Christmas ... "

REMEMBER: LIFE IS A CELEBRATION—MAKE THE MOST OF IT.

TWELVE

Making Merry
Handcrafting a Merry Christmas

Each morning sees some task begun
Each evening sees it close:
Something attempted, something done,
Has earned a night's repose.
—Henry Wadsworth Longfellow

Does it always seem like *everyone else* is making clever hand-crafted gifts and decorations for Christmas? Do you struggle with the notion that a good old down-home Christmas mandatorily includes needlepointed stockings, hand-painted rockers for the new baby doll, personalized ornaments for the tree, and something incredibly clever and unique for all the neighbors, teachers, friends, and family? Have you ever wondered if you might like to try your hand at some crafting yourself?

Do you absolutely, positively have a healthy desire to try something new this year?

If you are so inclined, you *can* do it, you know. You don't have to be an artist, a highly-skilled craftsman, or even a graduate of a six-week night course to know how to create something yourself, something you might even be proud of.

The first step is this: remind yourself, repeatedly, "I am *not* an idiot!" Too many people are intimidated by hand-craftsmanship. If it will help, think back to the good old days, when most people *had* to make things themselves or do without. Surely they were no better equipped than you are. Necessity was the mother of their invention. Let self-extension and the promise of genuine satisfaction be the mother of yours. Let your creative spirit come alive at Christmas.

"But I wouldn't know where to begin!" you say.

Begin here ... at THE BACK OF THE BOOK. Here is the crash course in handcrafting that you have always wanted to take. Once you are familiar with the methods and materials, you can experiment, practice, and develop skills to the extent of your own interest and determination.

Try something new. Be innovative with your imagination and your

The Back of the Book

Welcome to THE BACK OF THE BOOK. If you find yourself suddenly swept away by a newly-discovered fervor for making things with your hands and imagination, don't stop here.

Instructions in a Christmas book do not a master craftsman make. Consider other sources of information, instruction, and ideas: the public library, craft books and magazines, catalogs, gift shops, hardware stores, art supply stores, craft fairs, night courses ... Live and learn. Learn by doing, by asking, by researching, and by PAYING ATTENTION. Don't be afraid to try new things.

If the spirit is willing—make it this Christmas ... and Make Merry!

Art used to be definable as what men created. Crafts were made by women and natives. Only recently have we discovered they are the same, thus bringing craft techniques into art and art into everyday life.

—Gloria Steinem,
from *Outrageous Acts and Everyday Rebellions*

hands, constantly armed, however, with a healthy dose of patience. Be on the lookout for the many ways to put a new twist on old techniques. Choose your "own thing" and go for it.

BEFORE STARTING A PROJECT

1. Become familiar with the entire craft process *before beginning.* Read all labels, manufacturer's notes, and craft instructions carefully. Consider researching techniques to sharpen your knowledge and awareness of various skills.
2. Gather all the tools and materials you will need. Prepare a work surface to suit the project (old newspaper, piece of Masonite or plywood). Arrange materials for easy accessibility and maintain adequate ventilation when necessary. Wear proper clothing and gloves as needed.
3. Work slowly and carefully, proceeding one step at a time. Avoid foolhardy shortcuts. Be patient. Do it right the first time, even though it takes longer. Said Chaucer, "There is no man, whate'er his trade may be—who can work well, and do it hastily."
4. Use caution with innovation and improvisation, especially the first time you try a technique. But don't be afraid to experiment with a well-thought-out idea—you can practice on scrap materials first.

BETWEEN WORK SESSIONS AND WHEN YOU ARE FINISHED

Clean all materials thoroughly and arrange neatly for convenient resumption of your craft. Keep all tools and toxic materials out of the reach of children and pets.

Make notes of innovations and ideas still fresh in your mind that come to you during the creative process.

Don't take on too many projects at once. You won't be able to concentrate sufficiently on any one, and will usually end up frustrated and frazzled.

Plan ahead for long-term projects and begin early, allowing ample drying, setting, or have-to-do-it-all-over time (hope not!) to finish by Christmas.

Concentrate on one or two items or techniques each year, making several things from a single great idea.

Keep a file for craft-working notes, instructions, and projects. Cut out magazine pictures with interesting illustrations and ideas. Save pictures for guidelines to creating designs for handmade or printed materials. I have files on "animals," "greenery arrangement," "flower-arranging," "tree ornaments," "eyes, noses, mouths, and other facial features"(!) and other strange categories. It helps when you're stuck for an idea, or when you just can't seem to visualize an orangutan ...

DON'T BE INTIMIDATED BY TOOLS

There must be thousands of different tools to serve as helpmates in thousands of different applications. For the kinds of things you and I do, we are probably in need of only a dozen or so. We can handle that to start out.

Almost all the tools we will use are either extensions or adaptations of parts of our body. Your thumb and forefinger are a pair of pliers or a wrench. Your fist is a hammer. Your wrist can act like a drill (ever bore a hole in a lump of clay or dirt with your finger or fist by turning your wrist?). Your skin is a very fine file or piece of sandpaper. Think again of fingernails—as a screwdriver, saw tooth, scraper, knife, or chisel. Your teeth could be a saw or a clamp.

Over the ages, man has made many of our body functions and parts more efficient than they were—stronger, harder, larger, sharper, better leveraged. He did it with common things all around him—sticks and stones and bones, then metals. When electricity was invented, tools became more powerful and have brought us to where we are today.

So if some shaggy hunk of Neanderthal man or woman could work a tool, why not you?

To start with, find out what tools do what jobs. We are going to show and tell you about those we consider to be the basics. You probably will not need or use them all at the beginning, but as your skills and projects become more varied, you may want them all—and more.

These tools are easy to use and you can get any of them wherever do-it-yourself items are sold. A hint: If you are planning to use your tools frequently, get good ones. Tools are an investment and will become good friends.

The following are arranged according to the major functions they serve.

Meet Dave Fick

The "Tools" section of THE BACK OF THE BOOK was contributed by Dave "Dad" Fick. He made superior things with his hands and tried many different media, experimenting and inventing with every one. My Dad created a legacy of beautiful things: meticulous nature drawings scratched out of wild mushroom ("artist's fungus") or penned in ink on lovely papers, elaborately-detailed wildflower drawings with colored pencils, elegant art display boxes made of glass and dentil moldings, antiqued hand-painted old trunks, fascinating carved-wood walking sticks individualized for each recipient, and glorious little painted birdhouses — each with its own unique architectural detail, landscaping, welcoming doorstep, and flowers spilling out of windowboxes. We treasure all the gifts of my father's creative spirit ... and he will live forever in the art he made and gave, with great love and generosity, just for us.

Cut-Ups

This category covers and shows the tools used primarily for cutting things, that is, making small stuff from big stuff—one of the first things you do in so many projects. Use hand saws to cut wood, metal, plastics, plywood, Masonite, chipboard ...

Cross-Cut Saw: Use it to saw *across* the grain of a piece of wood. It takes practice to saw a straight line. Don't force it, go smooth and easy. The cross-cut saw cuts on the downstroke. Rub the blade (of any saw) with oil to prevent rust and to make the saw slide more easily through the workpiece. Never cut metal with this tool.

Rip Saw: Use it to cut *with* the wood's grain.

Coping Saw: A very delicate and versatile tool for sawing pieces of wood or plastic into odd shapes. The blade is very thin and cuts circles, curves, and notches. The blade can be rotated to change its cutting direction when necessary. If you want to cut a shape out of the inside of your

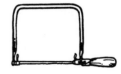

workpiece, drill a small hole in the section to be cut out, detach the blade, and insert it through the hole. Reattach it to the saw's frame and continue to cut. Follow your pattern lines very carefully and stroke softly. It is almost always easier when you clamp the work down on your table before sawing.

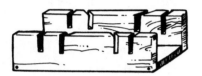

Back Saw: This saw has a rigid blade and is used for fine wood cuts, usually with a mitre box for straight or angled cuts.

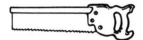

Mitre Box: There are fancier types than the one we show here, but this basic one will take care of most of your needs. It is made of hardwood and has pre-cut notches in it to guide the back saw in cutting either 90° or 45° angles. Hold the workpiece firmly in the trough and cut gently. Clearly mark on the work where you want to make the cut. Great for cutting picture frames. The guides help you keep your saw straight up and down.

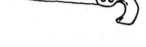

Compass Saw: A pointed blade lets you cut shapes out of the inside area of your workpiece when using stock too thick or too heavy for your coping saw. Drill a hole on the inside and carefully cut away.

Hack Saw: Use for cutting metals—rods, pipes, bars, and the like. Hack saw blades are quite thin, so stroke gently but firmly on the downstroke. Always put your work piece in a vise or clamp it securely to the table.

More Cut-Ups

Scissors: You know all about scissors for cutting paper, cloth, string, hair … Just keep them sharp and handy.

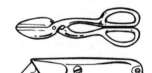

Tin Snips: Like scissors but used to cut patterns and things out of tin, soft sheet metals—aluminum flashing, copper, brass …

Utility Knife: A good tool for heavier cutting of papers, mat board, cardboard, corrugated board, leather, vinyl sheets, and thin wood sheeting.

X-acto Knife: A great and handy tool for general use around the craft room. Comes with many different size, shape, and special use blades and handles. Available in kits for general cutting and shaping of various craft projects. Every crafter should have one.

Razor Blades: The industrial type, with a rigid blade, is best and safest. Not only good for general cutting and simple shaping, but also can be used to scrape paint off glass. Avoid flexible blades.

When sawing anything, don't let the material you're sawing pinch the blade. If it does, you're in trouble and you won't be able to complete your cut. Bend the work down a bit to keep the "kerf" (the cut line your saw blade makes) open. There are several types of electric saws available to make any kind of sawing easier. Look into these when you begin to do lots of wood/metal work.

Grabbers and Pinchers

These are all hand-held tools that let you get a firm grip on things. They do the same thing your thumb and forefinger do, only better.

Slip-Joint Pliers: This is the common, everyday type of pliers most of you already have. They can be used to hold things tight so you can twist a stubborn pipe joint or bottle cap, loosen a nut, crack a pecan, crimp or bend something. The slip joint lets you open the jaws wider and gives more holding power.

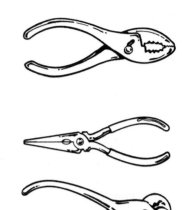

Long-Nose Pliers: The sharp nose gives you access to smaller areas, lets you hold smaller items. The rounded tops of the nose make bending soft wire and metal strips easy, and many of these pliers also have a wire-cutting area.

End Cutter: I call them "nippers"—they can nip or cut wire or nails. The rounded head allows nipping a protruding nail flush with the surface. It can also be used to pull nails out.

Tweezers: These come in many shapes and sizes. All are handy, not only for pulling out splinters, but for holding and picking up small and delicate craft items. Tweezers can be used as a clamp when gluing two small things together.

Beat-Its

The hammer is one of the earliest tools man created. He first called it a club, and it was not used primarily as a craft implement.

Claw Hammer: The head drives in the nail. If it goes in crooked, the slotted claw pulls it out. These come in many different weights and sizes. The claw hammer is basically used for nailing, but it is also handy for any use where a pounding or tapping pressure is needed.

Ball Peen Hammer: One end of the head is flat, the other rounded. The flat end is used for general hammering or flattening a metal sheet or bar. The rounded end is used for forming or texturing a metal material— like the dents in a copper bracelet or ashtray.

Tack Hammer: A lightweight tool for driving tacks, brads, or picture hook nails, one end of the head is usually magnetized to hold nails or tacks too small to be held in place with fingers.

Brass Head Hammer: The softness and lighter weight of brass helps to prevent surface damage to materials and implements being struck. These are for light and delicate striking only.

Twisters

These tools serve again as an extension of your hand, activated by a spinning wrist. They drive threaded screws and bolts into your work—

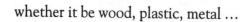

whether it be wood, plastic, metal …

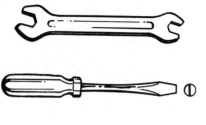

Wrench: A wrench grabs the nut that makes the bolt the powerful holding element it can be. This tool comes in sizes to adjust to the size nut you are using. Adjust the jaws to fit over the nut tightly and turn to wind over the threads of the bolt close to the piece.

Slotted Screwdrivers: A slotted head or straight-bladed screwdriver fits a screw with a straight channel in the head. Twist it with your wrist and you can join just about anything. This is the most common screwdriver.

Phillips Head Screwdriver: These do just what the slotted head screwdriver does, except maybe a little bit easier. The slot on the head of a Phillips head screw is cross-shaped, for a better grip by the screwdriver.

Jeweler's Screwdriver: For very fine screwdriving of tiny screws into the most delicate of crafts …

Hole-Some—But Boring

You have to make holes in things for lots of reasons. Consider Swiss cheese. Here are some of the most common hole-makers.

Awl: You may not know about this one. An awl is nothing more than a sharp, thick needle with a handle, great for starting holes in wood or plastic, preparing surfaces for nails, screws, bits, or augers. Because of the thick shank past the sharp point, this tool can be used for punching holes in many objects as well (like air-holes for caterpillar jars in the summer).

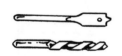

Hand Drill: This is tool drills holes in most anything pertaining to craft work. Turn the crank to twist the drill bit into the work surface using the hand-operated model, which is relatively inexpensive, or invest in an *electric drill*, which is a handy tool to have around the house. It works fast —use carefully.

Drill Bit: These you lock into the drill to bore different-sized holes. They are available in very small sizes ($1/16$") to very large (1" and over). Specific tips are available for wood, metal, glass, and even masonry. Ask your friendly hardware person for particulars in your specific project.

Auger Bit: This must be used with a brace, clamp, or vise. It is usually longer than a standard drill bit, so you can drill a hole through thicker wood (6-8").

Burrs and Mounted Stone Points: Additional attachments available for your electric drill that will carve, smooth, and polish workpieces. A hobby Dremel drill is especially useful for this type of craft technique.

 When drilling plastic, drill slowly, as the heat of fast drilling will melt the material and make a bigger hole than you intended. A heated awl sometimes works best in making a hole or slit in plastic.

Old Smoothies

There are not many surprises in this group of tools and implements to make things smooth, mostly by the method of abrasion. All of these are similar to a nail file (though I would not suggest using one of them on your nails). These prepare your work for final polishing and finishing.

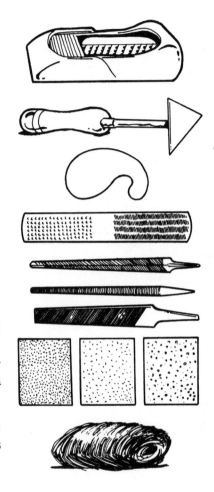

Surform Plane: This is a relatively new wrinkle on an old tool—the plane. The surface has a series of cutting blades with openings which prevent clogging. Surform tools come in a variety of shapes and sizes, and are highly efficient for trimming wood, plastics, and soft metals.

Shavehook: These come in various configurations and are used for fine scraping of flat and irregular wood surfaces.

Cabinet Scrapers: Handheld tools for even finer scraping of wood surfaces, these come with flat or curved shapes for woodwork of many kinds —cabinets, boxes, wood frames …

Files: Again, the principle of abrasion, refining the wood surfaces by rubbing out rough, uneven areas. Files can be very rough or very fine, depending on the smoothness of the piece, its configuration, and the final result desired. For frequent woodworking, you may eventually collect a broad variety of shapes, sizes, and abrasion factors.

Sandpaper: This is the most common abrasive material. Paper or cloth with a sand-like substance glued to it, the number of grains per square inch determines its coarseness or fineness. Use sandpaper in papier-mâché, decoupage, woodworking, preparing a surface for the final finish (paint, shellac, varnish), and many other craft projects.

Steel Wool: A gentler surface than sandpaper, steel wool comes in coarse to very fine texture, but won't cut it as fast as sandpaper. This is best for that last shining rubdown on your project.

If You Can't Beat 'Em, Join 'Em

Knowing how to connect one thing to another tightly and securely is one of the most basic issues of craftsmanship. Some materials can be adequately joined by glues or adhesives (see page 214), some require nails, and others need a good nuts and bolts approach to make a strong joint.

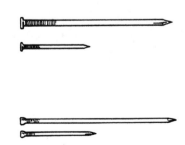

Common Nails: Nails are common to everyone, but "common" nails have a fairly broad, flat head, or striking surface. Nails come in "penny" sizes from 2 penny to 60 penny—the closest thing to a railroad spike. (This is abbreviated "2d", "60d.") The penny distinction comes from England and currently has little to do with the price of nails.

Finishing Nails: These also come in short to long sizes, though not as extreme as common nails. Finishing nails are the ones you use to surface finish a piece of fine woodwork. The heads are just a bit wider than the shank (or length) of the nail, so they can be driven flush with, or even "punched" below, the work's surface.

Brads: These can be nearly as thin and delicate as a piece of fine wire. They come in as many thicknesses (or thinnesses) as you will ever need. The length seldom exceeds one inch, at which point you would go to a nail for that particular project. Brads are used mostly for really fine work where the joints are often glued and then secured with brads.

Staples: Mostly used where they will be inconspicuous, such as on the back of a frame, under several layers of greenery, or for tacking down wire along a baseboard. Staples come in varying sizes, the largest effectively inserted with the use of a heavy-duty staple gun or light tack hammer.

Tacks: The broad head of a tack makes it good for holding down fabrics and carpet. Use a tack hammer with a magnetized head to keep fingertips and thumbs intact.

Screws: No nail can equal the holding power of a screw. Driven by a screwdriver, these can be as small as ¼" and as long as 4-5". Brass screws are available for fancy work, while steel is used for everyday projects. Screw heads come in flat, round, or oval, and are either slotted or Phillips type. The easiest insertion of a screw is by preparing the surface with a drilled hole somewhat smaller than the screw itself. Render the screw invisible by countersinking the head below the surface of the work; then fill the hole with wood dough. Sand and finish the entire surface when dry.

Bolts: The strongest holding unit available, bolts do not rely on the strength of the material being joined; rather they go all the way through the pieces to be joined together and are tightened on the other side by twisting a nut around the bolt's fine threads. The disadvantage to using nuts and bolts is their high visibility. Use only when strength is of dominant necessity and/or when the joint will be unexposed in the finished piece.

Clamp-Downs

Clamps are neat and of great variety. We are only showing a few basic ones here. They are very versatile tools and have a great number of uses. Use these to hold items steady when you are working on a project.

C-Clamps: These come in many sizes and all basically resemble the letter "C". They are good general purpose clamps for holding two pieces of material together tightly until glue sets. To prevent marring your piece, put a thin strip of wood or plastic between the jaws of the clamp and the object itself.

Spring Clamps: Also available in several sizes, these do a job similar to the C-clamp, but don't have the gripping strength, and are best for use when really strong holding power is unnecessary. Most of these have protective plastic over the jaws.

Hand Screws: I have two of these that my Dad owned sixty years ago. The jaw opening on these is wider than that of the C-clamp, and is handy for thick workpieces. Because the jaws have such versatile movement, they can clamp many irregular shapes and sizes of work.

Bar Clamps: For delicate craft clampings—doll houses, display boxes, balsa wood items — these can adjust to very fine requirements. The larger, longer type are great for clamping wide things like butcher block table tops, cabinet sides, bookcases, and other such projects.

Corner Clamps: As the name indicates, these are great for corner joints, such as picture frames, boxes, and many other flat mitered joints.

Vise: Put this on your work table for a really handy hold-down with lots of uses. Vises come in many sizes, strengths, and jaw openings, and hold down most things you could be working on—wood, metal, plastic, wire, odd shapes ... Remember to put something between the jaws and your piece to prevent scratching and marring.

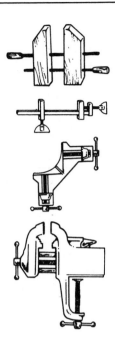

GLUES AND ADHESIVES

Knowing which glue to use in order to join two surfaces effectively is a key element of successful craftsmanship.

Adhesives have several properties: drying time, strength, ability to join uneven surfaces, flexibility, water resistance. Depending on your needs and the types of materials you are planning to glue, there are many adhesives from which to choose.

Tips on Gluing

When gluing any two surfaces together, consider these factors:

1. joint's exposure to heat, moisture, or cold
2. weight expected to sustain
3. snug joint or filler for an uneven surface joint
4. toxicity (accessibility to children and use in toy-making, as well as ventilation requirements when using)
5. environmental impact (fumes, waste ...)

- Make sure surfaces to be joined are clean and dry: dirt, dust, and grease free.
- Glue application: apply a minimum amount of adhesive onto both surfaces to be glued. Clamp, hold together, or apply pressure, and wipe off any excess glue. Don't disturb clamp until adhesive is completely dry.
- When binding a flexible material (such as fabric) to a rigid material (such as wood), apply adhesive to the rigid material only.
- When gluing porous materials: Apply glue to both surfaces, allowing it to become tacky. Apply a second coat to one surface and join.
- Avoid excess squeeze-out. Clean, using a cloth dampened with the adhesive's solvent (see manufacturer's label). Remove set glue with a putty knife or chisel. Sand glue stains.

- Clamping: Apply pressure evenly. For small jobs, use a paper clip or clothespin to hold pieces together. Wrap irregularly shaped objects with wire solder, string, or tape around the glued joint. Sometimes a wrench will serve as a clamp. For larger pieces, C-clamps come in a variety of sizes. Protect materials to be clamped with a buffer between the clamp and the object, to avoid damage to the craft piece.

TYPES OF GLUES AND THEIR USES

Glue	Special Qualities	Best for Gluing
White glue (PVA—polyvinyl acetate)	flexible, dries clear, fast-drying, non-toxic	wood, paper, fabric, leather, cork
Superglue (cyanoacrylate)	quickest setting glue available, requires no clamping, full strength in 24 hours (expensive, used only on non-porous materials, bonds skin and may require surgery to remove, so wear gloves when using)	china, porcelain, plastics
Epoxy	very strong, water-resistant, withstands heat, fills gaps between uneven surfaces (toxic)	metal, rocks/stone, ceramic, wood, glass, tile (just about anything)
Rubber cement (apply with brush or dispenser)	strong, bonds paper to many materials, dries quickly, excess easily rubbed away, rubber-cemented paper can be peeled away after use—patterns for cutting metal, glass, wood … (toxic, flammable)	paper
Spray fixative	one step easier than rubber cement	paper, fiberboard
Urethane glue	fills uneven gaps, strong, flexible, water resistant, expands as it dries	metal, plastic, glass, ceramic
Hot melt glue (apply with electric glue gun)	waterproof, fast drying, fills uneven gaps	wood, paper, fabric, plastic, glass, metal, ceramic
Acrylic medium	water soluble, non-toxic, waterproof when dry, can also be used as a varnish or protective coating	wood, paper
Aliphatic resin	grabs fast, sets quickly, resists solvents, non-toxic	wood (clamping necessary), paper, fabric, other porous materials
Silicone glue	flexible when dry, fills uneven gaps, non-toxic, water resistant	adheres objects to tile, glass, rubber, rocks, wood
Rubber latex-based	will withstand washing, dishwasher safe	fabric, vinyl, plastic

PAINTS AND OTHER COLORING MATERIALS

Knowing how to use paint, crayons, chalk, colored pencils, inks, and dyes brings the rainbow to your fingertips. Color can be added to just about anything, and these coloring tools create a medium filled with wonderful possibilities. There are many special qualities of these materials. As you use them, become aware of these properties.

Experiment with all of them, trying new techniques. The following guidelines will get you started. Again, pay careful attention to manufacturer's instructions, particularly regarding toxicity, flammability, and cleanup.

Tips on Paints, Painting, and Use of Other Materials

- Be sure surfaces are clean and grease-free before painting.
- Wear old clothing or a smock.
- Clean stained clothing immediately, before paint dries.
- Read labels and directions carefully.
- Two thin coats are better than one thick coat.
- Use lead-free paint for anything accessible to children. For toys, don't use any finishes containing lead, antimony, arsenic, cadmium, mercury, selenium, or soluble barium. Keep all paints and finishes out of reach of children and pets.
- Wood should be sanded smooth and sealed before painting. Priming or sealing prepares a porous or smooth surface to effectively receive paint or stain. Metal should be primed with a rust-inhibitive primer or Kilz spray primer.
- Put paint jar and can lids back on tightly and cleanly. Wipe excess paint away, and tap lid down tight with the side of a hammer or mallet.
- Clean brushes immediately.
- Clear spray can nozzles before putting away. Turn can upside down and spray two quick spurts to clear.

Painting Techniques

- Prime glass by painting with clear lacquer or gesso. Acrylics, tempera, or poster paints will then adhere better to the surface.
- To paint a straight line: Put masking tape around the object to be painted (glass bottle, egg, clay pot ...) and use this as a straightedge. Let paint dry 24 hours before removing tape.
- If you are not sure about your free-hand designing abilities, try transferring a design onto a surface with a light pencil, then fill in the design with paint.
- To give an antiqued effect to painted wood: Paint raw wood with acrylic colors in your chosen design, wipe on a stain when paint has dried completely, and finish with a varnish or shellac.
- Experiment with mixed media: India ink and watercolors, crayons and poster paint, ink and markers on fabric, chalks, watercolors ...
- Instead of a brush, use a sponge to apply paint for a textured look.
- Splatter paint with medicine droppers filled with different paints.

Design Your Own Christmas China

Look in the Yellow Pages for a good ceramic shop catering to the individual craftsperson. There you can find white bisque plates, cups, bowls, saucers ... and the china paints to color your own design.

Prepare the design carefully, practicing on scratch paper measured according to the pieces you will be painting. Test color combinations, proportions, and overall appearance—how the design will translate onto the dinnerware.

Take the painted ceramics back to the shop for firing and glazing. Check with the proprietor about dishwashing and general care instructions.

Consider personalizing mugs, plates, bowls, pitchers for wonderful gifts!

TYPES OF PAINTS AND OTHER COLORING MATERIALS

Cleanup: "S&W" stands for soap and water, "BC"—brush cleaner, "T"—turpentine, and "MS"—mineral spirits ... all are used to clean brushes of various paints, stains, and other finishes. See these initialed notations by each paint listed for clean-up. Follow solvent cleaning with a soap and warm water rinse.

Coloring Tool	Special Qualities	Surface Uses
PAINTS		
Watercolors (S&W)	transparent effect, non-toxic	watercolor paper, bristol board
Tempera/Poster (S&W)	opaque, solid bold color, water based, dries quickly, waterproof when dry	glossy paper, newsprint, gesso-coated surfaces
Acrylics (S&W)	fast drying, mixes to blend colors, non-toxic, water soluble, waterproof when dry, available in matte or glossy finish	paper, fabric, wood, rocks, papier-mâché, clay, baskets, eggshells, primed materials
Enamels (BC, T, MS)	smooth, durable, hard coat, dries quickly; flat, semi-gloss, high gloss finishes	plastic, primed metal, primed wood, ceramic tile, glass, clay pots, tree ornaments
Rust-inhibitive (spray or can, MS)	protects metals, spray paints easily, covers difficult areas	metals, woods
Epoxy enamel (T)	hard coat, durable	glass, plastic, laminated plastic, Formica
Oil-based (MS)	slow drying, hard finish	wood, metal
Lacquer (lacquer thinner)	hard coat, fast drying	glass, wood, porcelain
Latex (S&W)	water based, easy cleanup, comes in flat, satin, semi-gloss, and high gloss finish	wood, primed metal

TYPES OF PAINTS AND OTHER COLORING MATERIALS
(continued . . .)

OTHER COLORING MATERIALS

"Paint pens"	watercolor, acrylic, or enamel paint in a felt-tipped pen for easy, even application—great for personalizing objects	glass, fabric, plastics, paper, ceramics, wood
Fabric paints and fabric markers	water resistant, machine-washable colors, flows onto porous fabrics	most textured, non-glossy fabrics
Felt-tipped markers	permanent and watercolors, bright solid colors, mostly scroll tips available used for poster and commercial art, sharp to large tip, as well as calligraphy/scroll tips available	relatively non-porous paper (color may soak through and bleed)
Colored pencils	drawing tools, use short strokes to shade and tone	paper
Colored chalks and pastels	smudge and shading effects	charcoal, pastel, or velour-type papers with rough finish
Inks (India ink, white, gold, silver, and colors)	sharp, defined lines, vary line thickness with different nibs, or pen tips	paper (relatively non-porous), parchment
Crayons	wax colors, may be shaded by intensity and pressure, colors may be set with applied heat	paper, cardboard, eggshells, burlap
Gesso (acrylic emulsion, S&W), or "Kilz" spray primer	plaster-like substance coated onto a surface, provides a base to enhance brilliance of painted color, helps paint dry more rapidly, dries in 30 minutes to a receptive oil-proof finish	can be applied to prime most surfaces before painting: acrylic, wood, metal, terracotta, glass

❄ PAINTING WITH A SPONGE

Materials:

natural or manmade sponges
plastic bowl or plate
oil-based, acrylic, or latex paint
varnish

piece or wall primed for painting (a semi-gloss light color paint is recommended as an undercoat for acrylic and oil-based paints)

Pour a small amount of paint into the bowl or plate. Lightly dab the sponge in paint and brush against some newspaper to dry slightly. Sponge paint onto object (furniture, wood, baskets, metal, fabric, clay pots, walls ...). Apply evenly and lightly. If you plan to add a second color, allow first color to dry thoroughly beforehand. Varnish piece when dry (excluding walls).

Paint the Town

All the brushes shown here come in various sizes. Some can be as small as 3-4 hairs for fine detail work. Others come as wide as 4-6".

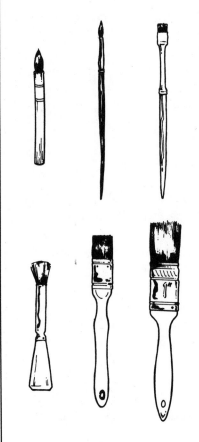

Oriental writing brush
sable brush
flat hog hair brush
stenciling brush
varnishing brush
standard paint brush

❄ SPLATTER PAINT ON FABRIC

An eyedropper or a medicine dropper works great for this; use one for each color of acrylic paint used. Droppers are available at a pharmacy.

Lay lightly moistened fabric flat over a plastic sheet (or old shower curtain). Drop colors onto the fabric and allow them to bleed into the moisture. Use small droplets or long strings of one or more colors, allowing paint to dry between colors. Dry flat. DO NOT HANG TO DRY!

This technique can brighten up T-shirts, sweatshirts, overalls, denim, bedspreads, curtains, napkins …

Care and Use of Brushes

There are several types of brushes and brush-on techniques:

Natural bristle: strong and absorbent, frequently used with oil paint and varnishes to apply thickly.

Sable: soft, absorbent "hair" brushes used for thinner coats, watercolor washes.

Nylon: less absorbent, easier to clean, good for latex, acrylic, and oil-based paints.

Stencil brush: thick, broad bristles used to "stipple" or dry-brush paint over a stencil.

Sponges, droppers: unusual tools for interesting painting effects (see above).

Toothbrushes, cotton swabs: good for painting very small areas, or for children to use for fun painting.

Brushes are available in various tip and head sizes. A broad, square head is for painting large, bold strokes; a short, pointed head is for fine detail work.

As you begin to collect an assortment of brushes for a variety of uses, it is a good idea to label the handles for specific purposes: "varnish," "enamel," "stain," "gesso," etc., and limit the brush to that specific use.

When using the same brush to apply many layers of varnish or lacquer, store the bristles suspended in turpentine to keep them soft and clean. Wipe turpentine off with an old towel or cloth before use during each application.

Never put benzine, turpentine, or other solvents in plastic. The plastic will melt. An old mayonnaise jar is better.

 When drilling into plastic, drill slowly, as the heat of fast drilling will melt the material and make a bigger hole than you intended. A heated awl sometimes works best in making a hole or slit in plastic.

STAINS AND SEALERS FOR THE "FINISHING TOUCH"

Before finishing a piece of wood, decoupage, papier-mâché ... with a stain, varnish, or other finish, make certain the entire surface is completely smooth: dust- and grease-free. Carefully read manufacturer's instructions, as well as the following ...

Types of Stains and Sealers

Lacquer: A very hard, glossy finish that dries rapidly. Lacquer does not flow on well over most paints or other finishes, and is highly flammable. Apply in several thin layers with a bristle brush. After the final coat, rub the piece with fine steel wool and apply a finishing wax after a two-day drying time. CLEAN UP with denatured alcohol or lacquer thinner.

Shellac: Used as a sealer to reduce absorbency (prime) before painting or staining, or as a final finish. Shellac dries dust-free and is ready for sanding in one hour. Apply freely with a bristle brush. Shellac will blend and smooth during the drying process. Sand, and polish with a paste wax for a warm glowing appearance. Store brush in denatured alcohol between coats and CLEAN UP with denatured alcohol as well. Shellac has a short shelf life, so purchase only as needed.

Varnish: A final coat, applied in flowing strokes after applying a sealer and giving the piece a thorough smooth sanding. Dry and sand lightly between coats, cleaning with a soft rag after sanding. CLEAN UP with benzine or turpentine, followed by soap and water.

Polyurethane: A clear, durable, water-resistant finish, which usually does not need sanding between coats if they are applied within the time specified in manufacturer's instructions. CLEAN UP using mineral spirits.

Stain: Add color and emphasize the wood grain. Wipe on with a brush or soft cloth, let stand a few minutes, then wipe off excess. Do not let stain dry and cake on wood. Always wear gloves when applying stain and other finishes. Test color on a hidden portion of the piece or a scrap of similar wood. CLEAN UP with turpentine. Apply one of the above finishes or rub with wax, oil, or polish.

Oils and Polishes: Give a rich luster to bare wood while being absorbed into the wood. These are suitable only for hardwoods, as the softer woods absorb too much of the oil. Rub over stained or bare wood with oil and a soft cloth. Two to three coats are usually sufficient. Make your own linseed oil for hardwood polish:

1 part boiled linseed oil (hardware)
1 part vinegar
1 part turpentine

Wipe off after 10-15 minutes to prevent linseed oil from darkening the wood. Let dry two days and repeat once or twice more.

Cleaning Brushes

Always clean a brush immediately after use. If you are using a solvent (turpentine, mineral spirits, benzine...), follow cleaning with a good washing in warm soapy water. Never let bristles stand on the bottom of a can or bucket. Suspend the brush, as shown, if soaking is necessary. Store with bristles upright, hang by the handle, or wrap dried brushes in foil and lay flat on their side.

If you have some *hardened brushes*, use a mixture of:

4 oz. trisodium phosphate (from the pharmacy)
one quart of hot water

Soak brushes until soft, suspending in the solution. Rinse thoroughly in clear water. *Always* wear gloves when handling the solution, being careful not to splatter.

Antiquing

There are various techniques to give woodwork an "antiqued" look:

1. Brush or wipe on a stain. Wipe off excess.
2. Make an antiquing glaze. Mix well (using old measuring spoons, not from the kitchen!):

    3 T. turpentine
    1½ t. raw umber
    3 T. clear varnish

    Flow glaze onto the piece and wipe off with textured paper towels, coarse net, or fabric.

3. Distress wood with light beatings using chains and scrap metal to effect random scratchings. Paint and/or stain.

    Add a final hard finish (varnish, shellac, polyurethane) to these "antiqued" pieces.

Working with Wood

You don't have to have a lot of sophisticated tools to work with wood. For simple ornaments and decorative shapes, use soft pine that can be cut with a hand-held coping saw, or balsa wood (available in sheets) cut with an X-acto knife and #11 blade. A hand drill can make holes for hanging, or an awl or a sharp needle will pierce balsa for threading to hang.

    Dye, paint, stain, wax, or cover wood cutouts with interesting papers (gift wrap, wallpaper, tissue paper ...) for decoration.

Paste Wax and Clear Shoe Polish: These are best for fine grain softer woods, such as pine, poplar, and willow. Sand the piece until it is very smooth and clean. Rub wood with wax or polish, coating evenly for a smooth, clear finish. Use non-toxic wax for toys and puzzles. Buff to shine with a clean cloth.

Household Dyes: Household dyes can be used to stain wood. Mix colors of dye to create various shades. Dissolve one package dye in one pint hot (not boiling) water. Test color on hidden part of piece. If color is too dark, add water; too light, add a bit more dye. After wood has been sanded smooth—and wiped clean and grease-free—apply dye with a brush, sponge, or clean cloth ... or immerse object into dye until proper coloring is achieved. Sand lightly and finish as desired. This dye is also good to use for stenciling projects.

Notes on Finishing

- Buy small quantities of finishes gauged to your present needs. These tend to harden and "glop" with age, and don't store well.
- Never stir varnish. Stirring creates bubbles on the project surface.
- Tap brush tip against inside of the can to shake off excess varnish. Never rub against the can's outer rim.
- Flow finishes on *with* the wood grain. Next, brush *against* the grain. Apply a final coat, lightly brushing again *with* the grain.
- When dry, sand varnish and other finishes lightly with fine steel wool between each coat, sanding *with* the wood grain.
- The number of coats needed depends on the nature of the project. Check manufacturer's instructions, project directions, and follow your own gut instinct. The more coats you apply, the richer the finish. Several thin coats are better than a few thick coats—always.
- Store all paints, stains, and finishes at room temperature, tightly closed, and out of reach of children and pets. Clean rim of can and lid of all excess paint or finish, using an old cloth. Place lid on can and cover with cloth to prevent spattering. Lightly tap lid down with the side of a hammer until closed.
- Remove old finishes with an appropriate commercial stain and varnish remover.

    As with any commercial product, carefully follow all manufacturer's instructions, paying close attention to surface preparation, number of coats needed, drying time, cleanup, and storage requirements.

WORKING WITH METAL

    With just a few tools and a little ingenuity, you could be making ornaments for the tree, a mobile for the kitchen window, a stand-up sculpture for your daughter's bookshelf ...

Materials

clean, empty tin cans or sheet metal (aluminum flashing, copper, brass, bronze ...)
tin snips, metal shears, or coping saw with carbide-tipped blade
round file, sandpaper, steel wool
pliers, awl, or punch
claw hammer, ball peen hammer, or rubber mallet
glue (epoxy, urethane, hot melt glue)
Kilz spray primer
paint (rust inhibitive, enamels, oils, paint pens, permanent markers)
acrylic spray (for finishing painted piece)

Cutting up the Can: Remove the bottom and lid with a can opener. Save these for other projects. With a continuous motion, use tin snips to cut down the seam of the can and spread it out flat. Cut away the rim.

Smoothing the Rough Edges: Place flattened metal sheet on a hard surface and smooth edges with a hammer. File and sand smooth.

Making Objects with Metal

- Always use a continuous motion when cutting to avoid slivers and jagged edges.
- Make a pattern with paper, attach to metal with rubber cement, cut around shape, and then peel off pattern.
- Beat piece with the ball end of a ball peen hammer to give it texture and shine.
- Polish metal with steel wool or buffing compound and clean chamois cloth. Give texture by rubbing with coarse sandpaper.
- Remove lacquer finish by wiping with turpentine, mineral spirits, or ammonia. Rub off gummy adhesive with lighter fluid.
- Or prepare metal surface with Kilz spray primer, providing an oil-free base receptive to paints and inks.
- "Punch" unbroken indentations with an awl or a punch to make a raised pattern. Pierce all the way through for eyes and pierced designs.
- Use the snips to fringe edges for an unusual effect.
- Bend metal over pipes, wood, balls, and other forms, hammering gently with a rubber mallet to shape. Use pliers for added support and to twist into shapes.
- Clean rusty metal with benzine and scrape smooth with steel wool.
- Heating makes metal softer and more pliable. Hammering makes it harder and more brittle.

PAPERS FOR CREATIVE USE

Papercraft includes such art techniques as origami—the ancient Oriental technique of folding paper to sculpt shapes; paper-cutting—intricate cuts made to achieve a silhouetted design; brass rubbings—reproducing a raised or engraved surface on paper by rubbing over the texture ...

Metalcraft Ideas

- Cut ornaments from sheeting and can lids in the shapes of snowflakes, stars, angels, gingerbread figures, and other Christmas shapes; also, hearts, houses, cats, dogs, ducks, bears, weathervane figures ...
- Make a metal mobile (dangling objects that don't touch).
- Construct a wind chime (dangling objects that do touch to chime and jingle with movement).
- Make cutout and pierced or punched wall hangings (trace weathervane patterns, quilt and cookie cutter shapes ...).
- Learn to use an electric solder gun and create standing sculptures, nativity figures, miniature accessories for a doll house or scene ...

Craft metals are available at hardware and craft stores in sheet and wire forms. Choose #18-26 gauge metals — the higher the gauge, the lighter and thinner the sheet or wire. Copper, brass, tin, aluminum, and pewter are popular craft metals. Use the library for more information on detailed metalwork: chasing, embossing, soldering, riveting seams ...

We like to give homemade gifts for Christmas. Would you like one of our kids?
— quoted from a Pam Marker cocktail napkin

We use paper to paint, draw, and color on ... to cut, fold, and shape ... to make collages, cards, and mobiles, mats, wraps and rolls ...

Types of Papers

Bristol Board: Comes rough or smooth at art supply stores in 1, 2, 3, 4, or 5 ply (thickness) weights. Takes ink, watercolor and tempera.

Mat Stock: Heavy board used to mat pictures for framing. Scrap is sometimes available at framers' studios. Cut against a straightedge, using an X-acto or mat knife. Good for mixed media (ink and watercolors).

Construction Paper: Varied colors available at art supply and other stores. Takes chalk, crayons, or colored pencils. Too porous for ink or paint.

Parchment: Available in light to heavy weights, has a translucent quality excellent for ink, calligraphy, scrolls, and fancy printing.

Vellum: Has a high rag content for a smooth, non-porous surface (good for ink), printer's stock.

Bond: Cotton fiber paper for stationery, notecards.

Stencil Paper: Semi-transparent oiled or waxed paper that can be used to trace and cut stencil designs.

Stencil Board: Flexible, oiled board-type paper with more durability than stencil paper, for use in repetitive stenciling projects.

Blotting Paper: Absorbs moisture, good for pressing flowers.

Tracing Paper: Translucent, easily erasable, in a smooth white finish.

Carbon Paper: Lightweight paper with carbon on one side for making transfers onto another surface.

Newsprint: Lightweight paper made of ground wood pulp and chemical pulp, best for dry art forms.

Tissue Paper: Light translucent paper which intensifies in color, producing interesting effects when layered and glued or varnished.

Rice Paper: Thin, textured paper in various weights and colors.

Parchment Effect: Rub both sides of bond paper with a small amount of salad oil on a cotton ball. Dry thoroughly, about two days.

Marbleized Effect: Melt colored wax crayons in a coffee can sitting in hot water (not *you*, the can!). Stir with a wooden stick. Use an old paint brush to coat paper lightly with melted wax. To prevent buckling, block by pinning paper, stretched tightly, to a piece of cardboard. Dry thoroughly. Press the underside lightly with a warm iron. This is a fun way to make gift wrap.

Other Papers Used in Crafts

clear or colored cellophane
colored and silver foil
Contact paper (clear, solid colors,
   and patterned designs)
crepe paper

gift wrap
gold and silver paper
handmade paper
recycled paper
wallpaper

How to Make (Recycle) Your Own Paper

Materials:
2 flat 8 x 10 wood frames
mesh screening
heavy staples, staple gun
duct tape
used paper
bucket
blender
plastic tub
newspaper

paper towels
sponge
dried flowers/leaves
natural dyes
white craftpaper
used paper scraps
(newsprint and glossy papers are
    not suitable for this project)

Shred or tear paper and soak pieces several hours in a bucket filled with enough water to cover paper adequately. To add color, use colored paper or add dye or natural color items (fresh flower petals, leaves ...). Use a separate bucket for each different color. Staple mesh screen to frame and secure with duct tape. Wrap second frame with duct tape to make an outline for the paper.

Fill blender halfway with water. Add a little soaked paper to blender and process. Continue to add and blend paper until mixture has the consistency of puréed peas. After blending the pulp, you can add other items for texture (dried flowers, thread pieces, leaves ...), sparkle (glitter, silver and gold stars ...), dimension (hole-punched contrasting color paper or confetti). Stir in textural additions. Empty contents of blender into a plastic tub. Spread flattened paper toweling on newspaper on the floor or table next to tub. Dip frames into pulp mixture—screen side up with stabilizing frame on top—and lift straight out. Shake to remove excess water and lift top frame off. Pulp should stick to the bottom frame. Carefully turn screening over and lay pulp side down on flat paper towel on newspaper. Press hard to squeeze out water and push sponge against back of screen to blot remaining water until mostly absorbed. Lift frame slowly, leaving pulp on paper towel. Turn towel with paper over onto white or brown craftpaper to dry, pressing again with a rolling pin if thinner paper is desired. Slowly peel off paper towel and let paper dry completely (one to two days). Keep a box or bag full of paper scraps until you have enough to do this.

LETTERING AND DESIGN

The art of hand-lettering has also seen a tremendous revival in the past few years. Take a course or teach yourself (practice makes perfect) to use the many pens and styles of lettering available.

Paper Terms

Deckle-edged — rough, torn edge in same or contrasting color

Tooth — roughness of paper fibers

Plate—smooth surface

Kid or Vellum—matte, or dull, surface

Ream—500 sheets

The weight of paper is determined by the number of pounds per ream.

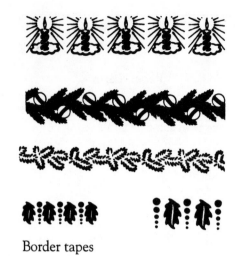

Border tapes

Pay careful attention to spacing, using a straightedge, precise measurement, and lightly penciled-in lines, or a lined sheet over a light box, as a guide. When preparing hand-lettering and designs for a printer, use a non-reproducible blue pencil (available at art supply stores) to line up your work.

Tools Available for Lettering and Design

Calligraphy Pens: Available for dipping in ink, using with ink cartridges, or in felt tip. Various "nibs" (points) produce wide to narrow strokes. Special pens allow you to do fancy scrollwork, double lines ...

Tracing Folios: For tracing curved lines. These come in many sizes and shapes.

Templates: Metal or plastic pattern plates. With these you can trace uniform shapes (stars, ellipses, curves, circles ...) with speed and accuracy.

T-Square: For drawing parallel lines and 90° angles.

Protractor: For measuring and drawing any degree angle.

Compass: For drawing precise circles of various radii.

Letter and Number Stencils: In numerous shapes, sizes, and styles, for tracing uniform letters and numbers.

Peel-Off or Rub-On Lettering: Available in a variety of sizes, colors, and print styles.

Border Tapes: Adhesive border in multiple designs and sizes for setting up camera-ready copy for reproduction by a professional printer.

There are also several basic camera-ready design aids available (stars, snowflakes, hearts, entire snowy village scenes ...) for making greeting cards, printed invitations, and other printed materials. Look for these in art supply stores or ask printer.

How to Enlarge or Reduce a Pattern

To Enlarge: Make a tracing of the pattern. Mark off the tracing with squares (¼" for small designs, ½" to 1" for larger ones) in a grid pattern. Make a copy sheet with squares enlarged in the proportion you wish to duplicate. (Example: If your original is marked off in 1" squares and you wish to double the size of the tracing, mark off your copy sheet in 2" squares). Carefully reproduce the lines and curves of the original design onto the corresponding squares of the enlarged copy, one at a time.

To Reduce: Reverse the above process, using proportionately smaller squares on the copy sheet.

How to Trace and Transfer a Design

Use tracing or lightweight bond (typing) paper. Lay paper over the pattern to be reproduced. Tape to the page to hold in place. Trace outline of desired design with a sharp-pointed pencil. Remove the tracing paper.

To transfer the pattern to another piece of paper, fabric, or other flat surface, rub over the back of the tracing paper with a soft-leaded pencil, covering the entire design. Tape the tracing (soft-leaded side down) to the surface onto which you want the design to reappear. Trace over the lines on the right side of tracing with a sharp pencil. The soft lead underside will transfer onto the clean paper or surface.

To transfer a design to a dark surface, use dressmaker's chalk instead of the soft-leaded pencil on the back of the tracing. Follow the same technique.

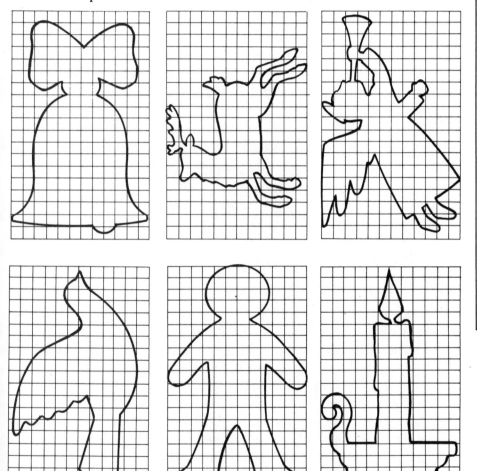

Sample patterns for wood, metal, paper, or fabric cut-outs

Build a Birdhouse or Bird Feeder

Birds get *hungry* — especially in the winter, when the ground is frozen (which is one reason God put berries on bushes during the cold season!). But imagine how many calories it takes flying all over the place looking for those berries. There is tremendous pleasure to be found watching all kinds of different birds come to your house for dinner. You can make bird feeders or houses with so many different materials — from plastic milk jugs cut with a heated awl and filled with seed to meticulously hand-painted and varnished dollhouse woods and moldings. Some of the nicest are the very natural open ones made from rough wood — a base to hold the seed, with two end-pieces to support a slanted roof. Drill holes at the top and twist in a curved piece of 18 gauge wire for hanging, fill with seed, and stand back! Make several for gifts, but keep at least one for yourselves.

 A light box is constructed by putting a source of light (bulb) inside a cardboard or wood box cut to hold a slanted translucent glass or acrylic writing surface. Different-sized lined sheets serve as guides under writing paper—the light makes the lines visible to the writer.

Craft Workbasket

These basic tools and supplies will get you through most handicraft projects:

aluminum foil
awl
brayer
brush cleaner
cheesecloth
clear plastic spray
cloth diaper rags
clothespins
coping saw
decoupage scissors (manicure)
denatured alcohol
epoxy glue
eraser
floral tape, clay, wire
gesso
gloves
hammers
ice pick
long-nosed pliers
masking tape
measuring tape

(continued …)

How to Transfer Magazine or Newspaper Prints to an Alternative Surface

For color or black and white prints, mix:

4 oz. water	2 oz. turpentine
1 squirt dishwashing liquid	

Shake mixture thoroughly in a jar. Brush mixture over the picture to be transferred. Blot gently with paper towels. Place white paper flat and lay the moistened picture face down on top. Rub evenly with a spoon. A reversed copy should appear on the blank paper. This is a fun "scientific" trick for making gift wrap and greeting cards.

KIDSCRAFTS

Guiding children eager to learn into the world of arts and crafts is as fine a gift as you can give. Stimulating curiosity and imagination, encouraging invention and innovation, and introducing little hands and minds to a lifetime of thoughtful and creative production—what could be more valuable than this?

There will be times, perhaps many, when it just doesn't work. But when it does, and you share together in discovery, it's a memorable experience for you both.

Guidelines for Working with Children

To ensure a positive outcome of creating together:

- Allow plenty of time and energy to keep craft time fun, friendly, and relaxed.
- Be patient and positive yet gently encourage practice of skills. Too much praise does not encourage invention and improvement. Too little discourages. Period.
- Explore the many possibilities of a tool, craft procedure, material, natural resource. Allow self-initiated experimentation. Experience together the many different shapes, textures, and colors of the world. Enjoy the materials and tools that you use.
- Advocate good clean fun and responsible creativity: keep craft materials in reasonably good order, teach safe and efficient use of tools, and clean up the high-spirited mess *together*, even if it takes longer.

Making a game of working with craft objects makes learning fun and skills longer lasting. Try some of these.

 If neither you nor the child is into this kind of thing—forget it. Find something else you both can enjoy together.

Introductory Skills for Experimenting and Initiating (For All Ages)

Sort nails, screws, nuts, and bolts by size and category.
Tear, crumple, and twist paper into shapes.
Punch holes into various papers (and save for New Year's Eve confetti!).
Glue together various objects.
Use scissors on flat and folded materials.
Hammer nails and turn screws into scrap wood.
Sand, file, and/or plane wood and rusty metal.
Lace yarn through punched paper cards.
Mix coloring media.
Drill various-sized holes with a hand-drill.
Measure, draw, trace, stencil, use templates and folios.
Shape clay.

Exposing a young person to these and other basic skills will be the foundation upon which to discover and nurture talent and creativity—at Christmas and all through the years. A more life-enriching gift you could never give.

CRAFT MEDIA

You don't have to spend a lot of money to make things. Be creative with what you've got—make something of it! Recycle everyday objects found around the house, such as:

airline miniature bottles	old picture frames/glass
baby food jars	pantyhose eggshells
balloons	paper scraps
baskets	pine cones
broken toy pieces	pipe cleaners
cardboard boxes	plastic berry baskets
chicken eggshells	plastic milk jugs
clay pots/broken ceramics	ribbon
cork	rocks
detergent bottles	seeds/beans
fabric	socks/stockings
glitter	spools
golf/tennis/ping-pong balls	straw brooms
interesting bottles	string
makeup sponges, brushes, pads	Styrofoam blocks, balls, cones
milk/oatmeal cartons	tin plates/cans
mirrors from old compacts	wine bottles
mushroom boxes	wooden blocks
old glassware/flatware	yarn
old greeting cards	atrocious objets d'art and other
old jewelry/jewelry pieces	yard sale salvage(!)

(continued ...)

nails, screws
newspapers
notebook/file box
paintbrushes
paints
paper clips
paper cups/juice cans
paper towels
pliers
popsicle sticks
rubber bands
ruler
sandpaper
scissors
screwdrivers
sponges
stains
steel wool
string
varnish
white glue
wire and wire cutter
X-acto knife

Organize a workshop of hanging peach baskets, old mugs and cups, and other nifty containers filled with these craft supplies for easy accessibility. Store sharp tools inserted in cork or a piece of Styrofoam.

Plaster of Paris Molds

Making "sculpture" from plaster of Paris is inexpensive and easy. Buy the dry powder at a hardware store and mix as directed.

To color plaster, add one packet of household dye to one quart of hot water. Mix 4 oz. or ½ c. dye to each pound of dry plaster.

To mold plaster, lubricate rubber, plastic, aluminum, or wood molds with liquid soap or shortening to prevent sticking. Pour in wet plaster and scratch in signature, date, and other impressions on the surface while plaster is still wet. Allow plaster to dry and gently tap out.

For hanging: make a hole with a straw set in the plaster piece while still wet.

Paint dried plaster with watercolors, acrylics, or enamel paints, and varnish for extra sheen and durability.

Keep a large craft box or bag stored away for continuous hoarding of recyclable materials and supplies. The more you work with these things, the more possibilities you will see in everyday "junque!" Make something new from something old, or create works of "ART" from interesting "found" objects.

MAKING CRAFT FACES AND FIGURES

Many times throughout *The Christmas Lover's Handbook* I have advocated the use of figures and miniatures in holiday decorating.

The fascination with "little people" begins when we are small. We collect dolls, Star Wars figures, Ninjas, and toy soldiers ... and when we get bigger, some of us still enjoy collecting figures and miniatures — Kathy has an assemblage of bears, E.J. loves clowns, Renie furnishes dollhouses ...

Collecting miniature characters, animals, and other little creatures is made even more fun by learning how to create your own, using a diversity of materials and techniques. Make tree ornaments, people your nativity scene or electric train village, decorate packages or wreaths, or create a new generation of collectors by giving your handily-crafted miniatures as gifts. Look what the imagination of Mr. Marvelous Jim Henson did for the Muppets!

Apples—Apple Head Dolls

Hard, late fall apples are best for this craft. They need to dry out over a three- to five-week period, so begin in mid-November or sooner for holiday decorating.

 Winesap, Red Delicious, and Rome apples are best. Golden Delicious gives skin a lighter appearance, as does soaking the apple in lemon juice after carving.

To make a standing figure, carefully insert a wooden chopstick or heavy wire loop up ¾ of the way through the core and surround with a sturdy wire armature to be dressed or covered with papier-mâché.

For hanging as an ornament, leave the stem and tie with a ribbon or cord.

Stand or hang apple heads in a warm, dry place for three to five weeks. The face will shrivel when dry to reveal a wrinkled, leathery old soul.

Peel apples carefully. Using a paring knife, fork, or baby spoon, carve features into the apple, cutting fairly deeply. Triangles make delightful wrinkled old eyes, slits form eyebrows. Carve out the sides of a nose, cheekbones, and a pointed or dimpled chin. A curved slit makes a smiling mouth, while a straight cut gives a more serious countenance. Use a fork or fingernail to create lines and wrinkles, more of which will appear with the drying process.

If you like, insert whole cloves for each eye and use rice for teeth. Beans, beads, and seeds also add dimension and interest.

Standing Wood-Cuts

Yellow pine 1-2" thick may be cut with an electric jigsaw or a hand-held coping saw to make many Christmas shapes and figures.

Draw a simple design on the wood or transfer a pattern from a magazine or book. Weathervane figures are popular designs. Cut with the saw, following lines carefully. Use an awl or a drill bit to make eyes or pattern indentations in your figures. A chisel carves away shavings to add more texture. Sand finished wood pieces with a fine grade sandpaper until very smooth. Pine is a lovely white wood, and a clear finish is often best to highlight its natural beauty.

If desired, use white glue to attach paper or fabric clothing or texture to your figures and varnish over all as you would with decoupage. Several coats of varnish will make the decoration appear part of the wood. Fake fur can be glued on figures to make animals and other hairy creatures. Insert wire or broomstraw for various appendages or porcupine needles … Or simply paint and finish with a protective varnish.

Carved Plaster of Paris

Mix equal portions of dry plaster of Paris and vermiculite (available at garden supply stores). Add water slowly until mixture is the consistency of thick cream. Pour into an appropriately-sized container (wax milk cartons are best) and allow to harden overnight.

Peel away the carton when completely dry. This soft carving material can be shaped with kitchen tools—a table knife, spoon, fork …

For color add food coloring to the plaster while mixing, or paint with acrylics when carving is completed.

How to Empty a Raw Egg

Make a small hole in the top of the egg with an ice pick or a large needle. Invert the egg and make a somewhat larger hole on the bottom, carefully puncturing the membrane and yolk. Gently blow through the top hole, allowing egg to fall into a dish. Save this for baking, breakfast, or eggnog! Run a light stream of water through the egg to clean it out and set aside to dry in an empty egg carton until ready to paint or decorate.

Just a Few More Suggestions for Creating Characters

air freshener containers
bottles, jars, jugs
cookie dough
fruits and vegetables
pine cones
plastic pill bottles
nuts in shell
stiff papers and cardboard
Styrofoam balls
wood clothespins
wood spools and spindles
wooden spoons

Take an object, any object and, as if by magic, create a brand-new little being. Kids and grownups alike will enjoy the challenge of making something (or somebody) from "nothing."

Wire Sculpture

Heavy gauge wire can be twisted and turned to make lots of things, including standing figures. Use your pliers and wire-cutters to bend, cut, and connect pieces of wire along the lines of an Alexander Calder mobile or standing sculpture. You can staple the base (with a heavy-duty staple gun) to a painted or stained wood block to stand the character up on his/her/its own two (six?) feet.

Candles and Melted Wax

Using whipped candle wax (see page 194), spread and shape with a wooden spoon to cover a small votive candle or a large 3-4" diameter candle. Make a snowman or round Santa, gnome, or set of turtledoves … With different colors of wax or heated crayons, drip a few drops here and there, or add some craft accessory trimmings to create just about anything or anybody with wax.

Or you can pour melted wax into petroleum jelly-greased molds (candy or gelatin molds) to make other shapes. These will become candles you will never want to burn.

Eggs

Paint on clean emptied eggs using acrylics, enamel, or felt-tip markers. Glue on yarn, craft eyes, fabric … to make features and give dimension to your characters.

For standing figures, use a small amount of floral or modeling clay to stand egg upright on a base (an inverted cup or a small bowl) or glue on a stiff paper "collar." For hanging, glue a narrow ribbon around the egg lengthwise, leaving enough excess on top to hang. Or use a long needle passed through the top of the egg and out the bottom. Tie a small button or filigreed mount onto the bottom of a length of thread and hang with the excess thread tied at the top.

Rocks

Collect smooth rocks in the woods or mountains, or at the beach. Or buy select pebbles and stones from a lapidary or rock hobby shop. To smooth a rough surface, apply two or three coats of gesso or one spraying of Kilz before painting with acrylics, India ink, or felt tip markers.

Household cement, epoxy, or white glue mixed with sand (2 parts glue to one part sand) will effectively join one rock to another and also adhere craft trim to a smooth surface.

Make people, animals, paperweights, bookends, a candleholder, a unique centerpiece wreath, or simply an "objet d'art"! Every grandparent should have a handmade rock paperweight with "World's Best Grandma" or some originally clever saying inscribed thereon!

Corn Husks

Prepared corn husks are available at craft supply stores, or you can make your own. Use husks that have dried in the field, if possible, and complete drying on a well-ventilated screen until the husk is light brown. This takes about two weeks.

Soak husks in lukewarm water. You can tint the water with food coloring if you wish. Keep husks moist as you mold them into figures and shapes. Tie a bunch of corn husks together with string or yarn to create an armature or a body. Using an X-acto knife, cut and pull out portions of the sheaves to make arms, tying at the "wrist" for hands. Fold and curl individual husks and secure with craft pins to add dimension and design.

Add clothing, yarn, ribbon, or acrylic paint (or spray the entire figure gold) to give personality to your "husky" men, women, and creatures.

Corn husks are also good for making wreaths and miniature trees. Curl, tie, and pin onto Styrofoam forms to create many things with this early American craft material.

Corn Cobs

Cut all kernels off a fresh ear of corn and cut the ear into 1½" sections. Dry on a screen until hard. Use white glue to add eyes, cord, yarn, fabric hats, hair ... These can be the faces for corn husk figures, or use them to make a set of refrigerator magnets (glue magnets on back) or tree ornaments (glue ribbon around circumference).

Pre-Starched Fabric

This material is available in fabric and craft stores, or you can dip your own scrap fabric in liquid starch for a similar effect.

Dip pre-starched fabric in water just to moisten. Using craft or straight pins, pin fabric over a wire or Styrofoam armature, draping loosely and creating folds to give shape. Let dry and coat entire figure with gesso or Kilz. Paint with acrylics or spray paint all over. Glue paper toweling, fabric, netting, doilies ... over flat surfaces for texture. Finish with spray paint, clear acrylic spray, varnish, or shellac. This medium makes a lovely Madonna and Child for your mantel.

CANDLE-MAKING

When you "Deck the Halls" with candles, make them yourself. The materials are inexpensive and the possibilities for invention endless.

Think back to grade school and the ice candles you made in milk cartons. Weren't they neat? Just because you're grownup now doesn't mean you can't recreate the magic some December afternoon.

Use shape, texture, and color to make some conversation-piece candles for Christmas decorating and gifts.

Take a pre-holiday tour of the friendly neighborhood craft store to peruse every shelf for neat and new crafting materials. You won't believe what's out there ... and what you might do with it. But you will be inspired all the same. CAUTION: Plan carefully or you'll spend a fortune, often our eyes are bigger than our free time.

Pour leftover melted wax into miniature terracotta pots, insert a wick, and make little candle-pots to have on hand for electrical outages, summer evenings outdoors, and soft decorative lighting all through the house.

Materials

paraffin wax (available in bar form at the grocery store)
beeswax (optional—more expensive than paraffin, but a little of this added to your candles raises the melting point and gives off a wonderful scent)
stearine (available at craft stores, this makes your candles harder, more opaque, and slower-burning, but is also optional for the occasional candle-maker)
candlewick (also available at craft stores, or make your own)
coloring supplies (candle stubs, wax crayons, or commercial candle dyes)
coffee can (bend top to form a spout)
silicone spray or vegetable oil

Melting the Wax: The amount of wax you need varies with the number and size candles you make. Start small and work your way up to full-scale production. See page 233 for uses for leftover wax.

Chop wax into small pieces. Melt in the coffee can, which has been placed in hot (not boiling) water. Use a clean stick to stir the wax until melted. Add stearine at this point if you are using this:

3 T. stearine powder per pound of wax

Coloring the Wax: For colorful candles, add a small amount of wax dye (follow package directions), wax crayon pieces (2" crayon per one cup of wax), or chopped candle stubs (remove wick) to melting wax. Stir well, adding more color to darken, more paraffin to lighten.

Using a Mold: Candle molds are available in craft shops, or you can use your imagination with various household items: milk cartons, empty eggshells, juice cans, yogurt cups, old glass ball ornaments, kitchen or cookie molds … Oil molds with vegetable oil or silicone spray for easy removal when candle has set. Paper molds may be torn away. Eggshell and glass ball molds must be cracked and peeled off.

Making Your Own Candlewick: Soak 12' of soft cotton string in a solution of:

1 T. salt
2 T. borax

1 c. water

Hang to dry on a wire coat hanger. Coat with melted wax before using in a candle. Cut as needed.

The diameter of your candle determines the thickness of wick required. A wick that is too thick will smoke; one that is too thin will be quickly extinguished by melting wax. Follow these guidelines:

thin wick: candle is 2" or less in diameter
regular wick: candle is 2-4" in diameter
thick wick: candle is 4" or more in diameter

Pouring the Wax: After dipping the wick in melted wax to cover, tie it to a pencil, leaving a 2" excess at the top, and hang over the center of the mold until it touches the bottom. Be sure the wick is centered, taut and secure before pouring the wax.

Pour the wax slowly down the sides of the mold (to prevent air bubbles). Fill the mold ¾ full. Let candle harden overnight.

Removing the Candle: Tap sides of the mold and dip in hot water to release candle. Polish with a clean cloth and cut wick to 1" on burning end. Allow candle to cure at least one week before burning.

Decorating Candles

Use the warmed tip of a contrast color crayon or candle stub to drip a wax design onto the sides of your candle. Paint plain candles with acrylics. Or compose unique candles during the molding process with one of these techniques …

For Multi-Colored Layers: Pour one color of wax at a time into the mold, allowing to set completely. Then pour subsequent layers, for a rainbow effect, letting each color set before adding another. By tilting the mold, you can get interesting results with your layering.

For Unusual Shapes: Fill a container with sand, crinkle aluminum foil, and push it down into a depression in the sand. Pour wax into the foil. Allow candle to harden and peel off foil.

For Making Those Crazy Ice Candles: Pour a thin layer of melted wax into a wax milk carton. Insert a regular candle (of height equal to or less than that of the carton) into the melted wax base and hold still until set. Let harden completely. Add ice cubes almost to the top of the candle. Pour in remaining melted wax over the ice, leaving candle wick exposed at the top. Let harden. Peel away carton over sink, in order to drain the water.

For Adding a Wick to Wax Candles Already Hardened: Heat an ice pick and make a wick hole down into the candle. Insert a wax wick wired with #26 gauge wire. Fill hole with melted wax to secure wick. Wire will melt away during burning.

Uses for Leftover Wax

- Whip leftover clean paraffin wax to seal homemade jellies and preserves. Or spread whipped wax over a votive candle to make snowball or candle figures.
- Oil cookie molds and pour wax into the mold until half full. Let harden. Lay a string, wire, or narrow ribbon across the wax, leaving a 4" excess for hanging, and fill with more melted wax. Let harden and remove. Paint or decorate if desired and hang as a tree ornament.
- Paint emptied eggshells with melted wax. Dip into egg dye. Waxed portions will remain uncolored to reveal your design.
- Drip melted wax down empty wine bottles or jars for decoration, or to lend ambiance to your next Italian spaghetti supper!

Make it Easy on Yourself

Commercial papier-mâché pulp is available in most craft stores. Simply add water and form over armature as directed.

Other Papier-Mâché Projects

Papier-mâché decorates almost anything that holds glue

> covered boxes, glass, metal containers …
> jewelry
> lampshades
> masks
> miniature figures/scenery
> napkin rings
> picture frames
> puppets/toys
> sculpture
> terracotta pots
> trays and plates

PAPIER-MACHÉ

The French call it "chewed paper" and it is just that—shredded or torn paper, mixed with glue to make a paste suitable for sculpting over an armature.

Sculpting with Papier-Mâché

The armature is the base "skeleton" of the structure. Much of the skill in the art of papier-mâché is building an effective armature over which to mold the paper "paste."

One of the most common materials (remember grade school "planets"??) is a balloon. Cutout cardboard is another useful base material, as are wire mesh screening and molded chicken wire. Rolls and balls of newspaper, boxes, tin cans, milk cartons, Styrofoam shapes, cardboard tubes, drinking straws, bottles, jars, old clay pots … these and many more regular household items used individually or in combination make fine armatures.

Use masking tape, string, and wire to combine more than one item as an armature. Fill in gaps and shape with balls of paper, cotton, fabric scraps, and other soft materials. Wrap the completed form with tape or gauze to hold the shape together before covering with the papier-mâché.

Paste: Use powdered wallpaper wheat paste or make your own. If using the wallpaper paste, mix powder in a ratio of 10 parts water to one part powder.

To make your own paste, mix 1 c. flour and 1 c. water. Cook until bubbles appear and mixture begins to thicken. Cool before using.

Or simply mix ½ c. flour and ³/₈ c. water until smooth, the consistency of cake batter.

Put paste in a flat aluminum pie pan for dipping or mixing.

Papier-Mâché — Strips: Tear, don't cut, newspapers lengthwise in 1" wide strips. Dip strips in paste and begin wrapping over the armature to accomplish the desired shape and contour. Alternate the direction of strips to achieve a built-up effect. When the paste strips have dried on the completed form, use a brush to cover the object with two layers of white glue. Paint when glue has dried and cover with varnish.

Papier-Mâche — Pulp: This produces a smooth surface when sanded and is used for more sophisticated papier-mâché projects. Shred single pages of newspapers and moisten in a large pan filled with two quarts of hot water. Stir to separate paper pieces for even distribution of moisture. Soak overnight. Using a wire whisk or hand beater, beat the paper to a pulp (literally!) and strain or squeeze through fingers to remove excess water, leaving a soft, moist ball. Add 2 T. white glue and 2 T. wallpaper paste (or homemade paste) to pulp and stir to remove lumps. A few drops of oil of wintergreen will prevent mold growth and improve the smell. Spread onto armature to build up the sculpture. Sand when dry, paint, and varnish.

Tips for Papier-Mâché

- When using a form for molding that will not remain a part of the project (stainless steel bowl, football helmet …), grease the form with petroleum jelly or shortening. When papier-mâché dries, lift it off or cut the piece in half with an X-acto knife, and remove while still only partially dry. Reassemble, using freshly pasted strips to join.
- Lightly sanding a papier-mâché project when it dries will give a smoother surface, effecting better adhesion of paint and varnish.
- Combine strip and pulp construction for various projects—strips, to build up the body and secure shaped balls and rolls; and pulp, to smooth and add raised features and texture.
- Dry projects overnight or in a low (200° F) oven.
- Paint papier-mâché with any water-based paint. Finish with a clear acrylic spray or varnish (three or four coats).
- Colored tissue paper or paper towels dipped in glue or paste add color and texture to papier-mâché projects.

**Make it Easy on Yourself
Stenciling:**

Use a foam meat tray as your stencil board. Cut your design with an X-acto knife and stencil greeting cards, envelopes, gift wrap, giftbags …

Make a Piñata for Christmas Celebration

Cover a large balloon with papier-mâché as above, using two layers of strips or pulp—so piñata is sturdy without being impenetrable—leaving an opening in the back for inserting trinkets and treats. Tie a string to the top and hang to dry thoroughly. Pop and remove the balloon, fill with goodies, and cover hole with a few moistened strips of papier-mâché, masking tape, or glued tissue paper. Paint and/or use strips of fringed tissue paper to decorate.

Blindfold the holder of a bat or stick and let participants stand by to scramble for the treats when the "batter" finally strikes (everything) out!

For a Santa Claus piñata, make a cap of poster paper and trim with a fat white pompom. Use fringed tissue or construction paper, rolled cotton batting, or polyester fiberfill to make the beard. Take a picture—so you can keep your Christmas piñata forever, even after it has been smashed to pieces!

Remember to leave "ties" when cutting stencils

STENCILING

Why are so many of colonial America's now precious antiques stenciled? Because early Americans could neither afford nor import the expensive wallpapers and elaborate furniture available in Europe. Consequently, an ancient craft saw revival in the 18th century as an inexpensive decorative art.

Stenciling can be used from everything to putting cutesy heart and duck shapes on a nursery wall to dramatic "faux" designs and inlays on wood and painted objects. The stencil is merely the pattern for transferring the design or shape one or many times onto a receptive surface.

Materials

sharp cutting knife (X-acto with a #16 blade)
tracing paper
carbon paper
stencil paper (available in translucent, for direct tracing, or a heavier oiled "board" for durability in repetitive stenciling projects)
masking tape
acrylic or stencil paints (or household dye)
stenciling brushes (thick, stiff bristles for "dry" painting)
small brushes for detail work

Creating the Design: Trace a design you have copied or created onto thin tracing paper. Transfer the design, using a piece of carbon paper, face down onto stencil paper.

To create symmetrical designs, fold paper in half and draw half of the design on one side. Cut out the entire design and open the fold. For more complicated designs, fold the paper three or four times before cutting. Disconnected lines, called "ties," create an effective outline for stenciling projects. Tape your cutout design to stencil paper and trace. (You can also buy pre-cut stencils at craft and hobby stores.)

Cutting the Stencil: Attach stencil paper with traced design onto a piece of cardboard, wood, or glass with masking tape. Using a sharp blade, hold the knife perpendicular to the stencil and pull evenly toward the bottom edge of the paper. Turn the paper as you cut. Cut the small shapes first, larger ones last.

Painting: Tape the stencil to the surface being stenciled, using masking or freezer tape. When stenciling fabric, pin the stencil to the cloth, which has been laid flat and blocked on a large piece of wood or cardboard for stability.

Paint should be of a creamy consistency. Apply very lightly with an almost *dry* brush, achieved by wiping the brush onto newspaper after dipping to remove excess paint. Apply paint to the center of a large area first, brushing outward in light strokes. Keep ties pressed down with a penpoint to avoid seepage and smears. Work slowly and carefully, and wipe off stencil before taping to another surface when repeating a pattern.

Use a different brush for each color and stencil one color at a time, allowing plenty of drying time before painting one color over another.

Stenciling Tips

- Stencil onto a clean, smooth surface.
- Measure carefully for accurate placement before taping the stencil onto the surface.
- Use small paint brushes for detail work and tiny areas.
- Protect stenciling on wood with clear varnish or acrylic spray.
- Remember, a *sharp* knife for cutting, a *nearly dry* brush for painting.
- See page 243 for information on painting fabric.

Stenciling Projects

aprons/potholders
bed trays
canvas tote
chalkboard
Christmas stockings
clothing
footstool
peach basket
picture frame

Shaker boxes
sheets and bed linens
shower curtain
table linens
toddler rocking chair
tree skirt
TV trays
wood plaque
wooden spoons

CLAY MOLDING AND SCULPTING

This craft is fun, easy, inexpensive, and widely applied in gift and decoration making, besides being thoroughly therapeutic. You can use commercially available clays that dry or bake to a hard finish, or make your own out of simple flour, salt, and water. You're bound to have that stuff around the house!

Dough Clay Recipe:

4 c. unsifted all-purpose flour   1½ c. water (approximately)
1 c. salt

Do not halve or double recipe! Do not use self-rising flour!

Mix flour and salt in a large bowl. Gradually add just enough water to make a stiff dough. If dough is sticky, add a bit more flour. If it is slightly dry, knead with moistened fingertips. Knead dough for about 10 minutes until it forms a soft, smooth ball. Keep unused dough in an airtight container or a plastic bag. There is no need to refrigerate the dough over a one- to two-week period. But don't plan to save it much longer than this.

Commercial Modeling Compound

Types of commercial modeling compounds include Sculpey, Fimo, Cernat, and Promat (professional strength, made by Sculpey).

Knead clay until soft and pliable. Shape into desired form. Bake on non-metallic plate (a 13" x 9" Pyrex dish is good) at 275° F in a conventional oven for 10-20 minutes. Don't use a microwave for this. Check oven, as temperatures and time vary. Be careful not to overbake. Remove from oven and cool. Paint baked pieces with acrylics, coat with commercially-available glaze, or brush over rub-on metallics to highlight surface effects. Many clays come in a variety of colors.

Cutting Clay into Shapes: For flat objects, roll clay on a smooth surface or pastry sheet until all cracks disappear. If using dough clay, flour the surface and rolling pin; if using commercial modeling compound, dampen rolling pin to avoid stickiness. Cut with a sharp knife or cookie cutter. Smooth rough edges with a barely moistened finger.

Shaping the Clay: Roll balls and snakes. Make braids and twists. Use a potato ricer, garlic press, or recycle a Play-doh "tool" to make hair. To join two pieces of clay, moisten each piece with a wet finger. Add texture with forks, toothpicks, toweling, straws, manicure tools, hair curlers ... Press in seeds, dried flowers, leaves, coins ... and other found objects for design. Remove these before baking. If the piece is to be hung or strung as a bead, make a hole *before* baking.

Dough Clay Finishes

Coloring Dough Clay: To color dough before baking, mix food coloring, dry mustard, or paprika into the water when mixing. Or use strong tea or coffee instead of water as you make the dough.

Glazes: Various cooking substances create different effects on dough pieces. For *shiny light brown glaze*, brush on egg white, evaporated milk, or mayonnaise before baking. For a *darker glaze*, brush on egg yolk before baking, or baste piece once or twice with beaten egg while baking. For *color*, paint with food coloring before baking, or use one of the following to color baked and cooled dough clay pieces: acrylic paints, food coloring, shoe polish, felt-tip markers, watercolors, or enamels. A wood stain or rub-on metallic applied lightly and brushed with a clean cloth also highlights textures.

Baking Dough Clay

Preheat oven to 325° F. If piece is very thin, bake more slowly at 250-300° F. Cover thinnest parts of sculpture with foil to prevent browning. Use a cookie sheet that is even and flat. If piece puffs up during baking, reduce temperature 25° and prick puffy areas with a tooth-

Oil-based stenciling "crayons" are available and give excellent results on fabric, wood, and walls. Clean, neat, and drip-free.

pick. Allow approximately 30 minutes baking time for each ¼" of thickness, checking frequently, as ovens vary. The piece should be firm to touch and light golden brown when done. It is extremely important that dough clay pieces be thoroughly baked. You can dry the piece slowly in a 200° F oven for 6-10 hours, depending on the thickness, for more even drying.

Microwave Drying: Roll pieces out on waxed paper. Cut, shape, decorate, and remove pieces on paper directly to microwave after pricking each piece evenly with a toothpick to prevent air bubbles. Dry on full power 1-3 minutes. Watch carefully!

Air Drying: Place dough objects directly onto a well-ventilated screen in a warm, dry area. Let dry at least two to three days. Test thickest part for doneness.

When Dough Clay Piece Is Thoroughly Baked or Dried: Sand rough edges with sandpaper or a file, paint or color if desired, and seal. EXTREMELY IMPORTANT! Dough clay objects cannot withstand any moisture. They will squish, smush, and disintegrate right before your eyes. They also attract bugs. So it is *extremely important* to seal the piece completely with a clear acrylic, varnish, or polyurethane finish. Dipping pieces in polyurethane, drying, and repeating the dipping process three or four times should do the trick. Be sure to cover the piece front and back, top and bottom—*thoroughly*—to ensure proper strength, moisture, and bug resistance.

Items to Make from Clay

baskets
bread trays
button covers
candleholders and candle rings
finger puppets
jewelry (beads, earrings, bracelets, pins, hair clips ...)
mobiles

napkin rings
nativity figures/other miniatures
package or jar-top decorations
pencil holder
picture frame
refrigerator magnets
tree ornaments
wall decorations

DECOUPAGE

"Decoupage" is French for "cutting out"—the art of decorating a smooth surface with cutout pictures and heavily varnishing over the design to make the pictures appear to be part of the surface.

Materials

wood, glass, metal, or ceramic surface
decoupage or manicure scissors
white glue
magazine, card, gift wrap cutouts

Cellophane Collage

Decorate jars, bottles, glass plates and bowls, metal tins and cans with cellophane for attractive containers. The technique of layering the translucent colors creates a stunning effect.

Cellophane is available in vivid colors, pastels, and clear.

Materials:
items to decorate
various colors of cellophane
clear lacquer or varnish
brush
black permanent marker

Brush a thin layer of clear lacquer onto the object's surface. Place bits of cellophane over the lacquer, covering the object completely with a colorful pattern. Apply a second coat of lacquer and repeat layering to achieve a blending effect. Layer as much as you wish and finish with a final coat of lacquer. Use the marker to make stained-glass "lead" outlines, if desired.

The transparent nature of this technique over glass makes this an excellent craft for making candleholders. Put a votive candle into a cellophane-colored jar and watch the light dance through colors!

Never put colored cellophane in contact with foods. The dyes are toxic.

A Child's Artwork ...

can be a great design for appliqué. Cut pattern pieces to match colors and shapes of a child's drawing and appliqué the design onto a pillow, soft-sculpture toy, or wall hanging for her room.

varnish or polymer medium (available at craft stores)
brayer or drinking glass (for rolling smooth after gluing)
sealer, gesso, or paint (for background)
sandpaper
tweezers
dry cloth or old cloth diaper
paste wax

Preparing the Surface: The smoother the surface, the better. Sand boxes, frames, plaques ... carefully with fine sandpaper and wipe clean with a dry cloth or an old stocking. *Seal* wood with a commercial sealant before painting or after a stain has been applied. Brushed-on gesso or white glue, or Kilz spray primer provides a receptive surface for paint and/or decoupage.

Cutting the Design: Use a spray sealant or craft spray to coat the front and back of each print before cutting. Hold the scissor hand still, while moving the hand holding the paper to cut the outline first (this makes a smoother cut). Then cut out the small details with scissors or an X-acto knife (as you would cut a stencil). An emery board is great for sanding rough paper edges.

Gluing onto the Project Surface: Use a toothpick or cotton swab to apply small amounts of white glue to the backs of the small cutouts, a paintbrush for larger pieces. Tweezers are handy for placing tiny cutouts accurately on the design. Use a brayer (roller), drinking glass, or the back of a spoon to rub out all air bubbles and smooth down glued design. Carefully remove all excess glue as you work.

Varnishing: When glue has dried thoroughly, apply first coat of varnish. Allow 24 hours between each coat. Recommended number of coats varies from 4 to 5 to a maximum of 20. The number of coats applied will determine the depth and glow of the finished piece.

A polymer medium commercial decoupage finish dries more quickly than varnish and requires fewer (two or three) coats.

Sanding and Finishing: Clean the varnished surface well after it dries before applying another coat. Sand with a 320-360 grade sandpaper dipped in soapy water, rinse off the soap, and dry piece with a clean cloth (old cloth diapers are great!). Continue to sand after every third coat. Rub the final coat when dry with No. 0000 steel wool. Rub on a furniture paste wax to protect the piece and polish with a soft, clean cloth.

Tips on Decoupage

- Since the varnishing process can be a long one (up to three weeks), consider making several decoupage projects at once.
- Never overlap paper cutouts in the design layout.
- Tear a picture toward you for a feathered edge effect; or singe edges with a candle flame, if desired, continually moving the paper rim around the flame.

- For glass and other clear serving pieces, decoupage on the underside of the object.

Decoupage Projects

boxes
candleholders
clay pots
decorative jars or bottles
ginger jar lamps
glass plates, trays

lap tray
picture frame
shadow box
tree ornaments
wood plaques
wooden stools

NEEDLEWORK

For Christmas decorating, gift-making, and keepsake-creating ...

I think in some previous life I must have roamed the country as a pioneer woman. Words like "persevere," "new-fangled," and "ambush" are constantly creeping into my vocabulary ("I am *bushed!*"). While the predilection to be a spartan survivor (ever focused on the new and unusual) remains, I am afraid early American needlework talents were lost in the transmigration of this particular soul!

There is, however, still a warm place in my heart for the art and artistry of needleworking skills. My love of early American objects runs to lovingly hand-pieced quilts, crocheted lace, old loom-woven blankets, faded embroidered samplers ... the marvelous legacies of pioneering American women. Stories seem to leap out of the handwork as treasured gifts from the past.

There are a multitude of needlework craft forms and equally as many reference books, packaged kits, and art courses to get you started in one.

Consider using needlework in your Christmas creating. Keep a bagful of projects going all year long for twelve whole months' worth of terrific Christmas decorations and gifts, as well as future generations' worth of history and pleasure.

After all, what is it they say about idle hands?

Needlework Crafts: A Thousand and One Possibilities

Cross-Stitch: Many cross-stitch books and patterns are dedicated to the wonderfulness of Christmas. Use these or your own designs (charted on graph paper) to make a variety of holiday keepsakes.

Needleworking Notes

- Tape or zigzag edges of needlework fabric or canvas to prevent raveling during handwork.
- To block needlework: Stretch completed and moistened piece on a board, pulling even and straight on all sides, and attaching with tacks. Let dry, remove, and press well before framing or sewing into a pillow.
- Needlepoint and wool yarn crewel and embroidery pieces should be cleaned professionally.
- Wash soiled cross-stitch and cotton floss embroidery in cool water with mild soap. Place piece under a damp towel and press with a warm iron.

 Buy round flat magnets or magnet tape (with removable adhesive) to glue onto clay shapes and other decorative objects for unusual refrigerator magnets.

Making Fabric-Wrapped Cord

... for coiled bowls, baskets, placemats, trivets, napkin rings, pillows (leave selvage on outside for sewing into pillows), wreaths ... and other fabric accessories

Materials:
1½" cotton cording (or thicker) 2½" wide strip fabric cut on the bias to desired length (or of a width 1" wider than cord circumference)

Pin fabric around cording with right sides together. Stitch by hand or on the machine. Slide cording out until only 4-5" remain inside the fabric tube. Anchor this with a safety pin. Turn fabric right side out and pull back over the exposed cording. Remove safety pin and whipstitch edges closed.

Coil and shape as desired, whipstitching where needed to hold shape.

Cross-stitch on Aida, Hardanger (cross-stitch fabrics of varying colors, sizes, and weaves), gingham, checked fabric, knit sweaters ...

Most fabric stores and needlework shops offer a material called "waste cloth" which can be basted onto plain fabric to provide a cross-stitch grid for decorating anything: overalls, cotton panties, knits, nightgowns ... When the design is complete, moisten and pull out the waste cloth threads to leave a neat stitchery on the garment.

Quilting: I would love to have the time and know-how to hand-piece an old-fashioned quilt. Maybe, someday ... There are quite a few books on the subject available in bookstores and at the library. If you are the least bit interested, give it a try. Think of all the heirlooms you might eventually create!

Save old fabric scraps in a giant rag bag for craft projects, fabric gift bags, and that hand-pieced quilt in *your* future!

Crochet: A crochet hook and mercerized crochet cotton or yarn can make stunning lacy tree ornaments, starched baskets for potpourri and dried rose petals, tablecloths and linen trim, pillow covers, placemats, dressy collars, stocking trim ... If there is a bit of the Victorian in you, this may be your needlecraft.

Knitting: It isn't just for Grandma anymore. New threads, yarns, and patterns can make some of the most beautiful sweaters, mufflers, stockings, and vests you've ever seen. It's not as difficult as it looks either, yet the final product is a real joy. (Have you seen how much a hand-knit sweater costs these days?) Imagine making Christmas sweaters for the whole family ... or vests ... stockings? You might practice making a vest and cap for Santa Dog as your first project!

Candle-Wicking: This is a relatively "new" old art form currently seeing renaissance. The same wicking used to make candles (now packaged and sold in various thicknesses and colors) is pulled through fabric, stitched and knotted, to make textured designs. Create charming stuffed ornaments, dolls, pillows, table linen, bed linen, tree skirts ... Kits and supplies are available at fabric and craft stores.

Tatting: Tatting is the craft of making lace with series and groupings of knots made with a shuttle, cotton twine, metallic threads, or DMC crochet cotton, all available in needlework shops. Learning the tatting technique will find you making snowflakes, stocking and linen trim, placemats, fabric and clothing appliqués ... For more information, a good resource is *Tatting: The Contemporary Art of Knotting with a Shuttle*, by Rhoda L. Auld, Van Nostrand Reinhold Company.

Needlepoint: Needlepoint canvas is found in needlework shops by the yard, or in small blank or pre-printed pieces for making a huge rug or tiny tree ornament. Look for kits to make extra-special family stockings, pillows, and other timeless and enduring needlepointed items.

Crewel and Embroidery: These stitchings using gorgeous yarns and threads decorate many of the items listed above in other needlework categories, by giving design, texture, and color to a solid background fabric. Many craft books have complete illustrations of embroidery stitches, and these can be used in a number of crafts. Be creative, using the various stitches to make your own designs on doll faces, ornaments, home accessories, clothing ...

Working with Fabric

Fabric comes in many textures and colors for decorating and craft-making. Just walking through a fabric store can be a sensually stimulating experience. If you become stimulated to be creative with fabric, here are some techniques to help you along:

Transferring Designs onto Fabric for Painting, Applique, or Embroidery: Place a design under a piece of light fabric and trace lightly with a brown permanent fabric marker. For heavier, darker fabrics, use dressmaker's carbon or carbon paper placed between the design and the fabric, and transfer sharp lines onto the fabric, by pressing down and tracing the design with a ballpoint pen.

Painting Fabric: Add your own flair and color to a fabric background. Paint directly onto fabrics using a high quality acrylic paint (best when mixed with a fabric medium), fabric paints or markers, or India ink and a #1 Rapidograph pen (art supply stores). Use smooth fabrics with minimal texture or nap.

The same dry-brush technique used for stenciling will prevent excess moisture from bleeding into the fabric and spoiling your design. You can also use sponges to sponge on designs, or splatter-paint fabric with an eyedropper. Stretch the fabric to be painted, stamped, sponged, or splattered and anchor with heavy weights to flatten and straighten out all wrinkles. Create stencils for a repetitive pattern on one piece or several. When paint has dried, gently press the underside of the fabric with a warm iron to heat-set the color. Your design will be machine-washable. Hand washing is recommended, however, if the glimmer of shiny, glittery, or pearlized paint is used ... or if you add dimension with sewn-on beads, sequins, appliqués ...

Making Patterns for Fabric Cutouts: Trace or design patterns on interfacing cloth (for sturdy, reusable patterns) or newsprint. Pin pattern to fabric and cut, adding ¼" to ⅝" seam allowance.

Use cookie cutters, reduced or enlarged designs from books or magazines, and a little imagination in creating your own patterns.

If you are making tree ornaments, just one yard of fabric will yield 15-20 averaged-sized ornaments. Three to four friends together, each with a yard of fabric, can make and trade a fine assortment of these.

Cutting Fabric on the Bias: To make tubing, fabric-wrapped cord, and other craft projects requiring stretchable fabric—because cutting on the

Stuffings and Fillers

For loosely stuffed rag dolls, soft sculpture, toys, pillows ...

Polyester fiberfill — washable, soft, lightweight, non-allergenic.

Shredded foam — washable (air-dry), flexible, messy (clings!).

Cotton batting—less expensive than polyester but lumps; absorbent (good for baby items)

Foam pillow forms—sturdy (cover with muslin to line and protect outer covering)

• Use a crochet hook, pen point, or spoon to push filler into small areas.
• Other stuffing materials to recycle into fillers: old socks, stockings, feathers, hay, straw, beans, cut-up foam mattress (consider allergens).
• Add a small fabric bag filled with potpourri, scented balsam or pine needles, or kitchen spices to make your "stuffing" smell scent-sational!

❄

Pillow Construction

Measure the size pillow desired, according to finished needlework or pillow pattern. Cut a matching piece of fabric for the backing, adding an extra 1" on one side for the zipper, and allowing for ½" seam allowance on both backing and front piece.

Cut backing piece in half and with right sides together, machine baste with a ½" seam, installing zipper to fit.

If using a ruffle, cord, or other trim, pin around the border of the fabric, right sides together. Baste, then stitch carefully through all thicknesses, allowing a ½" seam. Trim edges and clip corners. Turn pillow right side out and insert form or stuffing. Fill small dolls, bean bags, and characters you want to have sitting or standing around ... with sand or dried beans. This will facilitate their arranging themselves in various positions of authority all through your Christmas home!

---

bias adds stretchability—fold fabric diagonally to make a 45° angle at the fold. Cut along the length of the fold and use this line to continue cutting as many bias strips as needed. Use a straightedge for accuracy.

Mixing Media in Fabric Decoration: Draw outlines with fabric markers, paint inside lines with acrylics, and add texture and detail with embroidery, appliqué, candlewicking, craft trim, eyelet, lace, contrasting prints and solids ...

Needlework Projects

aprons/potholders
baby bibs
backpacks/carry bags
bed linens
clothing
crib decorations/bumper pads
dolls/doll clothing
fabric table decorations

holiday ornaments
picture frames
pillows
shoe bags
soft sculpture
table linens
toys
wall hangings

"Faux" Quilting

A quilted "look" can be achieved in more ways than the most difficult one of piecing fabric together by hand.

One method is to pin painted, printed, or silk-screened fabric—with a layer of cotton batting in between—to an underside piece of fabric, and machine- or hand-stitch through all three thicknesses, outlining the major portions of the pattern on the top fabric. The edges may be finished with a binding or hem, or the entire piece could be framed or stretched on a wood frame as a wall hanging.

Use these "quilted" fabrics to make quilt coverlets, wall hangings, placemats, potholders, stockings, tote bags, pillows ...

How to Appliqué

In many places throughout this book, appliqué is suggested for decorating stockings, doll and children's clothes, tree skirts, table linens ... as well as to make wall hangings, children's gifts, and much more. How do you effectively apply one piece of fabric to another?

1. You can use glue, in some instances, when the piece will never be washed, such as with felt projects.
2. For most other fabrics, particularly those eventually destined for the wash, you will need a needle and thread, or sewing machine, to appliqué. Cut a pattern from newspaper and cut out fabric pieces, allowing a ¼" seam allowance. Stitch around each fabric piece ¼" from the edge. Clip curves and press under seam allowance for a neat turned-under border. Pin each appliqué to the background fabric and slip-stitch, top-stitch, or zigzag around the edge.

3. Use fusible webbing to attach appliqués. This heat-sensitive fabric, available at fabric stores, gives appliqué a better body and attaches directly to the fabric. Cut webbing pieces identical to each appliqué piece. Place webbing between the background fabric and appliqué and, following manufacturer's instructions, press with an iron to fuse the appliqué. Finish the outer edges with an embroidery stitch, slip-stitch, or zigzag by machine.

Putting Together a Pillow

Made from needlepoint, cross-stitch, appliqué, quilting ... pillows accent every nook and cranny of your home at Christmas or anytime. These also make welcome gifts.

Block, clean, and press needlework before making into a pillow. Also trim and tie off loose threads and, if necessary, stitch interfacing onto the back of the needlework for a lining between the stuffing or pillow form.

In addition to needlework, hand-painted pillows are all the rage these days ... from tiny little watercolor flowers and botanical motifs to bright and wild Picasso- and Matisse-like prints. Paint on polished cotton, chintz, raw silk, muslin, canvas ... The sun, moon, and stars are the limit. Make some for the holidays, one for each of the four seasons, or copy a motif of a favorite interior fabric and toss your imagination in too, for an extra bit of wit and sparkle.

❄

Rag Doll Body Construction

Hand-stitch across body joints to make doll bendable.

Simple Rag Doll Body and Soft Sculpture

Create all kinds of stuffed creatures and characters—dolls, ducks, dogs, dinosaurs ... using the following techniques.

Materials:

fabric—muslin, cotton, felt, parachute cloth, calico, satin, velveteen,
    lightweight burlap, fake fur ...
polyester fiberfill, cotton batting, old pantyhose ...
needle and thread
fabric paint, acrylics, and/or craft trim

Draw a doll body or other pattern onto newspaper or interfacing cloth. Cut two identical pieces from doubled fabric. With right sides together, stitch around edges, leaving an opening large enough to insert stuffing on one side. Turn doll right side out and fill with fiberfill. Whipstitch opening closed. Hand-stitch across body joints to make doll bendable (see illustration). Tie a double strand of embroidery floss or thread around the neck to give head a rounder shape.

Fabric Faces: Use permanent markers, acrylics, or fabric paints to paint on faces—silly, sad, happy, mad ...

Collect pictures of funny faces, eyes, noses, mouths ... to give you a few "feature" ideas ...

Embroider facial expressions using a satin stitch, French knots, running stitch, outline stitch ...

Use craft accessories and trim to glue or sew on a special face you

Soft Sculpture Techniques

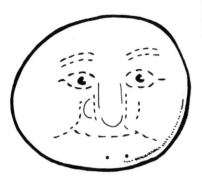

Each line represents a short running (or outline) stitch. Pull to tighten and shape; knot in the back of the head. Use tiny stitches for dimples if you like. Centers of eyes may be filled with paint.

can't help but love ...

Or soft-sculpture your "character's" face ...

Materials:

stretchy knit fabrics, cotton or nylon socks, or pantyhose (this makes excellent face material!)

polyester fiberfill

armature materials

thread to match fabric or pantyhose

fake fur, bent wire glasses, doll clothes, lambswool, trim, rouge, paint, old jewelry ...

Cut feet off pantyhose or socks to make a tube and draw top closed with gathers, tucking edges inside and whipstitching closed. If using plain stretchy fabric, simply sew into a tube and continue along the same procedure. Fill "head" with polyester fiberfill or scrap hosiery and tighten "neck" with gathering stitches to close and form a rounded head (see illustration).

Using a needle and thread, make small stitches to pull and push soft material gently into shaped facial features. Knot thread, and starting at the back of the head, pull needle through to make small stitches, one for each line drawn, or however you wish to design your "individual."

By pinching fiberfill up between the pulled thread areas, you give dimension. By pulling threads more tightly, you create indentations.

❄ INDIVIDUAL FEATURE TECHNIQUES

Eyes: Take small stitches around a circle or an oval and pull gently. Or use one stitch pulled from the back, then back in again from the front for tiny eyes (or dimples).

Eyebrows: Pinch up eyebrow over each eye. Stitch through, pinching from top to bottom across the eyebrow and tighten slightly before knotting.

Nose: Pinch up sides of nose from center front. Drawing needle under and through pinched form, stitch from one side to the other down the full length of the nose. Pinch out nostrils on either side in the same fashion.

Cheeks: Stitch small lines of stitches from the front to the back of the head for cheek lines. Push out filling to round cheeks.

Mouth: Run a gathering stitch in the direction you wish to pose the mouth (smiling, sour, unhappy, stern ...) and pull to tighten.

KNOT ALL STITCHES AT THE BACK OF THE HEAD.

Accessorize stocking faces with armature or rag doll bodies, craft trim, doll clothes, watercolors, acrylics, real makeup and permanent markers (for coloring and rosy cheeks), fake fur or lambswool, and other accents.

Doll Hair: Stitch a coil of yarn down the middle for a sewn-on hairpiece. Glue or tack yarn bits, braids, and buns onto the doll's head. Sew on curly hair with a large needle threaded with yarn and a loose loop stitch around the head.

Use fake fur or some of Dr. Scholl's lambswool for head and facial hair.

Making Doll Clothes and Dressings for "Little People" and Pets

Make sure dolls, bears, and handmade figures, not to mention Spot and Fluffy, are dressed appropriately for the holidays.

Making a Pattern: Patterns for doll clothes are found in pattern books at the fabric stores, or you can make your own. Study "people" clothing patterns for ideas and guidelines.

Measure doll or figure's sleeve length, arm circumference (at the widest point), shoulder and chest width, waist, inseam for pants, skirt length for dresses, neck circumference, and from the top of the shoulder to the waist.

Determine what kind of clothing (skirt and top, pants and shirt, sweater, vest, hat ...) you plan to make. Use a tape measure to figure these dimensions and then draw the pattern on paper, using a ruler and curved template.

Doll clothes should not be tight-fitting, as they will likely be taken off and put back on a minimum of 1000 times. Allow at least ½" extra all around for comfort and roominess, and another ¼" for seam allowance and hems (total ¾" extra around each pattern piece).

Cut fabric according to pattern. Use pinking shears, if possible, to limit raveling.

Fabric: Choose sturdy fabrics that can be washed. Recycle old scraps,

cut-up outgrown clothing, old sheets and toweling. Small prints look best on small figures. Consider cotton, calico, gingham, felt, fake fur, knits (sweater knit is great for Jingle Bear's Christmas sweater!), lace, satin, taffeta, velvet, velveteen ...

Sewing: Use a ¼" seam allowance and tight stitching to withstand wear and tear. Finish seams with a zigzag machine stitch, French seams, or pinking shears. Add snaps, hooks and eyes, buttons, Velcro strips, or fabric and ribbon ties for closure. Put on the finishing touches with fabric paint, embroidery, ruffles, lace or eyelet, ribbons, appliqué, braid, beads, sequins ... whatever best suits the occasion.

Make dolls and soft-sculpture faces in any and all sizes for tree ornaments, package decorations, mobiles, heirloom toys ... You can attach funny faces to lampshades in the kids' rooms, make them bloom from the center of a paper or silk sunflower, or arrange several climbing desperately out of a coffee can (Chock Full o' Nuts??) ...

HAVE YOU EVER WONDERED HOW TO ... ???

Cut into Plastic

For piggy bank slots and making things with pantyhose eggs and other plastics, use a *heated* awl, a darning needle stuck in a cork "handle," or an X-acto knife to make slits in plastic. Keep blade hot during the entire cutting process by running through an open flame (candle) or dipping into boiling water.

Craft Trims and Accessories

A needle and thread, glue, or craft pins attach the following to projects for accent and decoration, character, and personality:

beads
bottle corks
buttons
Contact paper cutouts
covered buttons
craft eyes
doilies
embroidery
eyelet or lace
fake fur
faux jewels
feathers
felt
filigree disks
glitter
iron-on patches/transfers
lambswool
pompoms
popsicle sticks (skis!)
rhinestones
ribbon/bows
rickrack
seed pearls
sequins
shells
silk cord
stars
stickers
yarn/string

Cut Glass

Colored and clear plate glass is available for use in framing, stained glass projects, shadow boxes ...

Before making a project requiring cut glass, practice cutting straight and curved lines on cheap window and scrap glass.

Clean glass with warm soapy water. Wipe glass cutter (craft supply store) with vegetable oil on a cotton ball, and keep cutter lubricated during the entire cutting process. Holding the glass cutter with your thumb pressing down and the handle perpendicular to the glass, score the glass in the pattern to be cut. Use constant pressure and one continuous motion. It's easiest to cut against a straightedge or template, or you can place a pattern underneath and trace with the cutter.

Tap glass along the score line and sharply snap into two pieces, applying equal pressure on both sides for a clean, even break. It is wise to wear thick, heavy gloves when working with glass. I have the scar to prove it.

Take Adhesive Off Just About Anything

Sticky price tags and stickers sometimes leave a residue that can be removed by rubbing lighter fluid on a cotton ball over the adhesive. Wipe clean with a soft, dry cloth.

Make Multiple Cloth Bags

Fill these with wrapped candies, jewelry, potpourri, hosiery, small gifts ...

Select a Christmas print, solid, plaid, stripe, or other fabric suitable to your tastes and purpose. Determine the size bags you will need.

Fold fabric in half, right sides together, and stitch across the middle. Then stitch up and down fabric in straight double lines, according to the size needed, leaving enough room between lines to cut bags apart. Cut and turn bags right side out ... and suddenly you have 8-10 small fabric gift bags for someone's special treats. Use pinking shears, a hem, or sewn-on ribbon or bias tape to finish edges. Decorate with lace, eyelet, fabric trim, iron-on name tapes, paint or fabric markers ... Tie with yarn, cord, braid, or ribbon.

If you accumulate lots of fabric scraps over the year, make gift bags whenever you are at the machine, and you will have a great assortment of recycled and recyclable "presentables" for Christmas and any occasion.

KIDSCRAFTS

Children can do most of the activities mentioned in this book, with a little supervision and instruction from parents. Here are a couple of things, however, for those who really think young! Make some for gifts and some for keeps ...

❄ HOMEMADE PLAY-DOUGH

A rainy day lifesaver ...

2 T. vegetable oil   2 t. cream of tartar
1 c. flour   1 c. water
½ c. salt

Heat oil in a saucepan. Put in remaining ingredients and cook 3 minutes, stirring constantly. Drop the ball of dough on a sheet of waxed paper until cool enough to handle. Add a drop of peppermint or wintergreen oil and knead well into the dough. Separate into smaller balls and knead in different colors of food coloring. Wrap in tied plastic bags and store together in a cleaned out milk carton in the refrigerator.

❄ FOREVER BLOWING BUBBLES

A warm tub "swim" after snow play is more fun with this bathtub-restricted activity!

4 drops light corn syrup   2 T. water
1 T. liquid dish detergent

Mix all together in an old bubble bottle or plastic baby bottle. Save bubble hoops from purchased bubbles and let the kids play Lawrence Welk celebrating New Year's Eve!

Whittle and Carve Toys and Decorations

Older children might try this old-time craft. Techniques and tools are simple and require mostly practice for an interesting product. Practice using a bar of soft castile soap ... shaving, rather than chopping, into shape. Blocks of soft balsa wood are also good for carving. Ask at craft and hobby stores about specific carving knives, chisels, and smoothing devices.

Make soapstone for carving small stocking stuffers:

    4 T. finely chopped castile
       soap or Ivory soap
    3 T. water
    2 T. chopped colored crayons

Heat soap and water in a coffee can placed in hot water. Stir with a clean stick. Add crayons when mixture is melted and stir until silky smooth. Pour onto wax paper to cool slightly. While still soft, press into molds (juice cans, wax cartons, yogurt cups ...). Dry and harden for 48 hours. Use a small knife and kitchen tools for carving.

Life is a celebration —
make the most of it!

Index

Other Books of Interest

Home/Family
The Christmas Lover's Handbook, $14.95
Clutter's Last Stand, $10.95
The Complete Guide to Recycling at Home: How to Take Responsibility, Save Money, and Protect the Environment, $14.95
Confessions of a Happily Organized Family, $10.95
Conquering the Paper Pile-Up, $11.95
The Greatest Gift Guide Ever, 2nd Edition, $8.95
How to Conquer Clutter, $10.95
How to Get Organized When You Don't Have the Time, $10.95
How to Have a Big Wedding on a Small Budget, $12.95
The Big Wedding on a Small Budget Planner & Organizer, $12.95
How to Have a Fabulous, Romantic Honeymoon on a Budget, $12.95
Into the Mouths of Babes: A Natural Foods Cookbook for Infants and Toddlers, $6.95
Is There Life After Housework?, $10.95
It Doesn't Grow on Trees, $2.95
It's Here . . . Somewhere, $10.95
Make Your House Do the Housework, $12.95
The Melting Pot Book of Baby Names, 2nd Ed., $8.95
The Organization Map, $12.95
A Parent's Guide to Teaching Music, $7.95
A Parent's Guide to Band and Orchestra, $7.95
A Parent's Guide to Teaching Art: How to Encourage Your Child's Artistic Talent and Ability, $5.95
Raising Happy Kids on a Reasonable Budget, $10.95
Slow Down . . . And Get More Done, $11.95
Step-by-Step Parenting, Revised & Updated, $9.95
Streamlining Your Life, $11.95
Unpuzzling Your Past: A Basic Guide to Genealogy, 2nd Ed., $11.95

Young Readers
The Admiral and the Deck Boy: One Boy's Journey with Christopher Columbus, $5.95
Becoming a Mental Math Wizard, $8.95
Breaking the Chains: The Crusade of Dorothea Lynde Dix, $5.95
But Everyone Else Looks so Sure of Themselves: A Guide to Surviving the Teen Years, $7.95
By George, Bloomers!, $2.95
Cadets at War: The True Story of Teenage Heroism at the Battle of New Market, $3.95
Codes & Ciphers: Hundreds of Unusual & Secret Ways to Communicate, $7.95
The Curtain Rises: A History of Theater From Its Origins in Greece and Rome Through the English Restoration, $14.95
The Curtain Rises, Volume II $12.95
Fiddler to the World: The Inspiring Life of Itzhak Perlman, $5.95
The Glory Road: The Story of Josh White, $7.95
Great Unsolved Mysteries of Science, $9.95
The Junior Tennis Handbook: A Complete Guide to Tennis for Juniors, Parents & Coaches, $12.95
The Kids' Almanac of Professional Football, $8.95
Market Guide for Young Artists and Photographers, $12.95
Market Guide for Young Writers, 2nd Ed., $16.95
Medical Practices in the Civil War, $6.95
Melvil and Dewey in the Fast Lane, $2.50
Mosby and His Rangers: Adventures of the Gray Ghost, $6.95
Music in the Civil War, $8.95
Roots for Kids: A Genealogy Guide for Young People, $7.95
Smoke on the Water: A Novel of Jamestown and the Powhatans, $6.95
Spies! Women and the Civil War, $6.95
What Would we do Without You? A Guide to Volunteer Activities for Kids, $6.95
With Secrets to Keep, $12.95
Woman of Independence: The Life of Abigail Adams, $5.95
Young Person's Guide to Becoming a Writer, $8.95

Miscellaneous Reference
College Funding Made Easy: How to Save for College While Maintaining Eligibility for Financial Aid, $5.95
Cover Letters That Will Get You the Job You Want, $12.95
The First Whole Rehab Catalog: A Comprehensive Guide to Products and Services for the Physically Disadvantaged, $16.95
How to Handle the News Media, $7.95
The Insider's Guide to Buying a New or Used Car, $9.95
Making the Most of the Temporary Employment Market, $9.95
Speaking with Confidence: A Guidebook for Public Speakers, $7.95